A TAR HEEL MARCHES

*The Story of a Berea Student Who Became
a Civil Rights Activist in Montgomery*

Fred Eli Epeley

A TAR HEEL MARCHES

ISBN-10:1983774731
ISBN-13:978-1983774737

Printed in the United States of America

Library of Congress CIP data applied for.

Books by the author:

Growing Up In Ottie's World

Don't Let The Green Wave Drown You

Front cover design: Drawn by Vyvyan Dunne, the cover depicts the beginning of the Montgomery march at Phelps-Stokes Chapel on the Berea College campus. A massive crowd crosses the Pettus Bridge in Selma and flows toward Montgomery, ending in an actual photo (by Mike Clark) of the Berea students behind their banner at St. Jude school. The author (circled in red) is visible directly behind the banner.

DEDICATION

A TAR HEEL MARCHES is dedicated to all the Berea College students and their adult supporters who marched in Montgomery. They understood the moral purpose of the college and, against all odds and obstructions, carried its spirit to Montgomery, Alabama, and to a greater world beyond. We were on the right side of history.

CONTENTS

Part II
Journey to Selma/Montgomery 171

ACKNOWLEDGMENTS

My editor and friend, Julia S. Pittman, once again made valuable suggestions for my book. I thank her warmly for her support.

Larry Harold Keagy is the person that drives the technology of publishing my books. He is dedicated and wonderfully supportive. Without his knowledge and expertise, there would be no finished book.

Several Berea students did the major work to bring about a trip to Montgomery. Their names are listed in the Berea archives. Among them one finds Roy Birchard, Danny Daniel, Mike Clark, Frank Corbett and George Giffin. I specifically knew and dealt with George Giffin. I extend a personal thanks to all the students. George inspired me to advocate for civil rights and his determination to go to Montgomery gave me courage.

Vyvyan Dunne, local, prize-winning artist, designed the cover and drew illustrations for the book. I express my thanks and appreciation to her.

Wayne Hambright, my sophomore roommate at Berea, proof-read the manuscript. He lived the Berea experience with me. I have always valued his opinion.

Dr. Dwayne Mack, Assistant Professor at Berea College, read my manuscript and made valuable suggestions. He has led a movement to preserve the history of the Montgomery march through his writings and teaching.

SPECIAL ACKNOWLEDGEMENT

Dr. Dwayne Mack was born one year after the Berea march to Montgomery. He could not be physically present with our group on the march. However, he has thoroughly researched, recorded, and archived interviews with original marchers. In addition, he has helped to preserve the history of the march in an article entitled, "Ain't Nobody Gonna Turn me around." It is through his promotion of civil rights on the Berea campus and elsewhere that the history of the Berea march to Montgomery has been preserved.

Dr. Mack is a man of passion and compassion. His dedication to teaching high values to his students is admirable. Because of his dedicated writings, research, and excellent teaching, I believe that he has earned the right to be a part of the Berea Montgomery group, if only in his heart and mind.

Resolved: I nominate Dr. Dwayne Mack to be an honorary member of the March to Montgomery group. I want to bring him home to us, as he has brought me home to Berea.

The author with Dr. Dwayne Mack at their first meeting in Morganton, North Carolina, in October, 2017.

INTRODUCTION

B erea College is a great institution. For one hundred and sixty years, it has served hundreds of talented young men and women who otherwise would not have had an opportunity to get a higher education. Its reputation for academics, liberal arts, and a Christian education is stellar. I came into Berea's class of 1961-65 by sheer bravado and I entered a doorway to a new way of acting and thinking. My experiences on campus changed my life profoundly.

No matter how great an institution is, it has flaws. Trying to hide dirty laundry, its members don't want to mention anything negative about itself. I have decided to tell my story of the years at Berea, because the college and I came upon an important event in the history of our country that challenged all that we had professed to be and all that we had believed. That event was the civil rights march from Selma/Montgomery, Alabama.

Berea was only ten years into its renewed experiment to offer higher education to minorities, because the college's purposes had been blocked and thwarted since 1904. Doubt surfaced among Berea's leaders as they butted heads with a group of idealistic students advocating equality and civil rights for all.

Intelligence and emotion do not play on the same field. The extremely bright, talented students who had entered Berea when I did had not yet dealt with their own attitudes and their society's treatment of minority students. In their heads they knew that their society was wrong. Many were afraid to break away from attitudes that their society had instilled in them.

While a student, I transformed myself from a quiet mountain person to a firebrand filled with courage. I owe much of my transformation to Berea's teachings and its moral code. Then, like a delinquent child, I turned on my college family and pushed everyone to a breaking point.

In an attempt to paint a wide canvas of life as a student in one four-year period, I have written about events that are amusing, revealing, sad, and disrespectful. Keep in mind as you read that the Berea College of today is not the college I experienced. We are fifty years removed from my experiences. Remember, too, that I was a young adult, impetuous, foolish, a person searching for a sense of belonging.

My stories are based upon real events. I experienced some, I observed some, and I heard people tell about others. I have used these events to paint a moment in time. I especially chose to give a personal narrative of what it was like for me to go to Berea. I have explained my reasons for going to Montgomery, to march, to risk my life for causes in which I fervently believed.

Every student who participated in the march will tell a different story from his own perspective. My experiences will not necessarily agree with theirs, just like two witnesses to an automobile crash will not give identical testimony. We live our lives individually and see events from an individual perspective. I do not profess to speak for any other Berea student or participant in the Montgomery march. No other student experienced what I did on campus and on the march. No other student can speak for me. I urge all those who went to Montgomery to write about their own impressions and experiences of the trip so that a total, rich tapestry of the event can exist.

If one searches the list of students who participated in the march, he will not find the name of Chloe, one of the main characters of this book. I intentionally created a character from a composite of all the African-American students whom I knew. I had to reconstruct dialogues with characters because I am remembering over a vast period of time---fifty years. I have presented events as I remember them.

In order to understand the events of this book, it will be helpful for the reader to read my other books, GROWING UP IN OTTIE'S WORLD and DON'T LET THE GREEN WAVE DROWN YOU because they explain my background and they lay the foundation for my Berea experience.

I want to recommend that the reader consult a short history of the Berea students' march to Montgomery, "Aint Nobody Gonna Turn Me Around," written by Dr. Dwayne Mack, presently professor of African-American studies at Berea. He has written the most accurate, thorough, and well-researched account of the event. I personally thank Dr. Mack for his invaluable work. He was accurate and fair. I know because I experienced the history personally.

I wove the college alma mater, "Berea Beloved ," written by William M. Cable '29 and Wilfred Johnston '29 throughout the book because that song expresses beautifully the spirit of the place and the events that were unfolding in my life. I warmly thank Berea College for permission to use it.

In writing this book, I have exorcised my demons from youth. For these fifty years I had not even unpacked my Berea diploma where it had rested since 1965. I had departed Berea angry, disappointed, and disillusioned. As I wrote this book, I came to realize how much I love the college and its people. I walked the painful pathway of past years and came to realize that my whole life had been lived by Berea's codes. Upon completing my manuscript, I took my diploma out of its box, brushed it clean, and then I proudly hung it on my living room wall.

ALL GOD'S CHILDREN

The author wrote this poem on April 5, 1965, after his return from Montgomery, Alabama. In it, Mr. Epeley expresses his feelings about civil rights in the America of his time. He was only twenty years old.

ALL GOD'S CHILDREN

All God's children gonna rise and shine

Cause all God's children ain't free

Gonna bend their backs no more to pick cotton

Cause slavery and segregation gonna soon be forgotten

And the lowest of all will be free.

All God's children gonna sing

All God's children gonna pray

Til they walk them golden stairs

In freedom day by day.

Goodbye cotton, goodbye Mississippi

Father of waters roll on to the sea

Hold high your heads and just keep a marching

Cause all God's children ain't free.

Sing it over

My body is weary and my back is bent

1

But my heart is strong in the Lord

In our great hope, in our great pride

Lies the goal we are working toward.

Hear Us Lord

Gonna march through the valley

Gonna march to the sea

Gonna march to Alabama

'Til we all gets free

Yes, brethren

Like waves of an ocean

Piled high with foam

We now got convictions

And we're moving along

Our King on earth

Our King in the sky

We move toward freedom

Ere we live or die.

Now hear me children

From Mother Africa we came in ships with chains

A painful place to be

Sold our mothers and our daughters

And our sisters and our brothers

Down the road to Montgomery

And Virginia

And Kentucky

And Carolina, too.

We wept, we begged, we suffered and we prayed

And freedom's not yet come through.

Gonna fix it!

Gonna fix it!

Gonna fix it!

For me and you!

Planters rose up to fire and sword

Their red banners flying on high

From Maine to Mississippi

And ends of the earth

Rose up their dreaded battle cry

At Manassas

Bull Run

And Chattanooga too

Came the pride of the Union in their coats of blue

Laid waste to Alabama, laid waste to Atlanta

Waycross and Charleston town

Bugles and banners, dying and manners

The chains of slavery come down.

March to the rhythm of the men in the field

To the shout of one, two, three

We must fight, we must die,

We must suffer and bleed

Cause all God's children ain't free

Silence at Appomattox.

A silver-haired man, time etched on his face

Surrendered his army for the dignity of a race

Closed down the cannon, laid down the sword

Surrendered his Southern Nation

To the mercy of the Lord.

Appomattox lay silent and still.

Blood is shed! There's hatred in seed!

And all God's children ain't freed!

All God's children must rise and shine

Cause all God's children ain't free

Gonna sing

Gonna shout

Gonna pray and say

We Shall Overcome Someday!

With a song in our hearts

And a prayer on our lips

We march this joyous morn

We rise

We shine

We take our place

A new life, a new world is born

Cause freedom will ring this day

And all God's children will be free!

(Fred E. Epeley, April 5, 1965, age 22.)

THE AUTHOR AT AGE 20 (AT BEREA) AND TODAY AT AGE 74

Fred Eli Epeley

Fred Eli Epeley

Part I

Journey To Berea

A TIME FOR DEPARTING

The time for departing had come. It had rested heavily on my heart for many years, but in the past, I had been able to push its reality to the back of my mind. Today it was real. I stood with heavy heart in the middle of the living room of our humble house and drank in for one last time what had been my home. An old, yellow, worn suitcase sat on the floor in front of me. My entire life's possessions lay within. It contained my clothing, two shiny buckeyes my brother Willard Worth had given me for good luck, a picture of my family, a worn photo of my grandfather Elkanah Smith, and a pack of Oreo cookies. I chuckled as I remembered what Grandpa Smith had told me one day, "He who travels light, travels fast." I was traveling light. I wanted to travel away from Ottie's world at the speed of light. In this moment of departing, I was venturing forth, hoping that luck would carry me to a new family in a new world.

I must take care for what I wish.

I looked carefully at the contents of the room. A worn, vinyl couch the color of faded mustard sat against a smoke-stained wall. A blackened woodstove connecting to the front of the fireplace had painted the walls with black soot. A whitened square where someone had removed a picture was imprinted on the wall above the couch. Dusty yellow, plastic curtains hung limply on the sides of two floor-length windows. One window pane bore a long crack caused by a brick or rock that someone had carelessly thrown or maybe by freezing weather long ago. A rocking chair stood to my left and two cane bottom sitting chairs rested on each side of the black, iron woodstove.

I picked up my suitcase to leave and then, impulsively, I set it back down on the floor with a loud thud. Something was holding me here. My life had been inexorably rooted to this house and land. It exuded sadness, a sense of nostalgia that would not yet let me go. I began to wander slowly through each room of the old house remembering events and people that had passed through it. I remembered summer evenings when Ottie, my three sisters (Gertie, Justine, Callie) and I had gathered in the kitchen when darkness had fallen. Ottie had baked fresh, brown, buttermilk biscuits for us and we had eaten them with Duke's mayonnaise and fresh tomatoes from the garden. Outside in the darkness, cicadas had sung their shrill songs stirring the countryside with their winged symphony. I walked down the dogtrot that divided the house in two parts. Wooden stair steps led from the dogtrot upward to two rooms where Curtis, June Jr. and Willard Worth had slept when they were young. My brothers had gone away into their separate lives.

I opened the door to my bedroom and looked at the space where I had slept for eight years, a time in which I had grown from childhood to be a young man. I looked to the front porch where Willard Worth had napped each day after returning from hard work at the sawmill. I had wanted to go sit with him, to talk to him about his life and dreams, to be close with my favorite brother. But his loneliness, sadness, and anger at life had driven him to shoot at Eli and then flee like a wounded fawn seeking his refuge in the Missouri prairies which stretched endlessly toward the western sea. Losing him had wounded my life. Tears welled up in my eyes as I remembered him.

This house was no longer my home. At this moment, I was leaving it forever. I did not want any memories of my life here to go along with me on my new voyage.

It was a lonely departing. No one came to bid me farewell. Ottie was helping Bea do her laundry in exchange for a few dollars or for two quarts of home-canned tomatoes. My surrogate mother, Gertie, was a hair stylist in Danville, Virginia, and she seldom came back into Ottie's world. Justine had already left for Lees-McRae College where her brilliant mind had brought her scholarships to pay for an education. Callie and Louise were still enjoying the summer swimming at Optimist Park. I was leaving to study at Berea College in Kentucky and nobody cared. I picked up my beat-up suitcase, closed the door behind me, and walked down the front steps out of Ottie's world forever. Or, so I thought.

I took the unpaved road that ran eastward toward the Suburban Coach bus stop one mile away in the direction of Morganton. As I walked, I could see the rusted tin that covered the roof of our house sticking out above the treetops. Many times it had been a beacon leading me homeward toward all that I valued in life. Now it was a place to avoid, a place to let go of. My throat grew tight and I felt the pain of departing as I passed landmarks of my youth: the Bridge, the Country Store, the church on the hill, and the cornfields lining the highway.

I walked slowly through the hot August sun. I knew for certain that when I boarded the bus going to Kentucky, that I would never come back to this place, to these people, or to the unhappiness of Ottie's world.

At the bus stop, Suburban Coach Bus Company had erected a small shack that served as a shelter for anyone waiting outside in the elements. It looked like a country outhouse and smelled worse. This bus stop was located in the black part of the county. Corpulent, black men sat around upturned barrels playing checkers, shooting dice, and sniffing glue at a local hangout near the bus house. They were enjoying their lives. Maybe my good life was just beginning.

The gray Suburban Coach bus rattled along highway 70 past small farms and white, wooden houses, past the high school where I had graduated only three months earlier. It ploughed its way among factories belching smoke and past gasoline stations offering gasoline for twenty-nine cents a gallon. Bus riders pulled the stop cord setting off beeping near the driver's seat alerting him that they wanted to get off. Others boarded the bus and took a seat. White people sat at the front while black people sat in the back of the bus. My ride ended beside the rock wall bordering a courthouse built in 1838. Passengers disembarked, whites first followed by the blacks, and scurried across the busy main intersection in the direction of banks, five-and-dime stores, or shoe stores. I picked up my suitcase and walked two blocks past the shoe store where June Jr. had stolen his shoes from the old Jewish couple, to the Greyhound bus station. It seemed as if I were the only person moving on from this town.

In the bus station behind the ticket window covered with black, iron bars there sat a little old lady who looked as if she had appeared from another time. She had twisted her black hair around the top of her head and had pinned it with a jeweled hairpin. Layers of makeup dripped from her face and I could not locate her mouth; neither could the tube of lipstick.

"May I help you?" she asked with no interest in me at all.

"I want to buy a one-way bus ticket to Berea, Kentucky, please," I said softly.

"Did you say 'Arrears' Kentucky?" she asked with a puzzled tone.

"B-e-r-e-a," I spelled out slowly.

"Never heard of a place like that," she mumbled.

"It's a college," I proudly announced to her.

"I don't care what it is," she snapped. "I just sell bus tickets to it."

She took a thick tome marked "Bus Routes" from a shelf behind her. Licking her gnarled, witch-shaped finger with a lizard-like tongue, she flipped through some pages and then stopped at a line written in dark ink. "Asheville, Knoxville, London, Corbin, Crab Orchard, Renfro Valley, Berea...."she read off the stops along my route.

"That will be $12.95," she purred through her heavily painted lips. "You will change buses in Asheville and Knoxville. The bus gets into Berea around ten o'clock tomorrow morning." She took out a segmented ticket, dipped a hand stamp into black ink, and slammed it on each part of the ticket. I paid her the $12.95 and reached under my shirt to check the white envelope that held the cash for my first semester. It was the legacy from my Grandpa Smith.

Over the door of my waiting room were the words "Whites Only." On the opposite side of the ticket window was a second waiting room with the words "Colored Only." These two signs bothered me because I felt in my heart that I was not superior to anyone. My family was as poor as any black family here. The signs reflected the times in which I lived. I had not built my society; however, my whole life lay ahead of me and I could help build a new one if I chose. Next to my waiting room door was a water fountain with a sign reading, "Whites Only" and above another fountain were the words "Colored Only." I went into the "Whites Only" room and sat down. A Negro man came in and took my suitcase to the window and checked it through to Kentucky.

The Greyhound bus was late. I climbed aboard behind an old crippled man and two fat ladies. I walked down the aisle and sat in a middle seat next to the window. The bus was filled with mothers and their babies, unkempt adults, and a crowd of noisy black people at the back of the bus. As the bus cranked its engine and backed out of the parking space, my heart raced in panic. Fear overcame me. I wanted to run to the door and jump back out into the horrible life that I had known for years. Though difficult, that life was my only security.

I wanted my mountains and streams, my Spruce and Hemlocks, my winding paths through green meadows, the howling winds down from Oaky Knob. I wanted Willard

Worth and Gertie and Ottie. I wanted to go back to the safety of my poverty life, to the only home that I had known. It did not matter how bad my family and its situation had been, I belonged with them.

Where am I going? Where shall I roam? In this new life I will be standing alone. I don't know where I'm going. I don't know if I can put together a new family who will stand beside me or guide me. Fate had dealt me Ottie's family. I was embarking on a journey now to create my own new circle of friends and family. I hoped that Berea would not disappoint me in my efforts. Darkness swept over me like a bottomless pit. I folded my body into a fetal position and sat quietly thinking. I fell asleep.

The wobbling, slow gait of the bus straining to pull Old Fort Mountain shook me awake. The Negroes in the back had quieted down. Babies had been fed and no longer kicked up a fuss. Some people leaned back in their seats snoring. I looked out at the mists rising from the Blue Ridge Mountains. It seemed as if I were staring into the distant forever. Somewhere over those distant mountains was Golden Valley. The ashes of my youth were scattered there and my only souvenir was a beat-up suitcase, riding in the bus compartment beneath me, filled with virtually nothing.

"I cannot live in the past, I thought through the aching in my head. "I will wrap my memories in my heart and lead with my common sense."

The bus reached the summit of Old Fort Mountain and sped down the hills toward Asheville. In the distance bright lights beckoned. In my mind my thoughts urged, "Don't be afraid to dream. Look to the rainbow and, without fear, be a color in that rainbow. A new world awaits you beyond these ancient hills. Those who will help you change your life are waiting for you in Berea. You will become a son of Kentucky."

WON'T DO YOU NO GOOD

A voice at the Asheville bus station blared out over the loudspeaker, "Bus to Knoxville is now loading on track fourteen. All passengers please board at this time." I rose from my seat and followed a line of passengers heading in the direction of the bus platforms. The passengers went through a heavy, glass door to an area where several Greyhound buses sat idling in their assigned stations. Their engines belched out heavy, black diesel smoke around the area. Someone in the crowd began coughing and ladies quickly dug into their purses for lace handkerchiefs which they promptly capped over their noses in order to block the acrid stench swirling around them.

The driver of bus fourteen came out of his office and sauntered over to the bus door. He wore a gray uniform jacket and trousers. A gray cap, folded up in front, rested snugly on his head. One set of silver wings decorated the front of the cap and he proudly wore a second set of silver wings on the left side of his chest. He smiled amiably at the small cluster of passengers anxiously waiting the next leg of their journey.

"Tickets, please," he crooned in a deep voice that instilled confidence in his passengers that he would get them safely to their destination.

The line that had formed in front of me moved quickly. When my turn came, the driver read my ticket and tore off the second segment that read "Asheville to Knoxville."

"Change buses in Knoxville. Take the one going to Cincinnati," he said to me pleasantly.

I followed a fat lady up the steps and down the aisle to the middle of the bus. She squeezed her two bulbous hips into a seat leaving her love handles hanging in the aisle. I sat alone at a window seat. When everyone was seated, the driver closed the heavy bus door, pulled the bus into gear, backed out, and headed westward along Highway 25.

There were few interstate highways in 1961. The Eisenhower system had just begun to build roads in 1957 in our area, so we were relegated to two-lane highways that wound around impossible mountain curves, through gorges, into backwoods communities, and sometimes to places filled with potholes that made the ride seem like a broken roller coaster. The bus made stops in Canton, Clyde, and Waynesville. Although no passengers got on or off, the bus had to go there anyway. This was the only long-distance transportation link for isolated towns. Mine would be a slow journey.

I leaned back comfortably in my seat and watched our steady climb up the mountains to Hot Springs. Signs along the way read "Hot Spas" and "Relax in our Healing Waters" and "Put a Little Mud on your Face." Hot Springs was a tiny town with a gigantic heart. The bus station amounted to a simple gasoline station. Boxes wrapped in dark brown paper tied with white strings and cheap suitcases were scattered haphazardly everywhere. The lone station worker had left them sitting where he had thrown them. One passenger boarded our bus here and sat down in the seat beside me.

He was a tall, lanky mountaineer. He wore a long-sleeved muslin shirt, suspenders, dark pants, and heavy work boots. His dark hair hung around his neck just above his shoulders. He had dark, piercing eyes that looked right through a person. He smelled of tobacco and fried potatoes. Maybe his wife had fried the potatoes for his supper just before he had left his home. I assumed he had a wife and family who loved him dearly. These mountain people were clannish and blood kin meant more to them than life. Despite his outward appearance, he obviously had people around him who cared for him. I envied him. No one had fried potatoes for me when I had left home some hours ago, and there was no certainty that fried potatoes would be waiting for me where I was going.

With nicotine stained fingers, he took a Camel cigarette and a wooden match out of his shirt pocket. He struck the match against the sole of his boot causing a flame to flare from the end of it. He placed the cigarette in his lips and applied the fire at the end. Blue smoke shot up from the cigarette. He breathed deeply and then exhaled the smoke, sending a great puff of blue air out across the seats in front of him. The sweet smell of burning tobacco quickly permeated the air in the entire bus.

"Want a cigarette?" he said out loud without even looking at me.

"No, thanks," I heard myself say. This was his way of opening up conversation with me so that our ride together would not be so tense.

"Headed to Knoxville?" he said in his slow mountain twang. Before saying these words, he had already taken another breath of smoke into his lungs, so puffs of smoke blew my way with each word.

"Berea," I managed to mumble through a fit of coughing.

"What's up there?" he curiously wanted to know.

"It's a college. I'm going to college," I heard myself explaining.

"Won't do you no good," he said prophetically, returning to enjoy his cigarette.

This man was making me angry. What right did he have to interrogate me about my journey and how it would affect my life? It was not his questions that angered me. It was the fact that I could not answer them for sure.

I was on a journey looking for a home and life that I had never had. It would be among new people, but I considered a new start among strangers to be beneficial. Berea was a beacon to so many students looking for a new beginning. I imagined it filled with loving people with wise old eyes who knew that all its children were damaged in some way. I resented the mountaineer's intrusion on my dream with words like "it won't do you no good." Besides, he couldn't even speak correct English. There was no way I could make this simple man understand the complexity of my life. I didn't want to talk about my suffering. What's the use?

"Why won't it do me no good?" I heard myself reply.

"How old are you, Sonny?" he asked.

"Well," I answered, "I turned eighteen on May 23," I admitted.

"You don't know nothing about life, yet, boy," he continued. "It is a waste of time sticking your nose in books."

"So why is it a waste of time," I shot back in anger, getting really irritated with him.

"Books talk about life, but they cannot help you to live life. Get married, have a lot of kids, build yourself the largest family you can support. Family is all there is. Enjoy your life daily with them. Have all the fun that you can have. Books will never give you a warm hug when you need one and they can't console you when you are lonely. A diploma will never fill an empty heart."

He leaned back in his seat and said no more.

I turned my face to the window. I did not want to debate the issues of my life on a Greyhound bus. I would lose the debate anyway. This mountaineer made me realize that I was not headed to Berea just to get a diploma; rather, I wanted to gather around me people who would form a new family of my own choosing.

The sun began setting across the mountains toward the west. I could see sparkling lights from tiny houses far below in the mountain gorges. Someone was turning on kerosene lanterns and lamps. The lights danced like happy fireflies in courtship across the trees. A gigantic orange moon hung low in the sky just above the silhouetted line of the fading mountain tops. Inside the bus, passengers turned on overhead lights in order to read or to talk to companions. Some were just afraid of the dark.

The bus headlights shone on a green sign along the highway. The sign carried the flag of the state of North Carolina...a white stripe over a red one against a vertical blue bar with the seal of the state emblazoned on it. "Esse Quam Videri" was written on a golden scroll at the bottom. The words, "You are leaving the great state of North Carolina" surrounded the flag.

"Yes, I am," I thought. "I'm leaving Ottie's world, North Carolina, and my horrid past. I'm going to give Kentucky a chance. How could it be any worse?"

The mountaineer was right. I was still too young to know that our issues are villains that stalk us wherever we go.

What had North Carolina ever done for me or my family? We were rag pickers here and no one gave a damn. The government did not assist Ottie and her eight children. They gave me no scholarship money to study. No officials in my high school ever spoke to me about going to college. At least a place in Kentucky was willing to give me a chance. I was tired of living off moonshine and hard farm labor. And I was tired of people implying that I would never get out of Ottie's world. It was as if I were a member of the Untouchables in India. I loved and hated North Carolina in the same breath.

The man next to me mercifully had fallen asleep. He leaned his head on his left shoulder which was tilted toward the aisle. His open mouth froze in a pose that imitated Munch's "The Scream." His snoring seemed to pour out the pain of his life.

The bus made a rest stop in Newport, Tennessee. I descended from the bus and purchased a cup of coffee for a nickel. The cool, outside air felt invigorating as I drew it deeply into my lungs. The dark mountains stood sentinel above me. When I returned to my seat, the man beside me had gone. I did not see him exit the bus. It is as if he had vanished through the luggage racks above our heads. I was glad to see that he was gone. He was out of place on my Greyhound bus journey. He was a son of the Appalachian hills, a stereotype mountaineer, and a mirage. And he dared to challenge my budding dreams!

The bus returned to the main highway and sped forward across Strawberry Plains toward Knoxville. We were now traveling on a four-lane highway.

I wondered about the mountaineer who had sat beside me and then had vanished so quickly from the bus. Who was he? I wished that I had asked. I did not even ask him a single question. His entire conversation had consisted of four questions: Want a cigarette? Headed to Knoxville? What's up there? Won't do you no good no way. In turn, my responses to him were: No, thanks. Berea. It's a college. It probably won't.

The mountaineer made me realize that a family is the most important thing in life. It costs no money. This stranger entered my world, challenged my mind, and then vanished. He reminded me that life is not always ours to command. There are times when life deals a hand and the recipient has to play it the best he can.

Berea was the hand now dealt for me. Would it do me "no good" as he had said? I wanted it to be a magic doorway through which I could exit Ottie's world to a world of respectability. How dare I hope! I was not even carrying enough money (gifted by my grandfather) to pay for the first semester of college, much less the entire year. Curtis had given me the $12.95 for my bus ticket. I had $1.25 in my pocket for food. It would purchase a pack of potato chips and a coke. Then what?

I began to reminisce.

My grandfather had given me much more than three hundred dollars. He made me promise to fill out a college application. I only did it for him. I had no hope that Berea would accept me into the class of 1965. A person had to have money to go to college, even Berea. Students did work for their tuition but it still cost $325 for one semester for classes and then one had to buy books and have money for personal expenses. I had none of these, yet the college accepted me as a student in June. Their letter said to come for orientation in August. The small inheritance from my grandfather was just a start. But he had given greater gifts. "Find a way or make one," he had said along with, "Love life and live it fully." I had promised to rise and make my valley proud as well as to honor his legacy to the end of my days.

So here I sat in this Greyhound bus surrounded by dark night. It could be a bus to nowhere or I could suddenly awaken from a dream and still be lying in bed in Ottie's house. The driver just might announce that the destination of this bus is Hell and that those who didn't want to go there could exit in Knoxville. I sat bolt upright just as the bus pulled into the station in Knoxville. Passengers jostled each other as they hurriedly exited the bus.

Descending from the bus at the station in Knoxville, I walked past a Salvation Army Band that stood on the platform belting out a heartfelt song:

"I am bound for the Promised Land,

I am bound for the Promised Land.

Oh, who will come and go with me

I am bound for the Promised Land."

I wanted to tell these musicians that theirs is a false hope. There is no Promised Land. Nothing is ever promised to us, and if it is, it is inherently false. Promises are not reality. Promises are hope and hope can stifle accomplishment. Making good decisions in present time is what it takes to develop an individual's life and one reaches goals by consistent actions and application. I was willing to take risks. That is the reason that I was riding northward on this Greyhound bus. The painful experiences of growing up in Ottie's world were driving me to go somewhere else to do something other than make moonshine with my life. Life could not possibly be more difficult at Berea than where I had already been. Kentucky would be no Promised Land. But it was a place where I could start over.

A NEW FAMILY

It came as a great shock to me to learn that all the seats on the bus from Knoxville to Berea were already filled.

"You can wait for a later bus," the driver informed me. "It will be a six-hour layover and you will get to your destination tomorrow evening. Or you can stand up in the aisle and hope that a passenger might get off. I'll let you decide."

I paced along the loading platform of the station, alternately staring at the bus and the waiting room. My world and my dreams were moving in slow motion. My exit from Ottie's world had come to a temporary halt.

"No seat on the bus," I heard myself say out loud. "But I have a ticket."

In order not to lose money, the Greyhound Company often oversold its seats, casting unlucky passengers like me out of sequence. Their philosophy implied that another bus would be along shortly. So what was the problem?

Disappointed, I moped around the waiting room. After a while, I sat down on one of the heavy, brown oak benches provided for travelers. Did I want to loiter around this place for six hours? This bench was an uncomfortable piece of furniture not suitable as a place to sit on or to sleep. The room was quite noisy with people talking, porters and workers tossing heavy luggage everywhere, and passengers constantly opening and closing the main door. The lady behind the ticket counter droned out endless departures and arrivals in a nasal voice...."Coach to Nashville boarding on Track 5.... Arrival from Asheville on time.... The Bus from Birmingham to Cincinnati is running late." The stale air, smelling of tobacco smoke and unkempt bodies, nauseated me.

The woman's nasal voice blared out, "Last call for bus to Cincinnati with stops in Jellico, Williamsburg, Corbin, London, and Berea. Please board now." I had never heard of these places and her calling them in unison made me nervous. I would have to pass through them to my destination.

I quickly made up my mind. I ran through the glass doors leading to the departure platforms toward the Cincinnati bus and yelled to the driver, "Sir, I'll stand up on the bus." I would be standing up on this bus for eight straight hours. Several more passengers were standing in the aisle with me. All seats were taken and some even had two people stuffed in one seat. No black people rode this bus for they had already been dispossessed of their seats earlier in Birmingham. In this era, black people had to relinquish their seats if a white person needed to sit. I found it amusing that I was standing at the back of a bus headed northward.

Out on the bus platform strife broke out. A frumpy black woman with streaks of gray showing in her hair came storming through the glass doors on to the loading dock. She wore a floral dress, made of cheap cloth, which showed wrinkles from her sitting a long time on benches in waiting rooms. A straw hat dangled on her shoulders where it was held loosely with a string tied around her neck. She charged into the line of people still waiting to board the bus to claim what standing room remained. She pushed roughly through the line of passengers and confronted the driver of the bus.

"Sir," she yelled in a pleading voice, "I've got to get on this bus!"

"So has everybody else in this line, lady," he snarled at her. "There's not enough room for those in front of you, much less for a colored person like you. You have no privilege here."

"You don't understand, Sir. I have got to get to Cincinnati. My daughter is sick and in the hospital there. This may be my last chance to see her alive."

"We all have problems, woman, and your issues are the least of mine. All whites have to have a place on this bus before you can even be considered. So get to the back of the line!" he ordered.

"Oh, please, driver, won't you have some mercy? I can't get there any other way. I have my ticket. I've paid to ride this bus," she pled her case.

Impulsively, I walked back to the bus door and started to get off, but the driver stopped me. "Stay on the bus!" he ordered. "I decide who rides my bus. Even if you get off, this woman will not get on. I have to take care of all the white riders first."

The driver ushered the remaining white riders on to the bus, took his seat, and closed the doors. The black lady pounded on the closed doors beseeching the driver to let her on.

"Get away from the door," he yelled. "I'm pulling the bus away from the dock."

He coldly drove away leaving the distraught woman lying on the loading dock where she had collapsed. "My baby, my poor baby," she wailed as we drove away into the night.

This brutal experience left me so stunned and weak that I had to hold on dearly to the overhead racks with both hands. I spread my legs so that my feet pushed up against the seats where they fastened to the floor in order to keep me from falling. It is hard to hold one's arms over one's head for a long time. The bus shook and swayed as it hit potholes and bumps along the roadway. My arms began to ache from the stress of being held upward and my thighs began to cramp.

What I had just witnessed made me sick to my stomach. I had just witnessed the effects of racism first hand. In all my life, I had not known any black people. None had lived in my valley and only a few had been allowed to even work there. I had only seen black people from a distance or when they walked past me on a city bus to take their seats at the back. I knew nothing about black people. I had only associated with whites my entire life.

What had just happened on the loading platform in Knoxville, however, was wrong and the hurt that I felt for that poor woman proved it. I had wanted to get off the bus, but the driver showed me that my action would make no difference. We had all been chained to a way of thinking and acting and the hearts of every person on that bus were devoid of compassion because of it. Social conventions took precedence over the biblical teaching to "Love thy neighbor as thyself" unless, of course, they were black.

This incident had burned itself into my memory and the effects of my seeing it in person began to make me think about who I am and why I am supposed to dislike people of other races. I could no longer excuse my upbringing or my actions. I now had to be accountable. I would give this incident much thought in the coming months.

When the bus pulled into Jellico, no one got off nor did anyone exit in Corbin. These passengers were hard-core travelers going to the end of the line.

My body became more and more weary. One man saw that I was about to fall asleep while standing up and he offered me his seat for a half hour. I thanked him graciously and slid into a comfortable position in his seat where I quickly fell asleep.

My mind wandered back to scenes of youth. I was swimming at the Mill Shoals with Kenneth and Melvin. We took one of Mr. Ingle's watermelons from the field and smashed it on the rocks in the creek and devoured the succulent flesh inside. We spat the black seeds with our mouths and tongues as far down the creek as we could. These were the sweet, happy, halcyon days of summers long past.

I saw myself walking home alone after dark from the Suburban Coach bus stop. Tall, dark pine trees lined the roadway, forming a foreboding gauntlet through which I had to pass. Fear of what may lie among the trees brought goose bumps to my arms. I was afraid of this road and this darkness. I began running and did not stop until I could see the lights shining from Bea's house.

I saw Ottie, Gertie, Justine, Callie, and me walking to church on a bright Sunday morning. The road was filled with dust. Our bodies formed silhouettes against the red clay. I walked ahead of the rest asserting my budding independence. My sisters looked like statues marching along toward Heaven. I longed to go back and walk this road once more with them for, at that moment, I had felt a strong sense of family, of belonging.

In my mind I looked southward from McDowell Church toward Burkemont Mountain. I took flight over the soybean fields, Silver Creek, over the roof of Melvin's house to a point where I could see the rusted tin covering Ottie's house. Below, Ottie looked like a tiny dot as she stooped washing clothes along the stream at the foot of a hill.

A hand tapped me gently on the shoulder and a soft voice said to me, "Your half hour is up." I returned the man's seat and resumed my uncomfortable perch between luggage racks and the floor. It was half past midnight.

The movement of the bus along the two-lane highway became hypnotic. It rocked back and forth as the road dipped in and out of the small hills and valleys. I leaned forward on the downward slant and backward as the bus climbed once more. On deep curves my body slid to one side then rocked back to the other. My aching hands held on tenaciously to the luggage racks like eagle talons grasping tree branches to keep the bird from falling. I moved in and out of a light sleep until the bus would make a sudden jolt, throwing me roughly across sleeping passengers in seats below me. Some growled at me quite rudely suggesting that I go somewhere and find a seat.

Around three o'clock in the morning, I was done for. My body was so fatigued that I had no more strength to stand. I went to the restroom, locked the door, and I sat on the commode. Once again, the rocking, rolling, riding motion lulled me to sleep. Passengers wanted to use the facilities and so they pounded on the door with their fists. I awakened with a jolt. This time I sat down in the aisle and leaned my head against a seat rest. Sometime during the night, I stretched out in the middle of the aisle.

When morning broke, the bus was in Mt. Vernon. I was in Kentucky. Signs reading "Berea crafts" and "Boone Tavern Hotel" began to appear on billboards. The land outside was different, too. Instead of the Blue Ridge Mountains, low-lying knobs formed of shale rock where inland seas roamed millions of years ago, marked the skyline. Some poverty was visible along each side of the highway. Shacks made of cheap wood and tarpaper ran along the gullies and knobs. Then atop one knob there stood a majestic mansion built by a family that had hit luck in horse racing. Kentucky was a land of stark contrasts and it would be my home for the next eight years.

Now, I was the only passenger left standing in the aisle. The bus came alive with the nasal clacking speech of the Kentucky folk waking up and wondering out loud when the bus would make it to their destinations in Richmond, Lexington, and Cynthiana. I really felt out of place. I imagined myself returning home speaking English with the accent I was hearing. I wondered, too, how I sounded to these people, because I spoke a form of old Shakespearian English from the Carolina hills. Would the people in Berea talk like them or would they be a collection of Yankees speaking an educational brogue?

Architecture along the way made me feel as if I were traveling in a foreign country. Each small town had built a unique courthouse in its middle forcing traffic to circle around it. They were very attractive. Many houses were built in federal style. I thought that Stephen Collins Foster might appear on one of their elegant porches and belt out a rendition of "My Old Kentucky Home." My body was so wracked with fatigue that my perception was probably flawed. I ached, oh how I ached!

When the Berea College campus came into view, my heart soared. The bus moved slowly along highway 25, and I strained to see the regal buildings lining each side of the road. The bus passed by the art building, the music building, the president's home, Phelps Stokes Chapel, Lincoln Hall, Fairchild Dorm, and the stately Boone Tavern Hotel complex that formed the heart of the campus. Each building was marked with a sign painted in blue and white. Giant trees formed a lush, green canopy above the buildings and dozens of sidewalks danced away in all directions.

The bus stopped near the college bookstore, and I heard the driver call out "Berea College." My nightmare journey had ended. On exhausted leg muscles, I staggered down the aisle and stepped off the bus onto Kentucky soil. Like monarchs of old, I wanted to bend down and kiss the earth, but I would not have been able to get up again because of fatigue. The bus driver set my suitcase on the curb and closed the compartment door with a bang. The bright morning sun stung my tired eyes.

"Are there any Berea College students in this group?" a kind voice asked. A young man stood there looking at me. He wore a name tag reading "Dave."

My thoughts raced: "Am I to answer this question in the affirmative? Do I have a right to be here with so few dollars in my pocket? Do I even have a right to a superior education?"

Exhaustion and fear drained me of my strength and delirium seized my mind as I collapsed on to the street curb. The world became a swirl of movement and colors. In my delirium, I saw my mother, Ottie, hovering over me just as she had done at the incident with the milk at Devil's Creek fork.

"Stay home! Get a job at the Carbon Plant! Give me some money!" she had railed at me. "Think that you can go to college, do you, you little shit? I won't let that happen!"

In my hallucination, I saw my mother begin to tear down all the buildings on campus. She flipped the Greyhound bus over on its side and began disassembling the windows of Boone Tavern Hotel. As Ottie wrought her havoc, a professor dressed in academic robes strolled by, looked directly at me and said, "Roll up the windows of the bus quickly. If you don't, someone may come along and throw a Berea diploma into each window."

By the time I had fully regained consciousness, Dave had lifted me under his arm and had placed me in a chair on the porch of Boone Tavern Hotel. Another helper had placed a coke and a sandwich in my hand.

"Are you feeling better now?" Dave asked.

In the distance, the chimes of the Phelps-Stokes Chapel began to ring out the hour. Its notes rang sweetly across the breeze bringing the whole campus to pause and listen. I would later learn that the chimes played these words:

"Lord, in this hour, be thou our guide, That by thy power, no foot may slide."

Ottie's voice rang through my head. "You will always be mine! Don't you dare try to get above your 'raisin'." I yelled loudly, "Can't I ever get away from you?"

"Why do you want to get away from us?" Dave enquired.

"Not you, Dave, my damn mother," I muttered looking up into his puzzled face.

FIND A WAY OR MAKE ONE

When I had regained my equilibrium, Dave led me across campus to my new dorm. I walked on unsteady legs under the canopy of huge oak trees with their thick green leaves casting cool shadows on the ground. Stately buildings in architectural styles of bygone years stood close to each other. The air smelled of summer, of new-mown grass, and warm sunshine. My eyelids drooped from lack of sleep and I looked out on my new world through a haze.

Dave led me to room 106 in Pearsons Hall which would be my home for the freshman year. Pearsons was an old, square, building whose dark bricks showed age. It was an ugly building with a front porch that looked as if it had been built as an afterthought. We pushed through a heavy, windowless door into a short hallway that contained just seven rooms. I learned later that Pearsons was the optimal dorm for freshmen and the first floor where I lived was choice real estate.

"I'm so exhausted, Dave. I've got to go to sleep right now," I told him, barely able to form the words.

"I'll get linens for your bed, a meal ticket, and a schedule of activities for orientation," Dave added. Then he left me.

I wearily climbed to the top bunk of the bed and fell asleep in my street clothes. It was not a deep sleep and lasted no more than two hours. My body jerked awake as my eyes focused on the ceiling not two feet above my face.

"What am I doing here?" I asked myself out loud. I did not feel that I had a right to be in college. Nothing in my life thus far had prepared me to feel equal to people around me. My muscles were so weary that they could hardly move on the mattress. I lay there immobile as my mind reviewed the heavy journey that had brought me northward to Kentucky. All my senses were dulled from my struggle. Nevertheless, I had to get up and talk to the Dean of Men to see if I could make a way to study at Berea. I climbed slowly to the floor, took a shower, dressed, and headed out of Pearsons Hall to find the office of the Dean of Men.

The sun was dipping slightly over the tree canopy when I descended the front steps of Pearsons Hall in search of the very man who held my future in his hands. Would he be a kind member of the Berea family like Dave, or would he exhibit the coldness of the Greyhound bus driver in Knoxville? What would I do if he turned me away? I hailed a student walking in my direction and asked him with apprehension, "Can you tell me, please, where the Dean of Men's office is?"

"You're almost there," he said in his nasal Kentucky accent. "It's in the Draper Building there to your right. When you go through the door, turn left. It's the first room."

"Thanks," I said in turn.

The design of the Draper Building was a copy of Independence Hall in Philadelphia. Its spire, the tallest on campus, pointed upward to a summer blue sky filled with white puffy clouds. I was about to commit to a union of students going back a hundred years, a union of mountain students marching up from poverty to respectability or I was on the verge of the greatest rejection of my life. Even the heavy doors of Draper resisted opening.

The hall inside was polished granite, so shiny and clean that one could eat off it. This polish was a testimony to the efficiency and standards of the Berea labor program. Above the first door to the left, was a large, professionally-lettered sign reading "Dean of Men." I walked up and down in front of the door, afraid to go inside. A condemned man could not have felt more angst. I rubbed my fingers together in a nervous gesture and I felt sick on my stomach. I could not stifle my yawning.

A lady stuck her head out the door and said, "May I help you?"

"The dean, the dean...," I stammered pointing my finger toward the sign hanging above the door. "Need to, want to...." I attempted to put together a coherent sentence.

"Do you want to see Dean Orwig?" she asked me directly, helping to salvage some of my dignity.

"Yes," I finally spat out the reply.

"Come on in. He won't bite you," she laughed.

I began to relax a little.

The lady disappeared through a huge mahogany door into an inner sanctum where few people ventured, while I slumped down in a plush couch and fell back into a light sleep.

A deep, nice voice awakened me. It sounded like a theatrical voice of God. "What is your name, young man?"

"Fred Epeley," I answered through my foggy brain.

"I'm Dean Orwig. Welcome to Berea. Come into my office and tell me how I can help you."

These kind words and his demeanor impressed me, for rarely in my life had anyone asked to help me when I was growing up in Ottie's world. Everyone I had met so far was supporting me.

I walked into Dean Orwig's office. It was tastefully laid out with an oversized mahogany, Henredon desk covered with books, pens, application papers, and letters, all disorganized. Reams of books lined the shelves along the wall behind his desk. A row of double windows arched upward from the floor to the ceiling. Heavy, red-velvet curtains draped around them. I sat once again in a plush, leather armchair that almost swallowed my tired body.

"You're a freshman, is that right?" Dr. Orwig asked me.

"Yes, sir, I just got off the Greyhound bus two hours ago and have had no sleep."

"Have you been to your dorm yet?" he continued.

"For a few minutes," I replied.

"What is the purpose of the visit with me?" he finally got to the question.

"You see, sir, I am not here to beg, nor am I asking for charity, although I am a charity case. I don't have enough money to pay my expenses for the semester, much less the entire year."

"Do you have any money at all?" he enquired.

"I have $300 my grandfather bequeathed me when he died. Sir, I read in the school catalogue that Berea does not turn away qualified students for lack of money. I'm obviously qualified for I have this acceptance letter for the class of 1965 here in my pocket. But I have no money."

"Tell me about your aspirations, Mr. Epeley," Dr. Orwig inquired with interest. "Why are you here?"

"I want to leave forever my mother Ottie's world filled with want, lack, and poverty. I want to establish a new life of my own choosing. I want to awaken each morning knowing that I will have adequate food. I want to open my mind to learn all I can about all that is. I never again want to be ashamed of who I am or what my circumstances may be. I've just made a tough journey from North Carolina to this new place." I lowered my head and stared at the floor.

Dr. Orwig looked away toward the huge windows on the opposite side of his office. Then he got up and walked to the windows, where he could stare out at the centuries old oaks outside. For a moment he seemed to be in a reverie, as if he was, himself, reviewing some event in his life. Turning, he walked back and said to me, "Mr. Epeley, please stand up." I felt then and there that I had failed and he was set to usher me out of his office.

"Look, Mr. Epeley, you and I are about the same physical height. We stand eye to eye. Today, however, I judge you to be a giant of a man. You have the courage to speak up for yourself. You have told me of your dreams and plans. There is no doubt in my mind that you will go as far in life as you choose. You are exactly the type of student that we want to come to Berea. Therefore, I'm providing for you a voucher for all expenses for the first semester. If you will visit my office each month, I'll provide for your personal needs too."

It was so simple. He left me standing like a granite statue in the middle of the room. He went to his desk where he wrote out the vouchers, and then he returned and shook my hand. I barely remember beyond that moment. I heard him say to his secretary, "Nancy, please welcome Mr. Epeley to our Berea family and see that he lacks for nothing."

I walked out of the Draper Building into the approaching evening. The smell of freshly-mowed grass blew on the cool wind from the Pinnacle. I rode on an air of disbelief. I sat down on a stone bench and breathed deeply of the history of the stately buildings surrounding me. These ancient trees and ivy-covered halls seemed to smile. I relaxed for the first time since leaving Ottie's house.

I wondered what Ottie had felt when she had returned from Bea's house and had realized that I was gone forever. Had I left no trace behind? Did my sisters have empty hearts now that I had gone? Did anyone miss me? Today, my old family had vanished and my new one had just begun.

I looked at the sky that was turning into evening. I had not realized that the Dean and I had spoken for a long time, for now a few stars were revealing themselves above the distant pinnacles. I felt so alone. My thoughts turned to my grandfather, Elkanah Smith, the man who had pushed me forward to this moment. I murmured softly out loud, "This is a new beginning. Help me, Granddad. Help me to rise up to make my family and my valley proud!"

Elkanah (Canie) Smith
Though illiterate, this proud mountain man, my grandfather,
urged me to get an education.

THE FIRST DAY

I did not sleep deeply that first night at Berea. I tossed and turned in my bed as the chimes of Phelps Stokes Chapel rang every fifteen minutes. Students walked up and down the hallway of the dorm going to the restroom or getting a coke from the machine in the lobby. Quarters jingled down the machine slot and metal cans clank as they fell down to the bottom where thirsty students retrieved them. One electric light bulb buzzed like an angry hornet ready to sting. At five o'clock in the morning, a distant train made a mad dash down its tracks on the outskirts of town. It roared like an in-coming tornado. The tracks ran beyond the college pond less than a mile away. My roommate had not yet come to sleep on the bottom bunk which I had left for him. Roommates for other students in our dorm kept arriving all night long, though. After the train had zipped past, then I fell asleep.

It was past eight o'clock in the morning when the door to my room flew open, and in walked a person who would challenge all my perceptions of life. His name was Bashir, he was an Arab, he was not American, and he was not white. He was very noisy. He plopped his suitcase heavily on the wooden floor and its noise made my head hurt. He pushed open the only window in the room with a bang and then slammed the door shut behind him.

"Were you raised in a barn?" I yelled out with great irritation. "Be a little more respectful. I'm trying to get a little sleep here."

"I was raised in Palestine, not a barn," he smiled through a row of perfectly white teeth.

"Palestine, Kentucky?" I asked. I knew there had to be one. There was a London and a Paris. There just had to be a place in the state named Palestine.

"No. Palestine is in the Middle East. It is a part of the modern state of Israel," he beamed with pride. "Who are you?"

"A very tired, sleepy Fred," I muttered.

Without warning and with great strength, he rolled me up tightly in my bed sheet, set me down on my feet on the floor, and belted out, "Well, Fred, let's go have some breakfast!"

This roommate had his nerve to be so casual about noise making. But I did not suspect at that moment that we would be friends for life. What chutzpah, what nerve, how full of life he seemed.

As we strolled across campus to the Student Union Building where the cafeteria was located, I began to ask questions about my roommate.

"Do you have a last name or is everyone in Palestine named Bashir?" I asked sarcastically.

"That's the only name we could think of," he laughed. "It's about like the name Smith here. My last name is Khalil and it is a very common name in Arabic," he told me.

"Fred Eli Epeley," I proudly introduced myself. "Fred is from the German word 'Friede' which means 'peace.' 'Epeley' is from the German 'Apfele' which means 'little apples.'"

"In Arabic your name 'Eli' is one word for 'God,'" he informed me. "So you are Peace God Little Apples." He found his own joke amusing. He burst out in fits of laughter.

"And you are Bashir Khalil, the Sheik of Araby. Why aren't you wearing a turban around your head with a sheet wrapped around your shoulders?" I teased him.

"In Palestine, we were civilized while you mountain people were running around over here with your asses painted blue. Remember, your Jesus lived where I did."

"You mentioned the name 'Smith' a moment ago. My mother was a Smith. My grandfather was a Smith. My great-grandfather was a Smith. And God himself has the last name Smith. God Smith. Jesus Smith. Mary Smith. Ha, ha, ha, ha, ha, ha! My grandmother's real name was Mary Smith." I couldn't stop laughing at my own joke.

"Do you know where Palestine is?" he asked me outright.

"We people from the hills are isolated, but we are not ignorant. I can read a map. Palestine is not a real country today. It is a concept. Palestinian people are spread out over Israel and Jordan."

"It existed up until 1948 when the Jews took over the land and created the modern state of Israel," he spoke with authority.

"The Jews needed a homeland, too," I foolishly interjected.

Bashir stopped in the middle of the sidewalk. He lifted his shirt above his shoulders and pointed to his abdomen which was covered in horrible scars. His left arm was missing half the muscle from the elbow to his wrist. A crowd of curious students gathered around listening to our conversation.

"Jewish soldiers did this. They attacked our home in the middle of the night and killed my mother, my father, and eight of my brothers and sisters. I survived by pretending to be dead. So please don't talk to me about a Jewish homeland. They suffered a holocaust, but they have inflicted one on me and my family."

The little group of students stood silently by, their faces flushed red from hearing his story. They were gaining a new perspective of history told from a personal experience. All the hardships of our lives paled when compared to Bashir's experience.

He left the group and walked alone toward the cafeteria. He was a sad picture of a sad and lonely man who, like us, was searching for a family. I ran after him and placed my arm around his waist. Several students joined me and we locked our arms around each other. We walked in this manner all the way to the dining hall. That night a fraternity of students formed deep bonds of friendship: Bashir Khalil, Fred Epeley, Wayne Hambright, John Vorhees, and Alfred James.

After dinner, all freshmen had to report to classrooms in Draper Hall for testing.

"Oh, my God," I thought. "I've been here just one day and they are already giving a test. What is this?"

I asked students around me. Upperclassmen in charge of testing explained that as its policy, Berea tested all freshmen in grammar, vocabulary, history, and math to determine if they were prepared for college level work. When I heard the word "math," I went totally dyslexic. I couldn't even remember my name. Math had been my curse since the third grade when I had failed to master reading problems. Now this!

I sailed through the vocabulary, grammar and history, but when I opened the cover sheet on the math test, I lost my brain.

There was no lack of experience with math since I had studied two years of algebra in high school and one year of geometry. Math made my brain sick and I regurgitated any and all formulas. Above and beyond being able to count my money, what value did all this hocus-pocus have? I never intended to build a pyramid. To me, the shortest distance between two points was the fresh grass I could walk across to get there. I might be a square in a circle, but I did not care if anyone ever squared a circle. Square of the hypotenuse? Get out of here! X+Y=baloney! If one train left Timbuktu with twenty passengers smoking weed and another one left Antarctica with six penguins dipping snuff, how long would it take everyone on both trains to get high??????? I wanted to tell them all what they could do with their square roots. Pi was something I ate with fresh coffee. E=mc or Irritation=Math Class. I could have studied math until Jesus came back and not have retained a damn thing, and I well knew it.

Results of said tests appeared in our post office boxes the next day just before we went to register for classes for the fall semester. I did well on grammar, vocabulary, and history. Across the math card there stood a gigantic red "F" with colors running down the page. In choice vocabulary words that I had just sailed through on the test, I screamed at my fate: "Do not calculate an increase in your juvenile poultry until the process of incubation has fully materialized."

I had to take two semesters, a whole year, of basic math with no credit. I felt like one of Berea's dumb students. My grade counted toward my average and quality points. It put me a year behind in my studies. Around me stood stunned students who had received news that they had to take four basic courses. Those who failed all the tests went to the back of the room to be sent home. If the brilliant kids that came to Berea were in this predicament, what must the surrounding colleges and universities be like? At that point, I began to take Berea academics very seriously. Many of us were returning to high school, to square one.

The following morning I walked alone to the cafeteria to breakfast. I was extremely hungry. I walked down the two sets of stairs into the dining room, turned left, picked up a tray, and started through the line.

Someone touched me firmly on the shoulder. Turning my eyes to the left, I spied three gnarled, wrinkled fingers with fingernails painted crimson red. Three expensive diamond rings swirled around the fingers implying they were still living flesh. I looked up into the face of what was surely a cartoon character out of a comic book. It was Mrs. Van Cleaveron, the dining room hostess. Her body was so old that, had I blown a kiss at her, her flesh would have melted and faded away. She looked strangely elegant in her expensive blue dress that was more suited to a cocktail lounge. Daily she wore a lace handkerchief pinned to her left side and in it there was an expensive brooch. At some stage of her life, she had most likely been somebody important, but now she was wasting away watching Berea students chomping food and struggling with their manners. She pounced on any student who made a mistake in etiquette or who did not follow the rules of the dining room.

"You did not show your meal card to the checker," she snarled at me through crooked lips painted slightly off target.

"What?" I stammered.

"You can't come into my dining room without showing the checker your meal ticket," she hissed at me. "Take off your cap and dress up a little better when you come back tomorrow." (She assumed that I had something better to wear.)

"I remember his number from yesterday," the checker told her. He pretended to write something across the bottom of his check sheet. I would discover that Berea students covered for each other in situations like this one.

"I'll be watching you, mister," Mrs. Van Cleaveron warned me. She meant it, too.

I found Wayne Hambright and John Vorhees and ate my meal comfortably with them. They were surprised that I had failed math tests. Wayne was so brilliant that he was signing up for calculus the first semester. That's a real bummer.

"What does your schedule look like, Fred?" Wayne wanted to know.

"French, Composition, P.E., World History, and basic math," I told him.

All freshmen were required to take composition, P.E., world history, and one elective. Since French would be my major, I signed up for it. Dr. Lumlum, department chairman, laughed when I suggested taking French 201 thereby skipping French 101.

"Not without taking a test in French," she snarled. "High school French does not count in our department. You have to prove yourself," she trumpeted.

Did a student have to take a test in order to defecate in this place?

"Well, Sacrebleu !" the thought ran through my mind.

Upon returning the results of my French test the next day, Dr. Lumlum cackled with laughter. "In addition to your piety, you are going to need a little bit of wit at this place. You flat out failed the French exam. French 101 is for you, buster."

This woman held a PhD in Latin, not French. Her studies were tantamount to going into a cemetery and rearranging old bones. How could a department chair rejoice in a student's failure?? I took an immediate dislike for her, a dislike that would explode two years later and catapult me out of the foreign language department.

Good Lord, this woman was department chair of foreign language studies and I would be in it for four long years with her. Maybe I could change my major to math! I regret terribly that I did not major in Hotel Management. I could have gone directly to France and learned the language in situ rather than endure this insufferable woman.

Nothing had prepared me for the peculiarities of some faculty or for the inanity of workers who populated various activities on campus. After four years on this campus, would I depart looking and acting like some of these people that I was meeting? Some of them made Ottie's world look classy.

I trudged back to my dorm passing a group of students on the porch having a jam session. They were discussing everything from the building of the pyramids to the second coming of Christ. I plunged through the group and entered the heavy metal door. Back in my room, I saw that Bashir was writing letters in Arabic to friends back in Palestine. I studied him carefully. He certainly was not a white man. People where I came from would not approve of my living with a person who was not white. He was such a nice person that I never noticed a difference in our skin colors. We became very close. He was just a good human being named Bashir.

"I guess I'm going back to square one in math," I muttered to him.

"You are not square," he laughed, "You are nice."

In time, Bashir would master the English language. I, on the other hand, would never master the art of math. But I would overcome barriers to loving and respecting him and Berea would expunge my backwardness and drive me to see that although I had left Ottie's world, in reality, I had become Ottie.

ALMA MATER TRUE

The chimes of Phelps-Stokes Chapel were ringing the three o'clock hour when I arrived at the front door of the building. As I entered, a college student worker handed me a program and a booklet containing all the rules freshmen were expected to follow. On the bottom of the inside page of the program, there was a perforated line and a one-inch space where I would sign my name at the end of the session. He instructed me to tear off this piece of paper with my name on it and return it to the worker before leaving the chapel. On my program the young man initialed the letter T in red ink.

"You are tardy for orientation," he smiled at me. "The college checks attendance at all sessions and you have to be on time. Dean Orwig will call this to your attention."

Berea was going to be tough on all fronts.

As I entered the chapel, over five hundred freshmen rose to sing the Alma Mater, "Berea Beloved." They had been practicing the song before my arrival and some were well on the way to mastering it. I walked down the main aisle and seated myself half way to the speaker's podium. I wondered why no one else was seated downstairs. Students in the balcony hissed and booed at me and motioned to the usher at the back. The usher explained to me that only seniors could sit in the downstairs middle section of the building. I wondered why I was sitting on the lower level by myself. My face turned crimson red as the student ushered me back down the aisle, up the stairs to the second level, where he seated me next to an attractive black girl who was wearing a light blue dress. Everyone in the freshman class had seen my mistake and so, I would forever be known on campus as the "would-be senior."

The girl smiled at me and whispered, "If that is the worst mistake you make at Berea, you are going to do fine." She went back to singing the words to the Alma Mater in a lovely alto voice.

I looked out across the student body. It consisted of a group of students from all over our country and the world. There was my roommate, Bashir, smiling and singing with vigor, though his young life had already been broken by tragedy. There was a girl beside me, out of the hills of West Virginia, a white woman who was rising above the situation of the coal fields and discrimination in her own state. I saw students with faces of hope. I saw students who were already homesick. As difficult as their lives had been, their homes were still home. I saw faces etched with a determination to succeed, for many knew Berea was their only chance.

This band of freshmen brothers and sisters, this varied group from towns and hills and hollows of Appalachia, these forgotten people were preparing to meet the world on their terms. In a few short years, many would have the title "Dr." in front of their names. Their talents would be a sweet perfume that would leave every place they touched more pleasant. They would not just live in their communities of the future, they would rule them.

I began to sing the school song off key.

"Berea, Berea Beloved, where friendships are formed fast and true, and all men stand shoulder to shoulder as brothers beneath white and blue." (Coble and Johnston)

I looked down on the sheet music and noticed that Raymond Coble '29 and Wilfred P. Johnston '29 were the authors of the music and words to the Alma Mater. They had sat in this very building some thirty-one years before me. Some fond memory at Berea had moved their hearts to pour out in song their feelings so that other students would sing her praises forevermore.

In this place and with these people, I could perhaps find a new beginning. Dr. Orwig had been supportive. My roommate Bashir reminded me of my brother Willard Worth. Wayne, Alfred, and John showed signs of interest in being my friends. Dr. Lumlum, who chaired my department where I would spend four years studying, was akin to Mrs. Lindendahl in Ottie's world. Mrs. Van Cleaveron intended to kill me on sight, I was sure. Mr. Rules and Regulations would grant no amnesty to any student. Four hundred ninety-eight students in this assembly had just scowled at me when I came in late. Did I stand a chance with them?

The singing continued: "Thy memory be enshrined in every heart, thy spirit be of us a part, and though we wander far away, thy chimes shall ring for us each day."

Ironically, in the steeple high above us, the Phelps-Stokes chimes rang out the half hour. People stopped singing and a hush fell over the auditorium. It seemed as if the music of the chimes was implanting itself along with the school song into every heart there. Mr. Holvey, the choir director, who was teaching us the song, flashed his wonderful Norwegian smile, and quipped, "You will remember these chimes long after the words to our school song have faded from your memory."

Now about these infernal chimes. I could expect to hear them play four times an hour every day, seven days a week, nine months out of the year for four straight years. At exactly fifteen minutes after the hour, the tower clanged out music. About a year after first hearing them, I learned what they were saying. They were an exact copy of Big Ben in London.

Fifteen minutes after the hour: Lord in this hour

Thirty minutes after the hour: Be thou our guide

On the three quarters hour: That by thy power

On the hour: No foot may slide

Then the clock would chime the hour, whatever it may be.

Dong! Dong! Dong! Dong! Dong!

We students took up the Alma Mater again with renewed vigor and purpose.

Dr. Holvey waved good-bye as he left the stage, leaving all of us hoping that someday he would be our teacher.

A dean of the college walked up to the podium and held up a huge sign reading, "Rules and Regulations of Berea College." We all laughed at his sense of humor. But he had no sense of humor. A short, wiry little man, he stood about five feet five in stocking feet. He wore a razor-line moustache across his upper lip and he had back-combed, light brown hair that tended to droop. His beady eyes looked out through eyebrows that dropped down almost covering the corners of his eyes. He was the enforcer of college rules. When the president or board of directors wished to punish someone or deliver bad news, it was he that was the bearer of bad news. A vision of Barney Fife floated through my brain.

"Please refer to your handbook as I present the more important rules that you will follow while you are here," he said in a high, crackling voice. "These rules and regulations are not up for debate or question. Berea is a private school which follows its own dictates. Memorize this booklet and check yourself daily to make sure that you are not guilty of infractions:

(I could just imagine myself getting up each morning, taking a shower, shaving, then referring to the rules booklet to make sure that I was in compliance.)

1. You are a student here by authorization of the board. For every student accepted here, one hundred are turned away. Remember that. If you do not behave properly, we can easily replace you.

2. You will receive liberal arts, Christian education here. Assembly on Wednesdays and Sundays is mandatory as is attendance in all classes. (You will have to drag this horse to drink in that water because he won't. You will have to drown the horse.)

3. You must maintain a "C" average in academics to remain here. (At that time, a C at Berea was equal to the grade of A at most colleges.)

4. Our student body is diverse. Respect all students and faculty regardless of race, sex, or gender. (God, did they have sex at Berea???? Weren't sex and gender the same thing? Maybe they were not here. My gender was male, sex had not yet happened!)

5. There is a $5 dollar charge for each flower that you pick on campus.

(Uproarious laughter)

(I had horrible visions of Berea students, armed with clubs, ravaging the campus, leaving it devoid of marigolds, zinnias, petunias, and snap dragons. You can touch my peaches, baby, but you better not pluck my plums!)

6. Every student must work two hours per day. You cannot be absent from your assigned work. Your pay is $.06 per hour. (I figured that I might be a millionaire in about ten thousand years.)

(Uproarious laughter)

7. You do not choose your work assignment as a freshman. It is assigned to you. (In my four years at Berea I got hired and fired by just about every department on campus.)

(Groans)

8. No Bermuda shorts allowed on campus, no lewd dancing, and women must be in their dorms by 9:30 daily." (I danced every day in the snack bar. Any dancing at Berea was considered lewd. The men did not care if the girls were locked up early because so many of the men were gay anyway.)

(Howls of anguish)

Mr. Rules and Regulations left the stage. In their minds, many of the students were already wearing Bermuda shorts, dancing lewdly, and some vowed to pick every flower on campus.

The Alumni President at the time stepped up to the platform and told a joke to relieve pressure that a discussion of rules invariably brought out with students:

"There was once a Berea student who could never get to class on time. Out of breath, she ran into philosophy class one day where students were already taking a pop quiz. The philosophy teacher called them his "little quiz-zicals." She plopped down in her desk, picked up his pop test, and asked, ' What is this??' 'It is one of his quiz-zicals.' Dismayed and not realizing what she was saying, she burst out, 'If this is one of his little quiz-zicals, I'd hate to see one of his little test-icles.'"

Phelps-Stokes Chapel rocked in waves of student laughter. We were grateful for his sense of humor and his willingness to share it with us. He waited patiently, letting us savor the lighter side of Berea.

"My task is to help you understand the history of the founding of Berea College. There is an outline of the history in the back of the rules book. Please read it and learn it thoroughly. At any time, in any class, a professor may test you on both the alma mater and any aspect of the history of Berea. The test will form part of the grade of the class in which it is given. Don't any of you be like the girl in the joke. Professors are not automatically compassionate. None I know will show you their quiz-zicals or test-icles." (Maybe a couple would).

(He was just a wonderful speaker. In honor of him, every student memorized "Berea Beloved" and studied the history of the school to perfection.)

"Please note these facts now: Berea College was founded in 1855 by John G. Fee on land donated by Cassius Clay. It was one of the first colleges in the South to accept black students. It practiced co-education based on the credo 'God hath made of one blood all nations of men.' The men and women who built this institution risked their lives in pursuit of their goals so that you could be present today. It behooves all of you to know their stories and to emulate what they did. You are now a part of this great school, of this neighborhood, this state, and this country. Carry yourselves, always, in a manner that shines a brilliant light on your own personal character and on our greater Berea family."

It was over. The Phelps-Stokes chimes rang the five o'clock hour. I tore the perforated piece from my program, signed my name, and gave it to an usher as I exited the building. The usher said to me, "We students help each other here at Berea. I am going to erase this tardy mark from your paper. My name is Clay. You will owe me a favor. I will call it in at some future time." He erased the red T and memorized my name.

The black lady with whom I had sat in the assembly, walked up to me and said, "I'm Chloe. Can we eat supper together today?"

"I'm Fred, the' I-can't-get-to-chapel-on-time guy.' Fred Epeley, the kid from North Carolina. I would love to chat over dinner and get acquainted."

"I'm Chloe Hinson from Tennessee. I hope they are serving steak and potatoes tonight."

"Fat chance," I laughed.

The prospect of Mrs. Van Cleaveron hovering over me in the dining hall made my stomach turn.

Chloe walked away sweetly singing, "Berea, Berea Beloved, where friendships are formed fast and true...."

I certainly hoped that her words would be true.

BUDDING FRIENDSHIP

Chloe was seated in a chair in the lobby of the Student Alumni Building waiting for me. I waved to her and she responded with a big smile as she extended her right hand in a warm handshake.

"Did you think I would not come?" I asked her out of curiosity.

"I knew you had to eat sometime," she joked. "We both look like fish out of water and I know that I could certainly use a friend, if only for dinner."

"I've met a couple of people in the last two days, but there has been little time to get acquainted with anyone," I said hopefully.

"Well, I've got your attention for the next hour," she laughed warmly, "unless you are capable of shoving food in your mouth for one solid hour without stopping. I really hope you are a talker."

"Hold on, Chloe, you might not even like me. I'm from the mountains of North Carolina. I have no manners, I have read few books (there were only two in our high school library), I shovel my food with my fork, I need a trough to eat out of, and I have to take one year of basic math because I failed my entrance test," I teased her. "Furthermore, I have never had a conversation with a person of color in my life."

"Well, Fred, I am from the hills of Tennessee from a family of six who live in a wooden shack with no inside toilet. I have never had a conversation with a person of color either, that is, of white color. You are the first white person I have met since leaving there, for no white people would live in my neck of the woods. I came a semester early because

I had to take English, basic math, and basic history before I could start college classes. You talk about feeling dumb! I'm not dumb. Schools in my town were that bad! Let's eat!"

"Are you looking forward to steak and mashed potatoes?" I teased her.

"It's meat loaf and mash potatoes tonight. I've already checked the menu," she remarked imitating a choking motion across her throat with her thumb and index finger.

"Would you please do me a favor, Chloe?" I asked with fear in my voice. "Would you peek down the stairs into the dining room and locate where a certain Mrs. Van Cleaveron is standing. That woman and I are already at war."

"What does she look like?" Chloe asked.

"She is a well-dressed, attractive, older lady with painted nails who scowls when she sees me."

Chloe disappeared down the steps leading into the dining room. I leaned forward stretching my neck as far as possible to see if Mrs. Van Cleaveron were in view. Suddenly Chloe came back in view and pointed with her index finger in the direction of the opposite dining room indicating that my adversary was over there. I quickly ran down the stairs, making sure to show my meal card number to the student checker. Then Chloe and I ducked into the serving line making ourselves as insignificant as possible.

Student workers, dressed in immaculate white coats with a red fringe, dipped food on to our plates. We placed our empty glasses in the milk machine, pushed the red button, and watched the glass fill with rich, white, creamy liquid. The dining room was all glass on the south side with a fantastic view of green fields stretching away to the knobs or pinnacles in the distance. These low-lying mountains had been formed millions of years ago by inland seas that had slowly deposited layer upon layer of silt until it had hardened into shale. Chloe and I chose a table that could seat four people. I sat facing the stairs descending into the dining room and she faced the back wall. The mountainous scenery presented itself to both of us. Chloe stared at me in wonder as I plowed headlong into the meat loaf and mashed potatoes.

"Don't you say grace before a meal?" she asked in a puzzled voice.

"I wouldn't know what god to pray to," I said, my mouth stuffed with food.

"Could I introduce you to my God of the Tennessee hills?" she asked as I continued to stuff my face.

"Just as long as he doesn't require snake handling as a worship requirement," I said through a mouthful of meatloaf.

She bowed her head and quietly said grace over her food. This concept of thanking God for what I had to do myself was incomprehensible to me. I could thank many people who had helped me get to Berea, but I didn't remember any certain god as being a part of it. God could have at least provided a seat for me on the bus from Knoxville to Berea. He could also have let the poor black woman board the bus in Knoxville, too.

"You are not a religious person, then," Chloe spoke with some disappointment.

"I'm a spiritual person," I explained. "Religious people annoy me with their platitudes and dogma that they use to excuse their discrimination against people who are different from them. I respect God; it is his fans I can't stand. I find your expression of faith to be a charming aspect of your character. Keep it. But it would not suit me.

Could I ask you a question that I have often pondered? How is it possible for black people to embrace Christianity for it was the Christians who bought and sold them into slavery? They found in their Bibles vindication for this dreadful act. Why didn't the slaves create their own god which would not embrace slavery?"

"It is the Christian teaching of love and forgiveness that appealed to the African slaves. That's all the slaves had. That's the only promise left for them. When I give thanks or pray, I'm addressing the highest belief in a loving and generous God. If white people misrepresented the Bible and God, then they must answer for it. So, you see yourself as different?" Chloe asked.

"I am different," I replied, "People view me as different. I don't fit in. My life in Ottie's world gave me unique experiences that do set me apart from people around me. From the time I was a young child, I saw ignorant people professing to worship God, yet they were mean, unkind, and gross hypocrites."

"You do know that the Dean emphasized that students get a liberal arts, Christian education at Berea and that we have to attend church lectures every Wednesday evening at Phelps Stokes? And two courses in Bible are required?" she reminded me.

"I can pick and choose my education. That is one way I am different. They will have to drag me kicking and screaming through those two required Bible courses. Besides, did you know that Moses and his group wandered forty years in the wilderness when they were only thirteen miles from the Promised Land?" I challenged her. "Couldn't they read a road map???"

Chloe took a bite of meat loaf on her spoon and deftly pushed it into her mouth using only the tip of the fork. As she ate silently, she scrutinized me with her sharp eyes. I knew that her astute mind was assessing whether or not she wanted to be my friend.

"It is better not to discuss people's tastes and their choice in colors," I explained. "I must add the word 'religion' because people never come to agreement about God and dogma. I'm a heathen. I can't be Christian. Love me that way."

My whole thought process went out the window as I saw the outline of Mrs. Van Cleaveron's body lurking among the tables opposite me. She looked like one of the water birds one sees wading in the shallows looking for food along the edge of the ocean. Instinctively, I knew that I was her prey. Chloe saw my reaction. In a heartbeat, Mrs. Van Cleaveron was standing beside our table, checking us for manners, dress, and probably lice. She said not a word. She stared at both of us with disapproval in her beady eyes. Then she walked away. I surmised that she did not approve. We could be brothers "beneath white and blue," but we had better not be any closer.

"Chloe," I said out loud, "do you realize that if people of my valley, people in my family, or anyone from Ottie's world knew that I was sitting in this dining hall with you, they would literally kill me? You are only the second person of another race that I have ever met in my lifetime. I met Rufus when I was five years old when my father had bought me a sandwich at Stan's Country Store. He was sweet and kind to me. My schools were all segregated. When I left home, there were signs above the bus station saying "Whites Only" and "Colored Only."

"Fred," she responded, "do you realize that if the people of my family back in Tennessee knew that I was eating supper with you, they would literally kill me, too? As your family and community did not allow us in it, we did not allow you in ours. Isn't it a small and terrible world from which we come?"

"My roommate is an Arab from Palestine. He has black skin and kinky hair. The only person who has reached out to me in friendship so far is you. What is going on here? It is evident that I am challenged to broaden my horizons. Should I pursue this friendship, my family and friends back home will disown me forever."

"My mother beat me unmercifully when she got drunk. Many times I ran away from home for days. The pain and sorrow of my life is legion. When I saw you come into Phelps-Stokes Chapel for orientation, so green, lost, bumbling like a fish out of water, I wanted to reach out to you, as I had wished someone would have reached out to me, to let you know that it was ok, that you were not a stupid kid, that you were not different. I want you to be my friend. We'll tell everyone that we are twins. Let them figure out how it happened."

Mrs. Van Cleaveron slunk back through our section of the dining room looking for the slightest of infractions so she could pounce. Looking at my plate, she snarled, "You didn't eat all your mashed potatoes."

Without a word Chloe scooped up the remainder of my potatoes and gobbled them down in one smooth motion. "Yes, he did," she smiled sweetly staring Mrs. Van Cleaveron down.

"Chloe, I have never been able to figure out why God is good to some people and very mean and nasty to others. Why was I not born into a wealthy family? Why weren't you? The two of us have been given (or chosen) a tough and painful road down which we travel. Why are the two of us not studying at Yale or Harvard? I am literally a charity case here at Berea. Where are God's abundance, love, generosity, and caring? Maybe giving you to me as a friend is worth infinitely more than these other things."

We placed our trays in the proper place and tripped lightly up the stairs to the lobby. As I looked back, Mrs. Van Cleaveron was shaking a gnarled finger at me as if to say, "I'll get you sooner or later."

"I've got your back," I heard Chloe yell to me as she pushed open the glass doors to the Student Union Building and disappeared into the coming evening.

I sat down on the steps of the Alumni Building to think over my situation. I had been brought up to believe that black people were no better than the animals in the field. I had never had occasion to have conversation or association of any kind with black people. Oh, what hatred and ignorance had been pounded into my head since birth! Now, when I desperately needed a friend to be kind, to support me, who stepped forth as my benefactor? It was a sweet, black girl who was intelligent, who had lived and suffered as I had. I could not allow the prejudice of Ottie's World to continue to dominate my life. I vowed to exorcise the demon of racism.

The campus was abuzz with students with maps in hand getting to know the new campus. Most said hello to me as they passed and I returned the greeting in kind.

I sat down on an old millstone artistically placed in a semicircle near Lincoln Hall and the Home Economics Building. Many stones from all over the ancient world had been embedded in this small shrine. I reviewed what had just transpired in my life. I had just eaten dinner with a black girl. I had just broken one of the strongest taboos taught me since childhood. I had thoroughly enjoyed the experience. This was my first act of rebellion against my upbringing and there would be many more. I had to kill Ottie's world and all its beliefs and practices in order to emerge into a life of my own.

I studied the bushes with white blossoms lining the outer section of the semicircle where I was sitting. Red and yellow zinnias poured out their fragrances from stalks and flowers. From my perspective, I could see the frantic activity of new students who did not know where they were or not much about where they were going. I knew for sure that I had just crossed over the river of no return. I would never be able to tell anyone in my old world about Chloe. I would be risking my safety if I even mentioned my roommate or fraternizing with people who were different. But, what difference did it really make? I was so damned different myself!

French would be my major. People in most countries where French is spoken are dark-skinned. The very fact of speaking differently from my valley people made me strange and different. "Ottie didn't raise him right," they would say. "If he wants to learn foreign tongues, he ought to stick with glossalalia. At least he can use that if he goes to church." "What good is that going to do him anyway?" "He ought to learn something that will get him a job." And this nosy interference in my life would go on ad infinitem.

Poor Chloe, by virtue of befriending me, would be forever outcast from her family and community, too. But we both had already had our fill of these families and their way of living life. There was opportunity now for us to define our own lives. I would come to learn that many Berea students had maintained their prejudices, bigotry, hatred, and displeasure of anyone or anything different from themselves and I would reap the whirlwind of their wrath. I would also learn that at Berea, if a student did not make friends in the first few weeks, he would probably have no friends. The clannish custom of the mountains hung its ugly head; people tended to form cliques that shut everyone else out.

I stood up to go. Remembering Mr. Rules and Regulations and what he had said about the fine of $5 dollars for picking flowers on campus, I decided to commit my first act of rebellion against college rules. (The Devil made me do it.) This act of defiance set me on a new journey toward self identity and adult independence and was the first snapshot of my acting just like my mother Ottie. It was a down-right foolish choice.

I impulsively plucked a giant, red zinnia blooming among the white blossoms of the lower bushes. Pleased that I could finally disobey somebody's rules, I proudly stuck the zinnia in my shirt pocket. A student passing by blurted out, "That's a $5 dollar fine."

The Devil took complete control of me.

"Rat's ass," I shot back to her. "You don't even know who I am."

But I soon learned who she was.

She worked in Mr. Rules and Regulation's office.

(Oh, shit!)

WEAR SOME FLOWERS IN YOUR HAIR

Retribution for my act of attrition against the zinnia patch came swiftly. The following day a summons in the form of a three-by-five index card awaited me in my post office box. It had written upon it in red letters, "Please see the Assistant Dean immediately. No appointment necessary."

I held the card in my hands thinking out loud. What is that girl's reward for turning me in and how does she know who I am? My first adversary is Mrs. Van Cleaveron and now Mr. Rules and Regulations himself is on the war path. I have not even been at Berea a month yet. Will I endure?"

Taking the card with me, I went directly to Lincoln Hall where Mr. Rules and Regulations hung out in his lair. He intended to teach me accountability. When he saw me come up the stairs to his office door, he advanced to meet me.

"I'm told that your name is Fred, that your nickname is "Senior-Want-to-Be," he hissed and growled.

"Wow, information travels," I said sarcastically.

"Stand up straight, wipe the smile off your face, and drop the sarcasm. Your status as a student at this institution rests in my hands at this moment and I'm not feeling generous," he spat out through flared nostrils. "Rule No. 265 in the handbook explicitly states, '...A fine of $5 is accessed for plucking [oh, dear, he used the word "plucking"] any flower or bush on campus...' A student reported that she saw you pick a red zinnia last night and stick it behind your left ear."

"Yes, who was the snitch that had nothing better to do than spy on my private moments?" I asked bravely.

"Conscientious students obey the rules and help us enforce them against students who do not respect law and order," he said with his authoritative voice.

"The snitches and tattletales of this world ought to be tarred and feathered," I thought to myself. "In Ottie's world, where I come from, people don't hesitate to retaliate against informers."

"The tattletales, that snitch, that informer is none other than a sweet girl who works in my office. That is her labor assignment. Her name is Vixen. She is my extra set of eyes and ears wherever she goes. If she tells me that you plucked a zinnia, by George, you plucked a zinnia."

Here again I hope he had used the word "plucked." I wasn't hearing well. I was beginning to feel like the proverbial snowball and its chance in Hell. In my foolish act of rebellion, I had impulsively acted like my mother Ottie would. Poor people have poor ways. In this situation, I was both poor and stupid.

I fell silent. How should I react in this moment of defeat? I had been caught red-handed. What would melt Mr. Rules and Regulation's heart? How could I extricate myself from this untenable, embarrassing event? I heard the worst part of myself, my obsequious, pandering, lily-livered, cowardly June Jr. self meekly blurt out, "Vixen is the prettiest girl I've seen on campus, and I'm sure every handsome boy on campus wants to date her. And, by the way, I love your bowtie."

My cowardly act had just shamed generations of proud mountain men and women who had battled the British at King's Mountain; women who had bravely faced adversity on the frontier; men who had sacrificed everything at Shiloh, Petersburg, and Bull Run. Where had my courage gone? Why was I afraid of this man and this rule? Why had I even gotten myself into this predicament?

I heard his voice answer me meekly, "Why, thank you, sir, for the complement for my office worker. My wife and I think she is quite nice. And, my wife picked out this bowtie for my birthday."

"Well, Sir, I want to tell you how sorry I am for picking that zinnia on campus. My dear, dead grandmother just loved zinnias, and I can't help but think of her every time I see one. I promise you that I will obey Rule 265 and never again pick a flower while I'm on the Berea campus if you let me stay. (I never picked another one.) I like the way you have decorated your office. It is warm and welcoming."

"Since you have apologized and promise to obey the rule, I can give you some slack. But there is a punishment. You are hereby fined $5 dollars for destruction of a zinnia. At $.06 an hour, working two hours a day, it will take you eighty-two hours (seven days) of work to pay for the flower. Furthermore, flower infractions require that you come to my office for detention and instructions twice.

He took out a ledger where my name had already been written. It seems that Mrs. Van Cleaveron had already laid out a case against me. He wrote my infraction in big red letters.

"What is the conflict you have with Mrs. Cleaveron?" he wanted to know."Your record follows you at this college, mister. We keep track all four years."

There seemed to be a hint of glee in his eyes. I thought to myself, "I hate your ugly, old bowtie and I think your office worker looks like Cinderella's stepsister." As I left Lincoln Hall, Chloe was waiting outside to greet me.

"Survival is a matter of brains, not foolish courage. You have to understand that faculty and adult workers are not your friends. They serve 'in loco parentis.' They are your parents away from home," she explained to me. "Many students are snitches, too. They try to ingratiate themselves with their labor bosses."

"Want to get a cup of coffee?"

"No, thanks," I replied. "I don't have any money."

"It only costs a nickel," she pled.

"I don't even have a nickel," I told her. "Besides, I got to get to class."

At that moment, the bells of Phelps-Stokes began to chime the nine o'clock hour. French class was awaiting my arrival. I would just die if the teacher was male and he was wearing a ludicrous bowtie.

When I entered the French classroom matters got worse. The first person I spied sitting on the front row was that sweet, little snitch, Vixen. She was wearing a red zinnia behind her left ear. On the way to class, she had plucked it at the same flower garden where I had gotten busted for picking mine.

"You'll be one of my friends before you graduate," she purred as she took the flower from her hair and handed it to me.

"I'm not that desperate," I retorted.

KEYS TO THE KINGDOM

I sat down beside Vixen and glared at her with angry eyes peeking out from underneath my   eyebrows. She smiled innocently and adjusted the zinnia behind her ear so that it shone more prominently against her face.

"Hi," she greeted me. "Maybe we can do French homework together."

"Like Hell. When pigs fly!" I thought to myself angrily.

Ignoring her, I looked out the window at the manicured lawns of the campus. Students scurried down the mass of crisscrossed sidewalks hurrying to class or to their labor assignments. This beehive was alive with people eager to begin their studies.

The sound of the classroom door opening and closing drew my attention back to the room. I knew that our professor had arrived. However, when I looked toward the podium, I saw no one. The empty podium stood there alone. The teacher was so small in stature that she had disappeared completely behind it. Then a petite voice called out from behind the podium, "Will two of you men please move this podium to the side of the room?"

I went to the podium and carried it myself to the back of the room. And there she stood. Our French professor was less than five feet in height. Her frizzy hair ballooned around her head. There was a faint touch of pink lipstick on her lips. Two circles of rouge, clown-like, swept along her cheek bones. She had beady eyes that shot daggers outward toward whomever she addressed. Time had been good to her. Her body was firm, shapely, and attractive.

Her name was Miss Laverne. She had served in the army as a radio operator during World War II. She told us with relish that she was operating the radio for American troops when news came that the great French author, Antoine de St. Exupery, had disappeared on a military flight over the Mediterranean. She had gained her knowledge of French by studying at the Sorbonne after the war. She called the roll (a requirement in every class at Berea) and then addressed the class in French.

She spoke dreadful French with an accent so American that a true speaker of French might doubt that she had ever studied in France. She read the first lesson with the class, explained some grammatical points, and then she assigned enough homework to jam up the Seine River.

On the way out of Draper Hall, Vixen sidled up to me, pushing her left breast into the side of my arm and cooed sweetly, "Isn't she such a wonderful professor. I love the way she speaks French."

"She speaks French like a Spanish cow," I retorted quickly moving my arm away from Vixen's breast. "She is about as interesting as a wet mop!" I snarled back at Vixen.

"By the way, why did you report me for picking a zinnia from the flower garden and now I see you flaunting a zinnia behind your ear?" I asked her angrily.

"My labor boss lets me have a flower when I want one," she said. "He knows that I won't destroy the patch."

"But you are a student like everyone else and all the rules apply to you, too," I reasoned.

"Oh, no, I am special. My boss is one of the deans. I do whatever I want to do. I can flaunt the rules, but you can't because you have no basis of power. That is how the world is."

"So you are a tattletale, a snitch, a rule-breaker, a flaunter of rules, and a tyrant because you have connections?"

"That is how the world works. If you were my friend, I could help you to get by with whatever you wanted to do. If you are wise, you will be friends with those who have some power," she said.

She made sense. In poverty no one has any power. In ignorance, one stays at the bottom of a caste system. Following moral guidelines does not necessarily lead to success or prosperity. Following established rules does not get a person what he wants. Rebellion is where success lies.

I decided to copy what Vixen did in her life. I began to flaunt, rebel, act without morals, and disdain college rules. One day I sent a note to Vixen at her dorm. It read: "I surrender. Meet me for dinner tonight in the cafeteria." She wrote me a response that merely read, "Grrrrrr."

At dinner she asked me, "Why did you say that Miss Laverne speaks French like a Spanish cow? That is not a nice thing to say about her."

"It is a true evaluation," I answered, "because that sentence is a translation of the expression, 'You are murdering the French language.' In French it is said, 'Vous parlez francais comme une vache espagnole.' That woman and I are not going to get along."

This French teacher reminded me too much of my mother and that would end up being costly to me.

When the evening meal was over, Vixen took me by the hand and led me across campus to the doors of Phelps-Stokes Chapel. The doors were always open, so we entered. She dug deeply in her purse and pulled out a set of keys. She looked like a jailor who oversees dozens of prison cells.

"I have keys to every building on campus," she gloated. "This one will open the doors to the cupola on top of Phelps -Stokes."

"Where did you get the keys?" I asked.

"I stole them. When labor bosses and janitors leave keys lying around, I make copies of each. Then, I ask what the keys are for. When they tell me, I write the information in my little black book. I can get you into any place on campus." She was such a braggart.

Vixen and I climbed a set of stairs to the doors to the cupola. When she unlocked the door, I saw inside a small room with a comfortable couch and two large armchairs. I walked in and looked at the view through the huge windows inside the cupola. I could see much of downtown Berea to west; the music building to the south; the library and Lincoln Hall to the east; and Draper Building to the north. I sat down in one of the armchairs and sank deeply into the cushion.

"Come over here with me on the couch," she demanded.

"Oops," I thought, "does Vixen have some hanky-panky in mind?"

I was disappointed when she took a plastic wrapper from her purse and extracted a thick cigarette from inside. She lit the cigarette, took a deep breath of its smoke, and then she exhaled, blowing a sweet-smelling smoke across the room. Handing the cigarette to me, she softly said the word, "marijuana." Oops! I had already smoked June Jr.'s special cigarette among the willows at the frog pond when I was a young lad. I knew what it was.

"Sit down next to me. I want to kiss you," she said without emotion.

My courage left me. This woman Vixen was a veritable black-widow spider. She would kill a person in an arachnid moment. I had to smoke this cigarette with her and give her a kiss or she would slay me in some way. I froze in place on the couch, but she slid over with puckered lips and laid a wet kiss on my lips.

I heard the words in my head, "You are kissing a pig."

"No, I'm not. I'm saving my life," I reasoned with myself.

The more we smoked, the more relaxed I became.

"You will come around to my view of life," she said. "No one ever gets what he wants by being nice like you. You have to be aggressive, mean, and brutal. Don't ever forget that I am that way. Then nothing that I do will surprise you."

"You are playing with me," I said.

"Actually I am," she responded. "But I only play with people I like. Remember that I have the keys to the kingdom. If you want to rule the kingdom, honor the king."

Whatever this stuff was that I was smoking was having no effect on me, or so I thought. I matched Vixen puff for puff. After a few kisses, she said, "That is enough for now. We should save some for later."

Whoever had heard of rationing kisses? What was this stuff we were smoking? Who was this girl Vixen and what was I getting myself in to?

"Let's go," she said. She extinguished the cigarette and carefully returned the ashes and residue to the plastic wrapper. She locked the door behind us. I took two steps forward and fell into the banister leading down the stairs. That event seemed so funny that I began to laugh uproariously.

"I suppose that you are craving some chocolate about now," she chided me.

"No, but I think I might be able to kiss that woman that speaks French like a Spanish cow."

"You should be ashamed of yourself. That is your new French professor."

"Whatever it takes, Vixen. I intend to have my own set of keys to the kingdom."

I stepped forward and staggered down the steps.

Phelps-Stokes Chapel

EARN WHILE YOU LEARN

In my first days at Berea, I made some very poor decisions. I was so desperate to get people to be my friends that I fell under the influence of individuals that were quite disturbed. I confused the idea of being an adult and having freedom with being rebellious. Fate placed me in the situations and my inexperienced life did the rest. Mrs. Kerfluffle was my first labor supervisor and she looked just like my mother. She acted like her, too. She brought out my conflict with Ottie and I began to respond to her as I had responded to Ottie. I had been assigned to work in the reference room of the library. It was a cushion job.

A creaky, outdated elevator carried passengers to the second floor of the library to the reference room where I had my labor assignment. I got inside it and pulled a metal gate closed across the opening; otherwise, the elevator would not operate. There were four buttons: second floor, first floor, second stacks, and first stacks. Books for the general library were kept in the stacks which were located two floors underground. I pushed the button for the second floor. I was in a real cage because the sides of the elevator were not enclosed. Cables lifting us upward stuck out on the sides. They swirled and piled in a heap as the leviathan moved upward. It came to a stop at the front desk of the reference room. I stepped out into a giant room with a high ceiling. All sizes of books lined the shelves. The room smelled of new books, paper, glue, sweat, and stale air.

A figure resembling one of the frost giants of Norse mythology came lumbering down the main aisle of the room. She wore a thick coat that draped on her shoulders like fur. Bushy hair swept upward on the top of her head, adding height to an already massive body. She glared out through thick-rimmed glasses. A 1930s style dress fell almost to her ankles, which stuck out of a pair of Red Cross correctional shoes.

She did not greet me. She simply said, "I thought I heard the elevator."

This lady did not acknowledge me at all. She walked directly to the desk and sat down in a swivel chair. Her lumbering body filled the chair to overflowing, and her muffin top jiggled over the armrests. Her curiosity had been piqued by the stranger in th elevator. I could have been Santa Claus and she would not have cared. The elevator was the surprise package that moved up and down all day long bringing the only excitement to her wretched work life.

"The reference room is my labor assignment or this year," I blurted out without being introduced.

"The reference room is your labor assignment for this year if I choose to accept you," she rudely corrected me.

"What library experience have you had in your life besides checking out a book?" this eccentric woman wanted to know.

"Checking out and reading a book, that's about it," I said nonchalantly.

"Work in here starts promptly at 7:00 in the morning every day except Sunday. Can you manage to get out of bed early enough to open the library at this hour?"

"Are there really people on the earth who are waiting at the door of a reference room to do research at 7:00 in the morning?" I heard myself say.

"There are. I, myself, have spent many seven o'clock mornings researching papers. My love of research led me to want to work as a reference librarian," she bragged.

The thought occurred to me that she probably lived (troll like) in the library, down in the stacks or underneath the building somewhere.

"If you are not willing to accept me, please say so, because I will have to return to the Labor Office and get another assignment."

"I will accept you on probation, on a temporary basis. You have to prove yourself to me. My standards are high, and I don't know if you have the mettle to make it in my reference room," she boasted, wiping saliva from her lips.

"When it comes to working in a library at seven in the morning, my standards are very low," I muttered inaudibly.

"Lady, do you have a name?" I dared ask.

"I am Mrs. Kerfluffle."

Dear Lord! I grabbed my throat with my left hand and placed my right one over my mouth to keep from choking with laughter. Her name and personality fit perfectly.

"Mrs. Kerfluffle," I giggled, "I will assess the working situation in this room and then decide if I want to work in your department two hours each day. At the end of the first month, if I am not happy, I will go elsewhere."

"Life doesn't operate like that at Berea, young man. Freshmen do not get to choose labor assignments at any time. You will be here for the entire year, like it or not. You should show pride that you can earn and learn while you study in college."

"Are they paying you a salary of six cents per hour, too, Mrs. Kerfluffle?" I had to ask.

In 1961-65, the labor wage at Berea was six cents per hour. At the end of each day, I had earned exactly twelve cents. In one week, I amassed a fortune of sixty cents, but I never saw any of the money. The college kept ledgers showing how much students earned each semester. I never saw one. I knew that there was not tuition and my work was in lieu of it.

The thought crossed my mind that Mrs. Kerfluffle was probably related to Mrs. Van Cleaveron and Mr. Rules and Regulations. She could be their older sister.

I pushed the elevator button in order to descend to the first floor because I wanted to get away from her.

"Don't push that button!" Mrs. Kerfluffle shouted at me. "The elevator is for my use and for bringing books from downstairs. You have to walk up and down the stairs," she croaked.

"We'll see," I mused as I ran down the two sets of stairs.

I felt as if I had spent an hour back at home with my mother, Ottie. Mrs. Kerfluffle and my mother was the same person. Both had a mean, nasty disposition. Both treated me as unimportant. I had to prove myself to each in order to have acceptance. It is no wonder, then, that I developed an immediate deep resentment toward Mrs. Kerfluffle.

Each hour I spent in the reference room was a consignment once again to the hell of Ottie's world. In my freedom as an adult to act without restraint, now I began treating Mrs. Kerfluffle as I had wanted to treat my mother. I wanted to lash out, to hurt her, to wring psychological pain from anyone who reminded me of my mother.

Mrs. Kerfluffle did not befriend college students. She used them as she labor program dictated, as worker bees to do work she found unpleasant. Ignoring the spirit of rules and regulations, she followed the letter of the law. I was required to re-make myself to fit her image. She made the mistake of stirring my old hurts, resentments, and past wounds. I intended to make her pay for it.

At the entrance to the library, I met a character as puzzling as Mrs. Kerfluffle. This person started me on a path of rebellion, which ultimately went badly for me. The Devil literally made me complicate my life.

Far better for me had I never met Lettie Desmayeux, a Cajun. What was a Cajun doing in Kentucky? Louisiana was outside the territory for acceptance at Berea.

"I see you met the bitch," is how Lettie first greeted me.

"Which bitch?" I retorted, "The campus is full of them."

"Mrs. Kerfluffle, of course." She pronounced the name with disgust.

"How do you know her?"

"I have been assigned to work in the reference room along with you this year. She told me that I would never make it through the year, so I should make an alternate plan," Lettie explained. "Where are you from?"

"Morganton, North Carolina," I said, knowing that she had never heard of my town.

"Plaquemine Parrish. You have a state mental hospital in your home town, right?"

"God, how would you know that fact?"

"My aunt, who used to live in Hickory, went insane and spent the rest of her life there," she said. "You must be crazy, too, to come to Berea and work in the reference room with that old hag and me."

"Actually, for the moment, I'm proud to be a Berea student. It took a lot of effort on my part just to get here. But I am puzzled at the unusual faculty and adults that work in this place, I said without excitement.

"It's all about money. The college doesn't want to pay professors much, so they get people who work cheap."

"Super intelligent people aren't ordinary," I suggested.

"It's always about money," she insisted. "If you live long enough, you will see."

"Qui vivera, verra," I blurted out ostentatiously in French. (If you live long enough, you will see.)

"Moi, je viens de la Louisane et je parle francais aussi," she shocked me by answering in French. (I'm from Louisiana and I speak French, too.)

"See you at work bright and early tomorrow at 7:00. Laissez rouler les bons temps!" (Let the good times roll!) I loved her reference to Mardi gras.

She disappeared like a mist from the bayou. "Let the good times roll," she had said in departing.

Lettie had not wanted to come to Berea. She had not wanted to be in any college. However, because of connections her father had had as a donor to the school, she had been given a dispensation to attend the school, even though Plaquemine Parrish was well outside the area for Berea.

Lettie was hostile toward everyone. Her life had been filled with hateful experiences. A veritable volcano, she could erupt at any second. I had hoped that her explosions would not come as we worked together in the library. She had told me, sadly, that in her youth, a gang of her father's drunken friends had raped her. She had dealt with her sorrow through rebellion against authority. She had loved to get cheap laughs at another's expense. "Let the good times roll" was a philosophy that had eased her pain temporarily. She could explode into violent rages at any moment. Lettie was at Berea to party and have herself a Mardi gras experience. There would be many wonderful times at Berea, but it was not a place one should come "to let the good times roll."

My work assignment with her was tantamount to making a pact with the Devil. I should have made a better choice than to let her influence me. My flaw was to need a friend, any friend, under any circumstances.

Mrs. Kerfluffle did not know, yet, that Lettie and I were her worst nightmare. We were lurking in the wings to bring unbearable grief to her life.

LET THE GOOD TIMES ROLL

There existed an uneasy truce in the reference room between Lettie, Mrs. Kerfluffle, and me for most of the first semester. Lettie and I reported to work on time, performed efficiently, and when finished, ran down the stairs to get out of her presence. Boss and students communicated primarily through written note except for an occasional confrontation over an infernal glue pot.

A glue pot, used for repairing damaged books, was the Holy Grail for Mrs. Kerfluffle. It sat in her holy shrine in a small room located to the side of the main reference room. Lettie and I often saw her next to the pot cleaning dry glue with her witch-like fingers. We suggested to each other that she was either sniffing the glue or eating it. But the exercise of watching Mrs. Kerfluffle play with her glue pot stopped being funny when she told us one day that we would be responsible for repairing all damaged reference books and we would have to use the glue pot in the process.

This was no ordinary glue pot. It was the glue pot from Hell. When hot, it threw out an odor like a rotting corpse. If one touched the hot glue, it would leave third degree burns wherever it landed. There was absolutely no way to repair a book without getting hot glue on one's body. Repairing a torn book in the reference room was like wiping someone's ass.

Lettie came screaming from the repair room one day with her hands glued to her face. I grabbed her by the arm and rushed her right into the restroom and stuck her head in the sink. She pried her hand from her left cheek leaving a patch of melted skin sticking to her hand. Lettie screamed in pain, "My good looks are gone forever."

"You were always ugly," I heard myself mutter. "The glue will just dilute it a bit."

She hit me with her left hand. Yes, Lettie actually hit me. In retaliation, I locked the door from outside and walked back to my work in the reference room.

I was vulnerable to the power of Lettie's wicked personality. She and Vixen were twin black-widow spiders. Wanting to be accepted as her friend, I followed her example in doing heinous acts that were not ordinarily a part of my nature. I felt powerful in my new adult freedom as a college student. I was proving that Vixen's philosophy was right. I had quickly forgotten what it took me to get to Berea. I saw Lettie and her actions as dynamic, cool, cute and exciting. I was very immature.

When she got over her mad spell, Lettie came to me with a proposal. It was her intention to assuage her built-up anger by taking action. She wanted to see how long we could keep Mrs. Kerfluffle trapped in the elevator when she arrived for work around 8:30 each morning. It would be easy because she never varied from her schedule. I went along with Lettie so that she would accept me as her friend just as I had done what Vixen had wanted earlier.

My common sense told me not to participate in disrespect to an adult teacher. But my desire to please Lettie and keep her as a friend overruled common sense. I was experiencing a new-found freedom. I was an ape with an atomic bomb.

The four levels of the library consisted of two above ground and two below. The first floor housed the main desk, reading tables, magazines, all sorts of periodicals as well as a listening room. We were on the top floor. Mrs. Kerfluffle had to enter the elevator on the first floor and ride it up to the reference room on the second floor. She always had trouble closing a heavy gate that slid in front of the main elevator door. One could hear the elevator door open. There would be a metal clanking as she closed the gate, then a pause as she pushed the button for the second floor. An individual could take control of the elevator by pushing one of the buttons first.

Lettie went to the lowest level of the stacks and waited. I went to the second floor of the reference room and waited by the elevator. At exactly 8:30 on the dot, Mrs. Punctual entered the contraption. I quickly pushed the top button summoning the elevator upstairs. I watched as each button lit up. Before Mrs. Kerfluffle could open the door, Lettie pushed the button summoning the elevator to the bottom floor. Down she went to the bottom floor. Lettie hid among the shelves in the stacks so Mrs. Kerfluffle could not see her. When I saw that the elevator was on the bottom floor, I quickly pushed the top button and Mrs. Kerfluffle rose once more as if she were on her way to Heaven. I hid in the glue room. Lettie caught the elevator again with the button in the basement. I ran back to the elevator and pushed the top button. This time when her royal carriage reached the reference room, I smiled and waved at Mrs. Kerfluffle as she rode the MTA from floor to floor. Up and down, down and up she went time after time. I heard her screaming, "Stop this thing. Get me out of here!"

On her eighth trip up, I yelled to her, "I'll save you, Mrs. Kerfluffle!" I walked into the electrical room and shut off the electricity, leaving her stranded between floors. Meanwhile, Lettie came back upstairs to the reference room. Students at the main desk had seen someone riding up and down in the elevator, so they summoned help. When the exhausted rider finally came into her office, she was huffing and puffing like an enraged bull. Lettie and I pretended to be busy by putting books back on their proper shelves.

"You two no-account rascals did this to me," she snorted. "I can't prove it, but I just know your did."

Lettie and I just looked coy. We referred to our escapades as "Let the good times roll." This particular one had been a rolling good time, for us, but not for Mrs. Kerfluffle.

Having been so successful at the first good-time roll, Lettie and I planned more. At 7:30 in the morning on April fool's Day dozens of reference books lay waiting to be shelved. Reference books lay strewn over the tables. Mrs. Kerfluffle demanded that we finish shelving books and tidy the room before her arrival. The two of us packed stacks of books on a wooden cart with wheels. Lettie sat in the middle of the cart with books piled all around her. As I pushed, she shelved them. We were running out of time and neither of us wanted a tongue-lashing from the master.

"Double-time your speed," Lettie yelled at me.

As we rushed down each aisle of books, Lettie shoved a book anywhere there was an empty space without reference to the Dewey Decimal System. There was no rhyme or reason to her filing system. "Get it done with fun," she howled with laughter. "Now it's your turn, Fred."

I took her place on the cart and gleefully threw books in random order, in any category. We thought that we had trumped the old monster. But at the end of the semester, we had to do inventory. She made us locate and re-file every book in the whole damn room.

A few weeks later, I felt a claw-like hand grab my shoulder and a banshee voice howling, "What have you done to my glue pot?"

"What glue pot?" I stammered.

"My damned glue pot," she cursed. No one had ever heard Mrs. Kerfluffle utter a profane word until that day.

"I don't do glue pots," I told her.

"It's gone, oh, it's gone," she wailed pulling her Medusa hair with both hands. "My blessed glue pot is no more."

It was as if she had lost a member of her family. I recalled having seen her lurking around the glue pot when Lettie and I thought she was sniffing glue.

Turning quickly, she assailed me with an incoherent diatribe of disconnected words and thoughts. "You...you...cause of this...stole my precious pot...oh, God, why did you curse me with this fool student?

Lettie was enjoying every minute of Mrs. Kerfluffle's award-winning drama. She peeked out from behind the water cooler, both hands covering her mouth to prevent her snickering. She was enjoying watching Mrs. Kerfluffle suffer as she had so often made us suffer.

"Mrs. Kerfluffle, I'm innocent of all charges. You seem dreadfully stressed. Maybe you would like to talk to the school nurse. I'll get the head librarian, Miss Milburn."

In defiance of her orders and directly in front of her, I entered the elevator, pushed the second-floor button, walked out the front door and went home for the rest of the day. I left Lettie there to deal with her.

Three weeks later a neat package arrived for Mrs. Kerfluffle. The return address was a house in Louisville. Someone had lovingly attached a sweet red bow on the top. She opened it carefully as if there were a bomb inside. When she saw the glue pot, she began to yell hosannas. She danced up and down in front of her desk raising her arms to Heaven. Such a sweet reunion had rarely been seen.

Her joy quickly waned and she turned with a fury on Lettie and me.

"You are fired! You will not work another day in this reference room! Get out! Get out!" She was beside herself with anger.

"Does that mean just me or Lettie too?" I enquired.

"Just you!"

"But you told me earlier that freshmen have to keep their work assignment for one year. I've grown accustomed to the reference room," I chided her.

Without thinking what she was saying she yelled, "Lettie can stay. I'm going to punish her anyway."

I went to Mr. Rules and Regulations and told him that my labor supervisor had fired me without provocation. The college gave her some time off.

At the end of the freshman year, I had been set free of my library labor obligation. Lettie and I had driven Mrs. Kerfluffle to the nuthouse. Lettie never returned to Berea after that first year and I never saw her again. But someone who worked in Louisville later told me that Lettie had ended up in Our Lady of Peace. She had been quite unstable since the day I had met her. There, she could "let the good times roll."

During the summer break I began to feel remorse for my treatment of Mrs. Kerfluffle. At no time in my life had I ever treated an adult, a teacher, a librarian with such disrespect. This mean aspect of my character frightened me. I was acting from deep wounds inflicted by authority figures early in my life. I was acting much like my mother would do. I told myself that I must change. Neither Lettie nor Mrs. Kerfluffle should influence me anymore. But I had to live with myself and take responsibility for my actions.

In an effort to make restitution, I went to the reference room and spoke with the new librarian that had replaced Mrs. Kerfluffle. I asked her if she needed an experienced worker. She told me that all positions had been filled for the year. I walked among the shelves and saw that all books were neat and correctly shelved. I desperately wanted a second chance to undo what I had done.

In a last ditch effort at self-redemption, I went to the librarian and asked, "Will you at least let me clean the glue pot?"

Frost Building
This building was the old library in 1961-65.

I worked upstairs in the reference room during the freshman year.

HILLY-HO-HO

Chloe and I sat comparing first semester schedules in the snack bar section of the Student Union Building. This snack bar had become my inner sanctum where I spent countless hours lounging, dancing, and socializing with anyone willing to talk. Sooner or later, every student at Berea would pass through this room on a daily basis. On the weekends, it was the center of all social activity. The dance floor was always packed with students releasing pent-up energy. They looked like Santa's reindeer dancing and prancing over rooftops. It is a wonder that the dance floor held together.

"You know, Fred, I finished all my basic courses and have registered for real college now. I bet we have the same courses," she explained.

"My schedule is as follows: Composition, World History, P.E., French 101, and basic math. They allowed me only one elective," I pointed out to her. "My schedule adds up to 16 hours but I only get college credit for 12. That basic math adds up to four hours and meets daily."

"Well, I have Composition, World History, P.E., Physical Science, and Music Appreciation. Fortunately, all my courses give college credit. You understand that we both have killer schedules, don't you. We have to spend two hours of study outside of class for every hour in class. That means that all the three-hour classes require eighteen hours of study. You must spend sixty-six hours of study per week outside the hours in class for your schedule. Don't forget that we also have two hours of work per day. This little school is no cake walk."

"Chloe, I've got to confess to you that I did some disrespectful things to Mrs. Kerfluffle, my labor boss, at the library. Lettie and I were cruel and immature. There is no way that I can apologize or admit what I did. They would throw me out of school."

"Don't tell anyone else about it. Change your ways. Go out of your way to show respect to everyone on campus, adults and students," she advised.

All my fears and doubts carried over from Ottie's world washed over me. Though my grades in high school were outstanding, they counted for naught here. Was I smart enough? Did I have the discipline to complete my schedule successfully? Upperclassmen had already told us that the sophomore year was the most difficult. Everyone had to take a year of humanities and the faculty gave only one grade of "A" out of the entire class of five hundred students. Had I made the bus ride for naught? Were my dreams and wishes misplaced? Should I have stayed in Golden Valley and worked at a saw mill like my brothers?

I had to be successful. The college had loaned me money for the year and they expected repayment in the summer. Gertie's words from long ago rang in my ears, "We have to make it on our own. There's no one to help. You can do it."

"Chloe, I'm afraid," I admitted to her. "This Berea experience is washing over me like the waves of an unsympathetic ocean. As divided as it was, I had a family in North Carolina that gave me some sense of security. I have found no place at Berea to drop my anchor. So far, you are my only friend. It would be devastating for me if you went away."

"Nothing has happened, yet. We are just looking at the reality of what we have chosen for our lives. Most classes meet on Monday, Wednesday, and Friday. You can discipline yourself to study eight hours per day. On the weekends there are endless hours for study. Don't make the mistake of getting behind in assignments or study. That would be academic suicide," she reassured me.

"Would it help to study together," I asked hoping that she would say yes.

"That would be the worst choice we could make. We would spend our time talking and socializing and we would get nothing done. After we have finished studying, we could meet to compare notes and discuss lessons," she offered.

"Composition scares me most of all. I hated writing in high school. Students tell me that teachers require a detailed research paper and that the school uses this course to weed out weaker students." I searched her eyes and answers for some morsel of reassurance.

"Calm down, Fred. I have Miss Streamer who is reputed to be the toughest in the English department. Former students say that her students learn superbly," she said with confidence.

"Do you know anything about Miss Kaulner? I've got her."

"Nope."

Chloe patted me on the shoulder like Gertie used to do. "Kiddo, we only have to maintain a "C" average to get a diploma from this place. Do you want to strive to be valedictorian at a place like Berea where most students were valedictorians of their high school classes?"

"Hell, no," I said out loud. "I'll get a diploma if I have to print my own."

Composition 101 met at 9:30 on Monday, Wednesday, and Friday in Draper Hall, the main classroom building. I entered the classroom and chose a seat in the middle of the room, third row from the windows. A dreadful hush washed over the twenty-five students anxiously waiting to meet Miss Kaulner. The bell rang but the teacher was not there. One student mentioned that we must wait ten minutes for a teacher holding a master's degree. Twenty minutes was standard for a PhD. I didn't want to wait at all.

I heard a jingling of bracelets, though, and the click-clack of high heel shoes coming down the hallway toward our classroom. Like Loretta Young in a 1950s sitcom, Miss Kaulner twirled through the classroom door. She wore a ring on the thumb of her left hand which held a long, multi-colored scarf for dramatic effect. She was a very attractive, older woman who was well preserved. She carried herself with elegance. Her salt-and-pepper hair was styled upward above a face filled with wrinkles from the fact that she never stopped smiling. Her lips were frozen in an eternal smile that never varied. How did she manage to talk without moving her lips?

"Good morning," she blurted out, all filled with enthusiasm.

No one responded.

"Have I been assigned a class of deaf mutes for the semester?" she enquired holding the frozen smile in place.

"Good morning," she repeated.

Two students mumbled, "Good morning."

She went down each row forcing every student to greet her. When finished, she took a deep breath and uttered the dreaded words, "Let's discuss the research paper you will write for me."

A sick feeling washed over the entire class. A girl began coughing at the back of the room.

"It's always like this when I talk about research papers." she smiled.

After giving instructions for the research paper, she wanted to know who we were. We gave our names and place of origin. When she got to me, I said, "Fred Epeley, Morganton, North Carolina."

"Oh," she remarked. "I got my M.A. degree in English from North Carolina. Nice place."

I noted her remark and placed it in my memory banks for future reference. I wasn't above using it to my advantage. Then I reconsidered. I would make an extra effort to treat Miss Kaulner with respect.

"I am Miss Kaulner. I've taught at Berea for several years. I live on the east side of town in a one room, two-story house that I call 'Hilly-Ho-Ho.' (Muffled laughter from the class) The name does sound silly I admit. But who has the wisdom to know the origin of the name? Have you read Shakespeare? I took the name from the falcon cries in his play 'Hamlet.' Look it up. When sending the falcons out to hunt, men yelled 'hilly-ho-ho' to bring them back to their perch."

Please, dear God, where did this school find such an agglomeration of unusual professors and staff? There was Mrs. Van Cleaveron, Mr. Rules and Regulations, Mrs. Kerfluffle, Miss Laverne, Vixen and now this. And only God knew who else lurked on the campus. Many years later, I came to love these professors and to understand that their uniqueness made Berea special. Despite their eccentricities, they were very good educators.

When I told Chloe about my experience, she laughed uproariously. Her composition teacher was four-feet-eight, wore her hair in a French twist, limped and had a bad habit of pounding her fists on student desks while yelling (bad breath not excepted), "You've got to dig. You've got to dig to pass this class."

As weeks passed, composition class went well. I wrote weekly papers for Miss Kaulner, and she returned them with a grade of check, check plus or minus in red ink. I even grew to appreciate her off-beat humor and eccentric ways. I studied her character and admired her beauty.

On a warm October morning, I resolved to visit Miss Kaulner in her Hilly-Ho-Ho home. I would reach out to her as I had refused to reach out to Mrs. Kerfluffle. I walked east of Berea past the Crafts building, where students made decorative brooms and wove mats, curtains, and bedspreads. I passed the White Cloud laundry where locals were busy washing clothes. As I hiked down a hill, I saw an unusual building to my right. It was larger than a standard living room and it stood two stories tall. Its natural wood hue harmonized with the surrounding trees. A cleverly designed wooden sign, cut in the form of a falcon in flight, bore the words "Hilly-Ho-Ho." I knocked on the door and waited. Miss Kaulner opened the door wearing her usual Ipana toothpaste smile.

"Good morning, Miss Kaulner. Please forgive my intrusion without calling. You piqued my interest with tales of your house. I intend to write about Hilly-Ho-Ho, so it was necessary for me to see it. My name is Fred in case you don't remember me." I was careful to be extremely courteous.

"Yes, Fred from North Carolina," she smiled. "Please come inside."

"I didn't mean to come inside," I apologized.

"Please be welcome," she insisted.

The interior was neat, clean, and stylish, just like her. Book shelves with a large collection of novels lined one side of the room. Her bedroom was on the upper level. The kitchen with stove and sink stood in a recessed nook just off the living room. Chairs of various shapes and colors spread out across the room. Something, however, was missing. She had no one with which to share her life and dreams. I imagined some love tragedy that had broken her life or maybe someone had betrayed her. I somehow wished that one of the falconers from Hamlet would appear and sweep her off her feet.

"In all my years at Berea, I have taught countless students and told them about Hilly-Ho-Ho. You are the first student to ever visit my home," she told me sadly.

Behind her outer facade, there lay a warm, lonely human being who had retained the title "Miss" due to some unspoken tragedy. Teaching was her life. Students were her family. Hilly-Ho-Ho was her private prison sanctuary.

Then she told me her story. "North Carolina holds a special place in my heart because that is where Carl lived. Yes, Carl. He was a sweet boy from the hills. I met him on the UNC campus and was smitten by his charm. I fell deeply in love with him. He lit up my life with joy. I finished my M.A. Degree a year ahead of him and came to teach at Berea. That's why I built Hilly Ho-Ho. We would marry and live here together." Her voice faded and she stared blankly at the floor, then she resumed her story. "He died. He drowned in the cold waters of the Nantahala trying to save his father who had accidentally fallen into the river. When I hear someone say North Carolina, it evokes a bittersweet memory of Carl."

She sat silently in her reverie and then she looked at me with her pasted-on smile. "When you have suffered enough, your life will ripen like a sweet fruit on a vine. You will understand more of life's purpose. You will feel the sadness of life deeply in your soul. I do hope that you will find someone to love, because it is in loving or losing love that life is accomplished."

She stood up signaling that the visit was over. I thanked her graciously and made my way back to campus.

Miss Kaulner was the first faculty member to welcome me into her home. Of course, I made the first overtures, but she did not reject me. There existed the possibility that this lady might become a friend. She had searched far and wide for a family of her own. I would accept her without question.

The next time I saw her outside of class was November and she was sitting at a table in the snack bar longingly staring out the clear windows at the distant pinnacles. I surmised that she was thinking of her lost Carl and the sadness of her life. She gazed at the spoon in her coffee cup as she stirred its contents, then she gazed back at the mountains. I walked toward her table, but she indicated with her raised right hand that she wished to be alone at this time. I nodded my head at her and smiled, letting her know that I understood.

Two days later I received a note from her asking me to come to her office at my convenience. When I arrived, she ushered me in and invited me to sit in a plush chair opposite her desk.

"Why are you befriending me?" she began. "What is in it for you?" "Are you trying to ingratiate yourself with me in order to get a better grade?"

"No, Miss Kaulner," I replied. "You are a classy lady. No teacher had ever invited students to visit in their home as you invited my composition class to visit yours. I was impressed with your graciousness and your willingness to share some private aspects of your life with me. Some part of me instantly wanted to tell you how hard my life has been, too, but fear overcame me because I did not want to be rejected again as had happened so often in my life. Please do not misread me, Miss Kaulner, because people always misread me and impute to me motives and impressions that are not at all true. Do you know that students on this campus already call me names and think that I am not of their sexual persuasion? For some reasons I seem to threaten them. I needed someone to listen to me and be supportive."

"On the day you visited me in my home, I was sad and lonely, too, and I wanted someone to support me," she said as she lowered her gaze to the desk in front of her. After a moment of thought, she jerked her head upward and boldly spoke, "So what are we two going to do about each other and life?"

"I can earn my own grade in your class, Miss Kaulner, but I'm not quite sure how to earn your respect and friendship. That is what I desire more than a grade," I spoke respectfully.

"You just earned my respect," she said with a slight smile on her face.

"Will you serve as my counselor while I am at Berea?" I asked her.

"It will be a pleasure," she responded.

"And will you be mine when life beats me down?" she asked.

"I will hear with an open heart," I heard myself say.

Miss Kaulner did a strange thing in December when the college dismissed students to go home for Christmas. The Berea students from North Carolina and points south had chartered a bus to Asheville. It would depart at 11:00. My class with Miss Kaulner ended at 10:30 in the morning. Most faculty cancelled classes on this day because of the excitement and students' inability to concentrate on subject material. Not Miss Kaulner. She scheduled a major exam for that departure day knowing that our passing her course depended on the score.

Anger, curses, blasphemous sentences flew from the mouths of her students. It was our first Christmas at Berea and freshmen wanted to savor all activities, not cram for a last-minute exam. All petitions to her to postpone the exam fell on deaf ears. She seemed to derive some sort of sadistic pleasure from our discomfort. Students in the class refused to study for her exam. Only two students passed it. I failed it, too. She never forgave me for not passing her exam.

After Christmas vacation, she grew cold and distant toward us all. Chloe and I wondered why she did it. Did she want to hold us to the high academic standards of the school? Did she hate Christmas? It was painful to consider that she sat alone in her one room, two-level house while students returned to the warmth and love of their own families. If I had been wise, I would have invited her to share in our campus activities.

At the end of the semester she left a note in my writing folder saying, "It is too bad that you will never be a good writer. You have not suffered enough, yet. You are too shallow. You have nothing to write about. My disappointment is great. I did so much want you to be a replacement for Carl."

MEET ME UNDER THE CEDAR TREES

Letters from my sister, Justine, sustained my morale and good emotional state during my four years at Berea. A letter per week came from Banner Elk, North Carolina, where she was attending Lees-McRae College. I ran to the post office daily hoping that a letter would be there. In our letters to each other, we gossiped, chit-chatted, and spoke of issues profound. We always found space to write words of encouragement to each other.

In one letter she wrote that her biology class was the hardest at the college and many students had failed it. But for her, it had been a challenge. She had spent three hours a day studying for biology. In the end, she had received and an "A" with a certificate stating, "grade given with honors."

I was required to study biology at Berea too. A grade of "B" was the best I could make. I teased her by saying, "Well, you don't know an angiosperm from an Echinoderm." "Shove it up your Xylem and Phloem," she retorted. For the next couple of letters we insulted each other through the medium of biology.

She encouraged me not to take events personally. "This, too, shall pass," she reminded me. Once she wrote the words,"Dum spiro, spero." (While I breathe, I hope.) I wrote back, "Spiro Agnew is not so dumb. He called college students 'worn out, effete snobs,' didn't he?"

In my sophomore year I took two semesters of Bible. Can you imagine? Two semesters of Bible! Justine and I debated the existence of God in our correspondence. Justine contended that He existed. I responded that She did not. No God would have inflicted our theology professor on us. He just happened to be from my hometown, Morganton. That horrid class met from 3:30-4:45 three times a week. We studied from the Bible as well as a text called THE BIBLE AS HISTORY AND LITERATURE. (And comedy and fairy tales).

This professor was so boring that he put himself to sleep. He would lean on his hand, which he propped on his podium, and drone like a plane engine stalling. Within thirty minutes, the entire class was snoring. I fell asleep when the Jews outran Pharaoh and waded through the Red Sea. I woke up when Jesus was ascending to glory.

I passed his class on the merit of my required oral presentation which I called, "God is female; she is black; she lives in Alabama; and, boy is she pissed at all of us." My presentation woke up the entire class and they engaged in a vociferous debate. The professor complimented my courage and originality, but privately, he told me I was going to Hell. Justine, too, said that I was probably going to Hell and that Berea was good training for that.

When she came to visit me at Berea, she noticed that many of my friends were either black or from a foreign country. "Some of your friends are black, aren't they?" she said sheepishly.

"I hadn't noticed," I replied. "They are good people."

"People back in North Carolina would not approve," she warned me.

"I don't need their approval," I informed her. "Have any of them ever been a friend to me? They are a bunch of hypocrites. They pretend to believe in God and can tell everyone what God thinks and believes. In the same breath they are judgmental, racist, condemning bullies and approve only of that which pleases them."

"But you will have to live with them if you go back," she told me.

"I have always lived among them," I said. "But I have changed. They haven't. What do I care what they think? I am responsible for myself, not them. I can be kind to anyone."

Justine and I remained close for most of our lives. Then she got sick, real sick. She was terminal. She went to live with my brother Willard Worth and his wife, Ruth, in

Missouri where they took good care of her until she passed away.

I picked up the phone and told my sister, Gertie, that Justine had died.

Devoid of emotion, I did not weep for her. I felt sadness that she was gone. Gertie and I chose to accept the viewpoint that Justine cared enough about us not to cause us suffering. We suffered not at all. We did not have to keep vigil as she faded away in pain. We did not lose her one piece at a time as the rest of the family did. However, I did not get to tell her good-bye.

Gertie and I decided to do our own memorial service for Justine, so I told her to meet me at the Mill Shoals, the small waterfall where we had spent most of our summers.

The murmuring waters of the Mill Shoals carried a healing quality for troubled souls who came for solace beside its ancient rocks and eternal waters and constituted a perfect place for a memorial service. I picked up a rock and threw it into the cascading stream. It struck some moss and catapulted into the deep pool at the bottom. I smelled the goldenrod and listened to bugs chirping in the drying grass. In the distance a cow lowed as a dragonfly droned by, its wings whirring like a helicopter.

Justine had come with us to this spot many times when we were young. In those hazy days of autumn, death had been far away and no one had thought much of it. We had swum in the pool below the falls. In a futile attempt to mimic a professional diver, Justine had dived in the shallow water, injuring two vertebrae which had pained her all her life. We had carried her on the way home.

When Justine and I had been in the fifth and seventh grades respectively, we had been very close friends. The giant cedar trees behind our house had become our refuge from the world. In the evenings after school, we had sat there and talked about the world, our dreams and aspirations. I had felt warm and reassured, listening to her lilting southern speech, each word sounding as if it were wrenched from a poem or a lullaby. She and Gertie had carried water from the spring. They had often sat to rest at the bottom of the hill, chatting with each other, forgetting about time, until Ottie would come looking for them. Under assault from a cold, hurtful outside world, I had felt comfort with her. She spoke up for me when others bullied me.

She had been a good friend to Gertie as well. The two of them had walked the long pathway to school together when they had been in the first and second grades. They had worked in the fields and had discussed boys, giggling as they shied away from meeting them. They had picked blackberries in July and had carried fresh milk to cool in the spring up Devil's Fork. They had gone to Sunday school together at the church, walking along roads filled with mud in spring and hot dust in summer. They had worn each other's clothes. They both had grown into elegant, adult women.

Justine, Gertie, and I had had some exciting fights. A fight would start over some trivial issue such as losing at playing the game of jacks. I had not liked to lose, nor had Gertie. Justine had been so good at the game that she rarely had lost.

"There she goes," we always had taunted her. "She can't miss." "She's taking them all."

Justine had taken all the jacks. Gertie had grabbed them from her hands and had hurled the stack across the floor at Justine. I had slapped Gertie, Justine had slapped Gertie and the fracas had been on. We three had rolled into a ball, hands and arms flailing in the air. As women will do, they had suddenly turned on me as if I had been the culprit, and had chased me around the outside chimney. A few minutes later I had turned the tables on them and had pursued them back around the house with a broom handle. I had intended to knock some sense into them.

At times, just the two girls had fought. Gertie had managed to get Justine in a headlock with her elbow. Gertie had twisted Justine's head in a circle and had rammed her head into the nearest wall. Justine had gone down seeing stars, as if having been struck by a jack hammer. Within a couple of hours, we had been friends again.

Later, when she had married, she had moved to New Jersey.

"Whoever moves to the North?" I had asked her in a letter. "Come back home."

I could not tell if she had been happy there. When she had returned, there had been a different person in her body, more Yankee and harsh. Life's experiences had hardened her. We no longer knew each other.

Gertie and I sat by the Mill Shoals thinking about her life and ours. We decided that whatever had taken her away would not dim our good memories of her. Gertie went home. I lingered by the gurgling water for a while. I sat and pondered the ebb and flow of life.

I would let the good live on. I chose to remember her sweetness and the joy years of our youth.

The water, softly gurgling across the rocks, reminded me of her soft, southern drawl which she had lost in New Jersey.

That voice whispered to me, "I am now in the great Forever. It is over. It is done. No regret for either of us. I am in the falling rain. I am in the blue sky. These daisies that bloom along the creek are me. Hang on to the sweet memories, the quiet talks, and the funny quarrels. I left you in silence for I could not break your heart as I lay dying. The pain was too great to inflict on you and Gertie, because you were special to me. When your life is over, come to meet me under the cedar trees and I will tell you all about it."

BREAK A LEG

I remember Lon Chaney playing that role once upon a time. You look like a forlorn vampire hanging by his teeth," Samuel shouted up to Dr. Parsons, who was clinging from one of the crosswalks that crisscrossed the ceiling of the Tab. Tab was short for Tabernacle which was our college theatre. Already stressed out, Dr. Parsons was in no mood for jokes. His usual irascible personality ratcheted up tenfold under pressure.

"When I get down from this ladder, I will show you some vampire teeth," Dr. Parsons yelled at Samuel.

Dr. Parsons disentangled himself from the Fresnel light that he was attempting to fix, deftly tiptoed along the catwalk, and slid down a light pole at the end of the walkway. He was fuming. He intended to take out his frustration of the broken light on poor, unfortunate Samuel who had made a bad choice in his type of greeting.

A small group of us actors were rehearsing a short play, "The Thief." When the shouting between Dr. Parsons and Samuel began, I melted away into the set and wings of the theatre. I stepped to the heavy velvet curtain that crossed the stage and wrapped the edge of the curtain around me, becoming invisible. Other actors hid behind the set; one went into a barrel we were using in the play, and another just sat down on stage and pretended to be a part of the decorations.

The confrontation grew fiery.

Dr. Parsons was a brilliant teacher, but he had a personality that kept people at a distance. He did not socialize with the faculty, and he usually sat reading his paper during their meetings. He would flap his newspaper loudly when he disagreed with them. If someone offended him, he would slam the paper down with a loud bang on the table, get up and make a dramatic exit from the room, making sure to slam any door loudly in the process. Somewhere in the past, he had gotten hurt deeply, and now he chose to keep anyone from coming through the gate to his personal heart.

Today, he was determined to drive Samuel away, and, maybe, he would toss him out of the Tab for good.

"Where did that little son-of-a-bitch go," he shouted storming down the aisle of the theatre, snorting and frothing at the mouth. In extreme anger, Dr. Parsons always had a white spit that covered his lips and mouth. We called it his "froth."

The room was silent. No one would tell on Samuel. Besides, no one of us wanted to divulge his hiding place and take the berating that was rightfully Samuel's.

"I'm going to kick your ass for disrespecting me, you little jackass."

"Well, come and kick it," Samuel challenged him as he emerged from his hiding place in the sound booth at the back of the theatre.

As Dr. Parsons stomped down the aisle toward the sound booth, Samuel slipped out the side door and walked down one of the outside aisles, trying to keep as many rows of seats between him and his adversary as possible.

Not to be outdone, Dr. Parsons hurled himself across several rows of seats in Samuel's direction. Samuel ran upon the stage where we had been rehearsing and grabbed a fake sword that was one of our props. Dr. Parsons grabbed a second one and they began a mock fight around and across our rehearsal space.

"I will teach you to respect me," Dr. Parsons informed Samuel.

"I was joking," Samuel said in his defense.

"Life and theatre work are no joke," Dr. Parsons responded.

"I'm sorry I called you a vampire," Samuel managed to utter an apology.

Dr. Parsons slammed the fake sword against the stage floor, stomped down the main aisle of the theatre, and exited through the swinging doors that covered the entrance to the auditorium. The doors swung back and forth dramatically flipping against themselves with a thumping noise.

Those of us in rehearsal waited until a dead silence reigned in the theatre before emerging from our hiding places.

"That man is a demon right out of Hell," Lucy observed. It was her first theatrical experience and would most likely be her last.

"He's not supposed to be cursing in front of us," John observed nervously. "I don't like people cursing me."

The swinging doors at the back of the auditorium opened gently and Dr. Parsons re-emerged and sat down in the last row of seats. He was here to observe our rehearsal. None of us could remember our lines or blocking as we felt his icy stare cast upon us. The rehearsal came to a dead standstill.

Dr. Parsons got up and walked to the edge of the stage and said to us very nicely, "I am so glad to have you actors in my theatre. I've been watching your rehearsal and I think you will have a very good show. Keep up your hard work. Break a leg."

Then he was gone like a shadow in the night. Stunned, we looked at each other in amazement. Did that monster actually compliment us?

"The Thief" went into production the following Tuesday. We were mediocre, but the audience responded politely. It was customary to have a critique at the end of each theatre production. Just my luck, it was Miss Kaulner of Hilly-Ho-Ho fame, who led the discussion. She pointed out that we were amateurs, had little talent and had produced a poor play and that we probably shouldn't count on continuing in theatre. I was devastated. She berated me in front of this audience of my peers and my professors. She had not forgotten that I had failed her Christmas exam and she evidently held it against me. Or was she being fair with honest criticism?

Out of the darkness of the theatre, there emerged the figure of Dr. Parsons, his skinny figure swathed in a short jacket and his wrinkles making him look like something out of "Sleepy Hollow." He cleared his throat loudly. I could see foam beginning to form around his lips.

"I wish to personally thank this group of fine students who have chosen to experience theatre. They are beginners. I do not have the same expectations of them as I have of professional actors. They have been to rehearsal every day for over a month. They memorized their lines; they directed themselves; they are developing a love of acting.

Let us not take that love away from them."

Miss Kaulner scowled at him.

He found something good to say about each one of us. Then, in his usual way, he exited the theatre leaving the swinging doors wildly flapping back and forth. I never went on stage again.

I became a volunteer in the theatre. I worked with sets, make-up, costuming, scripts, lights, and any other jobs that needed to be done in a play. I designed and printed programs. I took up tickets and worked as an usher. Whatever Dr. Parsons wanted me to do, I did joyfully. He rarely said a word to me, in anger or as a compliment. I thought that he was a mean, angry person that had no feelings in his life.

During the last regular performance of a play at Berea, I was sitting midway in the auditorium enjoying the production. When the lights came up I stood to applaud the actors with the rest of the patrons. Dr. Parsons came on the stage and asked everyone to be seated. He began to speak:

"There are times in our lives when we as professors have the privilege of teaching students who are worthy. The student of whom I speak never signed up for any of my classes. I never taught him formally. But I did teach him, because he was always at this Tabernacle doing whatever job was needed to make sure the show would go on. There is no aspect of theatre that he did not learn. This man probably knows more about theatre than many of my majors. Would Fred Epeley please come up on stage with me?"

"Through my efforts and testament to your knowledge of theatre, I present this certificate of appreciation in the Theatrical Arts to you. Furthermore, I formally induct you into the national theatrical fraternities of Alpha Psi Omega and Tau Delta Tau, in good standing and with all honors and privileges."

Dr. Parsons presented me the certificates and then drew me to him in a bear hug. This man, whom I had judged to be cold and aloof, actually hugged me in front of all the assembled people. He exited the stage, then, dramatically swept down the aisle, and pushed through the swinging doors, leaving them clacking.

The stage curtain closed, plunging me into semi- darkness. I worked my way through the crowd trying to go to Dr. Parson's office. But his office was locked. He was nowhere to be found.

I never saw Dr. Parsons again. The Dean told me that he had left immediately after the presentation to take a job at the University of Japan in Tokyo. It is just as well, for there are no words to thank this man for what he taught me. I see his ranting and raving now through the perspective of fifty years of teaching theatre and I, myself, have had rants and raves of my own through the years. I never took his classes; I never took any drama classes. I didn't need to. Dr. Parsons had already taught me what I needed to know. I established theatres wherever I lived and I established my own semi-professional group called The Stage Crafters. I hope I touched lives in the same manner as Dr. Parsons touched mine.

Dr. Parsons, wherever you are in this great universe, I hope you are still hanging from crosswalks, teaching the angels to play the part of vampires. I hope you are still snorting and frothing at the mouth, demanding excellence from everyone around you. And if, by chance, you are in Hell, I'm sure you will have the Devil playing the part of Hitler as you direct his memoires. You instilled in me a desire to strive for excellence. And you gave me a love for drama. Break a leg, Sir!

FAT MAN'S MISERY

Wayne, John, Alfred, Barbara, Chloe, and I stood in front of the Student Union Building waiting for wagon transportation to Indian Fort Theatre for Mountain Day celebration. We were dressed in dungarees and blue Berea sweatshirts. It was October and we were all ready for a break from the rigors of class and labor. Ordinarily students could not leave campus to go anywhere without permission and there were no cars to drive anyway. But this Mountain Day was a quaint, long-held tradition at Berea. I did not care a whit for it. I had grown up and suffered in mountainous conditions. Returning for a day in the mountains did not excite me; rather, it dredged up unpleasant memories. John had persuaded me to go.

A beat-up green tractor with a wooden trailer filled with hay and straw pulled up to the steps of the Union building. Our group piled into the straw like young children playing in leaves. We threw handfuls of straw at each other. Before the wagon pulled out on the highway leading to Indian Fort Theater, we all looked and acted like a bunch of hayseeds.

The tractor and driver pulled us out into the countryside past mail boxes with the family name "Pigg" written on them. John and Wayne got a kick out of that. Our group began to yell "sou-eeeee, sou-eeeee, sou-eee" out into the trees and across the drying fields. "Piggs" came to their front doors and stared at our trailer. "Dam, uppity college students!" someone yelled. A man catapulted a rotten tomato our way. It landed with a splash, spreading rotten juice all over Barbara, Chloe, Alfred, and me. Conflict with the country folk was always present, but it didn't matter today. We had a day off to play in the mountains.

The road we traveled was filled with groups of students who had chosen to walk the two miles to the theater. Some waved and yelled out, "You'll be coming round the mountain when you come." The double entendre sent us all into fits of laughter. "Now, now, Berea students behave yourselves," Wayne said sarcastically wagging his index finger at the group.

The tractor driver deposited us at the base of the trail to the Pinnacle. "Have fun," he waved as he drove back to the college for another joyful group of students. The lunchroom staff had put up a sign reading, "Lunch served between the hours of 11:00 and 1:00. Pick up your sack lunches here." Our group decided to eat lunch on our way back down.

The climb up the Pinnacle was steep and most of us were somewhat out of shape. The trail was dry and well-worn by hundreds of feet that had plowed up before us. We climbed straight up the path until it diverged into a thicket of pine and laurel, then doubled back on itself in a steep switchback. The shouts of student voices over and around the large rocks echoed down the valley. One group was singing "She'll Be Coming 'round the Mountain" at the top of their lungs. We walked past groups of students who had grown tired and were resting on boulders along the path.

"How far is Fat Man's Misery," Barbara called out.

"I don't know. I've never been here before," I replied.

"Just follow the long line of students," a voice called out from behind us.

Chloe developed a blister on the heel of her left foot. I paused with her while she lifted her left foot up and crossed it on her right knee, holding it there so she could examine the damage the blister was causing. She took a band aid out of the pocket of her shorts, opened it, and taped the middle carefully across the blister, which she punctured with a fingernail. After putting her foot back in her shoe, she gently rested all her weight on her foot to determine if she could continue walking. It worked. Our group continued its climb upward toward the Pinnacle.

Going through Fat Man's Misery was the high point of challenges on Mountain Day. Every student who had ever attended Berea went through it once, except me. I love to go spelunking and I have visited every major cave in America and Europe. But, the truth is, I have a bad case of claustrophobia. If I have a wide enough space on each side of a trail within a cave, there is no problem with my navigating it. However, if the path is narrow and one has to squeeze along between extremely high and narrow sides, my claustrophobia kicks in and I freeze in place.

Going through the Misery had nothing to do with being fat. Most fat people did just fine. It was the skinny people like me with claustrophobia that caused the problems.

A long line of students had formed at the entrance to Fat Man's Misery and the line snaked back up the hill toward us. Squeals, shouts, cries, complaints, and general bedlam emanated from the fissure in the mountain. It was composed of shale made from layers of mud placed there by ancient oceans that had once covered Kentucky. An ancient river had carved out the path through the mountain, leaving just enough space for an average person to walk through.

Savvy upper classmen were busy initiating freshmen into the experience of The Misery. One of them would form a line moving through the fissure, and they would encourage freshmen to follow behind them. Movement through the path was very slow. About three quarters of the way through the mountain, the upperclassman would stop, forcing the entire line to stop moving. Everyone was trapped inside Fat Man's Misery. Those with claustrophobia began to scream and complain. The back of the line continued to move forward pressing more and more heavily on those already in the fissure.

I stood staring into the crevice in the mountain wondering what I was doing at this spot on Mountain Day. These college students were gallivanting around the hills like pigs wallowing in slop. I had had enough of hills and hollows and mountain life. I had come here to elevate myself from my place of birth. This day was a horrible reminder of my early life. I did not want to celebrate my mountain heritage yet.

When our group entered Fat Man's Misery, I got trapped approximately one fourth of the distance inside. Bodies continued to press against my back. I looked upward and saw the sides of the rocks extending into a black ceiling. I could not even turn my body around. Fear and panic seized me. I began to yell that I wanted out of there. Everyone just screamed and laughed at me. No one can imagine the terror and horror of a person with claustrophobia trapped in a narrow space with a line of people pressing them from all sides.

I turned to face the incoming line.

"I'm coming out of here. I want out of here. Let me out of here," I screamed.

The line of students just screamed and cheered, "No fat man, no misery. No fat man, no misery."

The students thought that I was part of a joke.

I began crawling across the bodies of the students in line behind me. Grabbing hair, ears, faces, heads, noses, or whatever body part that would support me, I painfully moved back toward the entrance of Fat Man's Misery.

"You are going the wrong way," one girl screamed.

"I'm going the right way for me," I retorted.

Realizing the seriousness of my panic attack, students squatted down to allow me an easier passage across the line. I was gasping for breath when I raced back through the entrance. Students in the line I had just crossed bore shoe marks, bloody noses, cuts and bruises, and other reminders of their day on the mountain.

While the other members of my little group made their way successfully through Fat Man's Misery, I sought solitude on a lonely rock that provided a spectacular view of the pinnacles and the Bluegrass Country stretching to the north. The cooler mountain air made my breathing easier. Was I supposed to be ashamed of the spectacle I had just created? How does one cure his claustrophobia? In retrospect, my whole life was a case of claustrophobia. The events of my life crowded me, pushed me, and closed in on me until there was pain. Sitting on top of this mountain, I remembered the storms that used to come down from Oaky Knob and the gentle winds that used to rock Grassy Knob. There were no threatening fissures to enclose me on Ottie's farm. Even Devil's Fork was less intimidating.

Ottie's world was far away from me now on this day that was supposed to be fun and celebration. Its effects remained in my life. I looked northward toward Richmond out across the rounded mountains of shale to unending fields of bluegrass waving in the wind.

"Kentucky!" I thought, "This dark and bloody ground."

The Pawnee had made this majestic place their hunting grounds and had fought Daniel Boone and white settlers for the right to possess its riches and beauty. From this very mountain I can see the outline of the Wilderness Road over which thousands of hopeful travelers poured into Kentucky. Their weary, white-washed bones lined every mile of this ancient highway. Unlike those early sojourners, mine was an easier highway that I had taken to this land of Kentucky. They had been seeking a better life and I am seeking a better life. They had become sons of Kentucky as I will too, in time. My moment of reverie was a precious time in this Mountain Day. Perhaps, in a future time, the boy from Carolina and the man he would become in Kentucky would fuse into a happy person.

A peregrine falcon spread its wings and flew from the Pinnacle back in the direction of Berea College. White clouds stretched southward in the direction of the Carolinas reminding me from where I had come.

My friends made the trip successfully through Fat Man's Misery and caught up with me as I sulked back down the mountain.

"Don't be embarrassed, Fred, everyone has some phobia," Wayne consoled me.

"I don't like heights," Alfred chimed in. "I get seasick if I climb into the upper bunk bed."

"It was cool how you literally walked over twenty student bodies to get to your place of safety," Chloe whispered as she patted me on the left shoulder.

"Thank all of you for your love and concern," I said with gratitude. "I'm fine, but I will never come back out here on this stupid day. I don't give a damn about this tradition."

The sack lunch we ate at Indian Fort Theater was just dreadful. Berea lunches were generally bad anyway. The bag contained a peanut butter and jelly sandwich, an apple, a bag of potato chips, and a cookie. This standard lunch was served every Sunday of every week while I was at Berea. In order to give students who worked in the cafeteria a break on Sundays, students had to pick up a sack supper before departing the cafeteria at lunch. Cheap, just plain cheap!

On Mountain Day we would have a regular, hot meal at the school in the evening. I tossed the sandwich and cookie in the trash and ate the apple and potato chips.

"Take that food right back out of the trashcan," a familiar voice rang across the Indian Fort Theater. "Waste not, want not." Oh, my God, it was Mrs. Van Cleaveron!

Damn! Who would have thought that she would be monitoring Mountain Day lunch?

"Identify yourself, young man. Show me your student I.D.," she demanded.

I took my I.D. out of my pocket and showed it to her.

"I've got my eye on you. You will end up in my charm school class before you graduate. I can just see it coming," she warned me.

"She ran a charm school???" I thought. "It certainly had not done her any good."

"I would rather eat a horse paddy sandwich than that wretched peanut butter," I sassed her. "Ottie fed me better than this place does."

"Take that food out of the garbage can," she ordered me.

"You take a throw-away sandwich out of the trashcan and eat it yourself," I said bitterly. "I've already done that in my life."

My little gang of friends ushered me away from the Indian Fort Theater and we began the return walk to the college. No one said a word. We walked the entire two miles in silence. I wondered if they were reassessing their desire to be friends with me. I had embarrassed them all with the escapade in Fat Man's Misery and now I had made bad points for us all with Mrs. Van Cleaveron.

I was becoming more and more like my mother. I acted like her. I was angry and resentful. I had not even developed an ability to have fun like these students who were with me on Mountain Day. I had no warm fuzzy for anyone on this campus. Abuse and neglect had made me cold, unfriendly, and defensive.

Upon arriving at the campus, my little group departed in silence.

A BAKER'S DOZEN

Summer came. I found employment in Princeville, Illinois, working in the pea and corn-packing plants on the prairies. Through the Student Aid Fund, Dean Orwig loaned me transportation money to get to Illinois with the understanding that I would repay the amount from my first check.

In a flash, I found myself back in the real world of basic people of average intelligence, sweating blue collar workers, and fat Midwestern women who swore every other word and talked in a manner that would make sailors blush. Princeville is the first place I ever heard a female use the f-word. All the workers at the plant used the word in every sentence. They enjoyed tormenting me with their foul language and sexual innuendos.

A fat, bouncy, grey-haired lady sauntered up to me at the factory the first day and invited me to rent a room for the summer at her house. I said "yes" without even seeing it. She told me her name was Tillie Blank and that dozens of college students had roomed with her throughout the years. .

"I'll take the room, Mrs. Blank," I told her.

"Please call me Tillie," she smiled.

"Here is a key for you. If you lose it, you have to replace it yourself. Come and go as you please. You can't bring any girls up to your room, but from what I have observed over past summers, you will be so tired from working that you won't be able to think of girls."

That was it. I had a job and a place to stay. I really liked Tillie.

Knowing of my financial obligations, I spoke with Leonard Tilson, the factory boss, about work hours. He agreed that I would work from 3:00 in the afternoon until 11:00

p.m. Then I volunteered to work on the clean-up crew which added another six hours to my workday. Altogether, I would work fourteen hours a day and sleep eight.

One morning when I was returning home at 5:30, I looked down the street of the small town of Princeville and saw a man in his sixties, dressed in white t-shirt and white pants, struggling to carry some heavy boxes into a store. I casually walked down to him and said, "Sir, could I help you carry some of your boxes. My name is Fred. I'm a college student working during the summer at the factory."

"Oh, 'tank youse wary much," he replied in a heavily-accented German speech. "Youse have a nachname, last name?"

"Epeley," I said with pride remembering that my real father had a different name.

His face lit up with a gigantic smile as he repeated my name "Apfele."

"Youse are German. That name means "little apple grower," he pronounced agreeably.

"Well, I'm actually a Duke's mixture," I said shyly.

"Youse speak with accent," he said.

"Not me, you have the accent," I said laughing.

It had not occurred to me that I had a North Carolina accent. Adrian spoke with a Kentucky twang. Alfred had a yahoo accent from the hills of Tennessee. These two friends had come with me from Berea for summer work, too. We were singing flat in the choir among these corn-fed prairie people.

I looked inside the building to see what he was doing at 5:30 in the morning. He was a baker, specifically of doughnuts. He had a doughnut shop. I loved this adventure, but my aching body had to get some sleep.

"What is your name?" I asked him.

"Schneider," he answered as he disappeared into the back of his shop. "Youse can come to see me again."

I liked Schneider and Tillie Blank both. This was a neat little town.

As I walked home early one morning after clean-up shift, a man followed suspiciously behind me. I noticed his shadows darting from tree to building and back to trees. I thought that he might try to rob me. I walked very fast and the figure walked even faster.

I broke into a run, my heart racing with panic. I could not get my key into Tillie's door, so I jumped from the porch and ran in the direction of the lights downtown. Out of breath, I was ready to collapse when two powerful arms grabbed me and pulled me inside a door. The arms belonged to Schneider.

He grabbed a rolling pin and went back to the street yelling something in German that sounded like, "Du bloede Kueh, 'raus, raus, Arshloch, ich schmeise dein Gottverdamten Kopf." In the relief that I felt at being saved, I knew that I would have to learn German sometime. (When I returned to Berea, I enrolled in German class with Dr. Kogerma. Although I majored in French at Berea, I taught German in North Carolina public schools for seventeen years.)

Every morning thereafter, when I exited the canning factory to walk home at 5:00, Schneider stood leaning against a tree in the yard, arms crossed with a giant rolling pin in his hand, waiting to escort me home. We walked to his doughnut shop where he proceeded to bake some fresh doughnuts and prepare hot coffee which he fed me for breakfast. I talked with him for an hour as he furiously made all kinds of doughnuts. He pulled them from the hot, sizzling grease and sprinkled them with white gobs of powdered sugar.

Schneider became a surrogate father to me. He was kind and loving and appreciated my company while he did his lonely work early in the morning. He had endured a hard life in Germany before immigrating to Illinois, so he sympathized with my struggle to overcome the hardships of my life.

One day he said to me, "Success in life is a baker's dozen. When I sell a box of doughnuts to a customer, I always put thirteen doughnuts in it. I give them more than they ask for. It is my way of saying thanks. It is a symbol of good luck where I come from. So you, Friedrich, (that's what he called me in German) live your life as 'a baker's dozen.' Give people more than they ask for and always leave them in a good mood."

I learned to love this simple man with his heart as big as the ocean. He protected me from harm; he fed me; he counseled me; he found, perhaps, a lost son that he had never had. Schneider was a more powerful teacher than any of the learned people at Berea. He had no degrees, nor syllabi, nor final exams. And he never lectured. He was inspirational and ended all our conversations by handing me a doughnut. Professors everywhere could learn from him.

One morning I asked him, "Schneider, what do you see in me? Why do you look after my safety and protect me with your rolling pin?"

"You see, Friedrich," he said wiping clumps of white, sticky dough from his rotund fingers. "In Germany, I once had a family whom I loved dearly. My wife planted red geraniums in brown clay pots and set them along the sidewalk and in the window sills of our house. She made a place of beauty and peace for my son and me. She baked fresh bread and donuts daily for us and the neighbors. She eventually built her own bakery. She taught me how to bake."

"We had a son named Fritz. He turned eighteen in 1939 and the Nazis took him into their army. He died in the bitter cold at the siege of Stalingrad. Authorities told me that they had buried his body in the frozen tundra on the steppes of Russia."

Schneider ceased talking and his hands looked frozen to the dough he was kneading. His shoulders began to shake as heavy sobs shook his entire body. I saw some tears fall on the sides of the wooden bowl in which he prepared the morning baking.

When he lifted his head, he looked directly into my eyes. I could see the red veins in the white sclera. Hurt and sadness rested upon his shoulders like a great millstone. He wiped his eyes with the back of his left hand leaving a swath of white flour across his face.

"You are the exact image of my son, Fritz. He, too, had blond hair, blue eyes and medium build like you. When I first saw you in the early morning, I thought you were his ghost. I believed that my son Fritz had come home to me."

He paused again and wept softly.

"The war took my wife and son. She died in the firebombing of Dresden. After the war, I came to live with a German family in Peoria.

"You ask what I see in you, Friedrich. I see my son come back home to me. I have my family again if but for a moment in my dreams. My son was sweet and kind like you. Even if you are not Fritz, let me have my dream for a little while."

He returned to his baking. I rose from my seat, walked to him, and held him in a bear hug. We both wept for families lost and the sadness that had brought us together at this little donut shop on the Illinois prairies.

Before I left the shop, Schneider made me a special donut, covered with powdered sugar, which he called a "Schneeball."

"It was my son's favorite dessert," he explained.

In that precious moment, I was overcome with emotion because I had the father that I had always wanted and had been missing eternally. Furthermore, this sad, kind, broken man could embrace again his surrogate son.

In my friend Schneider, I once again saw what true emotional pain was. I felt ashamed and cheap in complaining about my circumstances in life. I had been complaining about having no shoes, when here was a man that had no feet.

By the end of the summer, I had repaid both loans from my freshman year and would return to Berea with a little change in my pocket. When I went to say farewell to Tillie, she had a mouth full of onions. They smelled so much of home that I wanted to kiss her. She invited me to come to stay with her again if I ever returned to Princeville.

Leonard Tilson did not want me to leave. He offered me a salaried job on the spot and told me that I would eventually have any office job that I wanted. But I looked at him and thought about his dead-end life. I would rather have another round with Mrs. Kerfluffle, Miss Kaulner, and Mr. Rules and Regulations than to be stuck for a lifetime just a few miles from where Carl Sandburg and Edgar Lee Masters were born. I was here for the money. My dreams lay elsewhere.

Saying farewell to Schneider was the hardest task of all. When I told him I was going away, he stopped his work and stared deeply into my eyes as if he wanted to remember something about me that was important to him. He placed both hands on my shoulders and drew me into a hug of friendship. "I'll miss you," he said in his German accent. He turned away and quickly threw fresh doughnuts into a paper box with a cellophane window on top. He thrust the box in my hand and murmured softly the words, "Auf Wiedersehen." Covering his eyes with his right hand, he exited through the swinging doors into his kitchen. My last image of him was his silhouette bent over a mixing bowl, like a priest at his altar praying over the communion wafer.

As I rode the Greyhound bus away from Princeville, I opened the box of doughnuts and, sure enough, counted thirteen. On top of the doughnuts Schneider had written these words on a white paper napkin, "Was nicht toetet, macht staerker." (What doesn't kill you will make you stronger.)

I thought of my Carolina home that lay far away beyond the pinnacles, the bluegrass, and the Kentucky laurels. I had not been there since Christmas and would not see anyone from Ottie's world until the coming Christmas. I wondered if anyone there ever thought of me. No letters had come. No news. It was as if I was dead or, perhaps, they were dead. I was homesick and I wanted to see Gertie, Justine, and Callie. Yes, I wanted to see Ottie, too.

Schneider had been my family for three months and now I was leaving him. My heart was filled with sadness, pain, and love.

When the bus crossed the Ohio River into Kentucky, I felt a warmth, a familiarity, a sense of returning to where I belonged. No one on campus mattered at this moment. It was the place that mattered. I felt pride that I was a Berea student.

Looking back in the direction of the Illinois prairies, I whispered:

"Sorry to leave you, my friend Schneider."

SHORT ARM INSPECTION

When Physical Education class ended at nine o'clock, I rushed back to Pearsons Hall to take a quick shower and get dressed for my French class at ten. I undressed from the sweaty shorts and shirt that I was wearing, picked up soap and towel, and walked stark naked down the hallway to the communal shower room. Few residents of our dorm ever wore clothing when going to take a shower and nudity was quite common at other times.

The cool water felt so good against my skin that I tarried a bit longer than usual, savoring the splashing from the shower nozzle. I dried off rather hastily, retrieved my soap from the soap dish, and stepped out into the hallway. It was such a gross error on my part to have forgotten that this day, a Friday, was dorm inspection day.

The Oxentine family lived in an apartment on the first floor of the building. They were resident dorm mother and father who kept a keen eye on the activities of all the students who lived in Pearsons Hall. Each Friday, Mrs. Oxentine teamed up with our dorm president and went to inspect every room in the building. She was German and very meticulous about how we men should live in her dorm. Wearing white gloves, she tested desks, window sills, and shelves for any sign of dirt. Offenders got a curt note informing them that "cleanliness was next to godliness" and that any future infraction would result in demerits.

She stirred around in our closets looking for smelly clothes and shoes. Our beds had to be made without wrinkles. The room must show signs that it had been swept and window panes must be washed weekly. Her keen eyes missed nothing. She did not hesitate to leave notes posted on the outside of the door (where everyone in the dorm could read them) detailing offenses.

Bashir and I won the gold ring for the most number of offenses during the year. We missed being thrown out of the dorm by two demerits. She even did double inspections on our room during the week.

Bashir was careless when he played sports. Sweat poured off him. After playing soccer, he would undress and throw his shorts and tee shirt into the closet, unwashed. They would lie there for a week until he had time to wash them in the washing machine in the basement. He and I got used to the smell and were not especially offended by it. Mrs. Oxentine, on the other hand, took great umbrage to the smell.

After one inspection, she left a note saying, "There is something dead in your closet. I have called the local undertaker to remove the body." By George, she actually did it. She was friends with a man who worked in a local funeral home. What shame I felt when the undertaker came out of the room carrying Bashir's soiled clothes in a body bag. Mrs. Fuhrer had intended to embarrass us so that we would consider mending our ways.

"Lady on the floor!" I heard Orville's voice echo down the hallway.

I was caught half-way between the shower room and my dorm room. I wore no clothing and no hope of getting any. I only had a bar of soap and my towel in my hand. I turned and ran back into the shower room hoping that no one had seen me.

Peeking out, I saw Mrs. Fuhrer and Orville open a dorm room with their pass key and disappear inside for her formal inspection. She did not stay very long in the room. She came back out, locked the door, and advanced on to the next room. Fortunately, the resident of the room was present and she engaged him in conversation.

I hastily looked around the shower room trying to find a place to hide. Other than the shower, there was no place. And the shower had no door!

Tiptoeing back to the entrance to the shower room, I overheard Mrs. Oxentine's conversation to whatever unsuspecting victim that she had cornered in his room.

"What are these funny stains on your sheets?" she asked him. "We have a heck of a time getting them out in the wash. Stop soiling your sheets!"

I was so embarrassed for that young man that I, myself, stood beet red inside the bath room. Merciful God, what would she say to me if she caught me naked?

Only one room stood between me and the inspector. I knew that she would come into the shower room and inspect every faucet, commode, wash basin, and tile. I knew that I could wrap the towel around my waist and walk by her. But, then she would know exactly who I was and she would never let the experience die. Every person on campus would know my story.

I leaned out the door and signaled to Orville that I was in the shower room. He saw me. He asked Mrs. Oxentine if the two of them could walk back down the hallway and begin inspecting the rooms on the other side of the hallway. She agreed. It was my plan to slip into one of the rooms that she had already inspected, provided the room was unlocked.

Wrapping the towel around my waist, I stepped hesitatingly into the hallway and started toward my room. Because it was wet, my towel slid from around my waist and fell to the floor. With quick thinking, I grabbed my towel and wrapped it securely around my head leaving only one eye visible. I walked directly past Mrs. Oxentine and Orville, naked as a jaybird. If I had wrapped the towel around my waist, she would have recognized me. Having never seen other parts of my body, the two of them would never recognize me again. To throw them off track, I opened my neighbor's door and entered room B8.

The two inspectors broke out in peals of laughter, not able to believe what they had just seen.

"He probably thinks that we are here for a short arm inspection today," Mrs. Oxentine snickered. "Unfortunately, there is not much arm there to be inspected."

News spread all over campus about the incident in Pearsons Hall. Students made a game of trying to figure out who the culprit was. My name never came up. Rumors circulated that maybe Orville and Mrs. Oxentine were having an affair. They had made up the story to distract attention from them.

From that day onward, we were all cautious when we walked to the shower room naked. Orville checked every room and shower ahead of time to make sure that no student would have to go through a short arm inspection again. As Mrs. Oxentine walked past students in our dorm, she smirked and wiggled her little finger in the air at all of us.

"SKOAD" ATTACK

"I need an escort from Anna Smith dorm to the library," my friend Candy told me on the phone. "I'm doing research for a term paper and I'm afraid to walk across campus after dark."

"Jim, Alfred, and I will be at your dorm in ten minutes," I assured her.

It wasn't so much that we three boys were being gentlemen. Rather, we were responding to a safety issue that had arisen in the last few weeks on the Berea Campus. There had existed an uneasy relationship between the college and residents of the town of Berea for a very long time. Some people blamed the conflict on the fact that the college provided utilities such as water, sewer, and electricity to the town. It also ran the fire department that sent trucks out in case of fire or injury. Some resented the power of the college to regulate their lives. Student workers provided much of the labor for all these enterprises.

Some of the residents in and around the town of Berea were poor and not well educated. Since students provided all labor, not many jobs were available for townspeople. They had to seek work in Richmond or Lexington. There was a general resentment of anyone associated with the college.

Verbal clashes erupted from time to time between townspeople and college students, but incidents generally remained non-violent. However, in the autumn of 1962-63, emotions got out of hand and events ended in physical attacks on students.

Berea students walked nightly to the All Night Restaurant, because it was the only place that stayed open all night. They also went to the movie theatre. Both these establishments were off campus in the downtown area. College students and townspeople mingled in the restaurant all the time. They eyed each other across the booths and swivel seats along a counter. Generally, they did not socialize.

Berea students shared some responsibility for the hostile atmosphere that developed. They did act superior to these country people. They had come from far-away places, bringing different ways of acting and thinking into a community that already had its way of living. Some were rude and quite sassy in their attitudes. Many Berea students had come from poverty, just like the people they were condemning, yet they looked down on them.

We called them "skoads." I searched in a dictionary and found that the word "skoda" can be found in the Czech language as well as several others. It is a pejorative term used to describe someone you don't like, someone you see as inferior. Among its many meanings are "bad person," "evil doer," and "criminal." The term was not new to me, because my family and neighbors had used it often to describe another town or groups of people who lived in the hills and hollows of Appalachia. "That group of skoads up on Pea Ridge," my mother, Ottie, said often, "Don't you go near them."

The reason we three men were going to escort Candy to the library was because of a physical attack that had happened the previous day against a student on campus. "Skoads" had poured out of their parked car on Highway 25 and had rendered a good beating to the Berea student.

Tensions rose.

Beat-up cars filled with two or three "skoads" rolled across campus every few hours. Those riding in the cars yelled vulgar curses and epithets at any college student they saw. Women as well as men were randomly accosted. Berea students began to yell curses back at them. That was a mistake. The "skoads" began hurling bottles, fresh and rotten eggs, cans, and rocks at anyone walking along Highway 25. Some "skoads" even got out of their vehicles and hid behind oak trees near Lincoln Hall hoping to get a close hit on any unsuspecting student.

The Student Government Association took action. They developed an escort system for any student that was afraid to navigate campus day or night. They recommended that students not go to the movies or the restaurant in downtown Berea. Howard Hall, my dorm, was paired with Anna Smith. Ladies could call Howard Hall any time and request an escort to the library, classes, or the Snack Bar. Whoever was available at the time went as an escort for the lady.

Close friendships actually grew during this time of trouble because of the nature of students supporting each other.

Jim, Alfred, and I met Candy at Anna Smith dorm. She was nervous because rumors had spread about the attacks. Of course, they were blown out of proportion.

"What will we do if we are attacked by 'skoads'?" Candy asked.

"The three of us will stand our ground and you run like hell," Alfred explained.

Candy called us after two hours of study, and we returned to the library to see her safely back to Anna Smith. It was nine o'clock at night. Women were locked up in their dorms for the night at nine-thirty. When she signed in at the dorm and said goodnight, we three sauntered in front of Union Church on our way to the Snack Bar for some late night socializing. As we crossed the road that runs beside the Student Union Building, the "skoads" got us.

A beat-up, red Ford sped up the hill from the small bridge located below the Student Union Building. We instinctively stopped to let it pass. Three passengers in the car simultaneously opened the car windows and hurled a barrage of rotten eggs at Jim, Alfred, and me. Alfred got the brunt of the attack. Smelly, rotten egg yolks oozed down his overcoat and dripped on the ground.

"You sons-of-bitches," Alfred yelled in a fury.

"Fuck you," one "skoad" yelled as he peppered us with a second round of eggs.

"Goddamed skoads!" "Pieces of shit!" "You low-life bastards!" we yelled in our best "college" vocabulary. Berea freshman composition teachers would have referred to our language as being in the vernacular or "quaint" or even "Appalachian." It was the language of anger. And we were certainly hoi-polloi, or worse, maybe Appalachian rednecks. We were behaving on par with the "skoads."

The Ford spun its tires as the driver took off, leaving wheel imprints on the pavement and acrid, blue smoke in the air. The driver went as far as the art building, turned around, and came back for a second attack on us. We ran toward the safety of the Alumni Building. They threw several more eggs which fell harmlessly to the ground in front of the Alumni Building.

Alfred took off his coat and tossed it back onto the steps of the Alumni Building. We all smelled terribly of rotten eggs. We didn't dare go into the restroom to wash off or into the Snack Bar smelling of rotten eggs.

Jim peeked through the glass in the front door, keeping watch lest the "skoads" return.

Though it wounded our sense of manhood, we three men needed an escort back to Howard Hall. I went to the phone in the building and called for assistance. Half the men in the dorm came charging across campus looking for a good fight with the "skoads," but they were long gone. Our dorm mates kidded us good-naturedly, and then they formed a wall around us as we all walked across campus back to the dorm.

Not long after my experience, my friend Mike was walking with a black, female friend back from the movie theatre, when a similar car sped by them on Highway 25. A passenger in the car hurled beer bottles at the two of them barely missing Ann's head. It was a blatant racist attack.

My roommate Wayne and a friend, Huddleston, were walking along the highway toward Indian Fort Theatre. They intended to spend a few hours hiking and relaxing in the mountains. Along that road they saw on mailboxes the family name "Pigg." They found the name amusing and talked about it in a loud voice. Some "Pigg" residents came out of their houses and began to taunt the two college students.

"Uppity college people," one young man snarled.

"A bunch of assholes, if you ask me," another hissed.

"What are you sons-of-bitches doing out where we live. This is our turf. Get the hell away!" another added.

"I'm walking a public highway owned by neither you nor me," Wayne hurled back.

"You're a cocksucker," the first young man to speak insulted Wayne.

"You're a damn pig," Wayne shouted without thinking.

A pregnant silence reigned for a few seconds. Both groups were deciding how to react. Wayne expected that he would have to fight them. But everyone present got the joke of Wayne's statement and they all burst out laughing. They really were "pigs" in both senses of the word.

"I'm Wayne H. and I'm from South Carolina. Have you ever been there?" he inquired.

"No," was their response.

"You'll have to come down some day, and I will introduce you to my family," Wayne spoke softly.

"O.K.," one of the young men answered. "Enjoy your hike."

The confrontation was over. The family went back into their house, and Wayne and Huddleston continued their hike.

Each time Wayne returned along the road to the Pinnacle, he would stop to engage that same family in conversation. They became friendlier and they never accosted him again.

In time, the "skoad" attacks ceased. However, students moved more cautiously around campus, especially after dark. Many ladies continued to call for an escort. Both men and women liked that custom.

No matter how much Jim, Alfred, and I washed our clothes, they always had the smell of rotten eggs on them, and the odor of "skoad" clung forever to our sense of manhood.

SANCTUARY

"The three of us are going to spend Easter vacation in a monastery," Josiah announced as he rushed through the door into my dorm room. "It won't cost us a penny, because the monks give sanctuary to anyone who wants it. They ask no questions about you or what you may have done. I do hope that you want to go."

He was excited like a kid at Christmas time when he is told that he can now open his presents. But I was not Catholic and did not share his enthusiasm for pageantry, monasteries, and nunneries.

"Are we going to go dumpster diving at the monastery searching for old relics, chalices, discarded hymn books and wafers?" I teased him.

"No dumpster-diving this trip. We will be at the monastery during high holy days and get to participate in rituals that are only carried out once a year. The bishop will be there and we will get to listen to devotionals written by Thomas Merton," he explained.

"Where is this heavenly hillbilly haven," I wanted to know. "Since when did Kentucky have monasteries?"

"It is the Trappist Monastery at Gethsemene. Guess what? They have taken a vow of silence! We won't be able to talk while there," Josiah was beside himself with enthusiasm.

I could not imagine Josiah remaining silent for five minutes, much less several days. I know that I can't keep quiet that long. I wondered how the monks communicated if they never spoke. Did they use sign language? Did they write notes to each other? Did they use smoke signals like the Native Americans? My questions would soon be answered.

"How will the monks respond to the three of us? " I asked Josiah.

"Stop making silly excuses because you do not want to go. Look, Fred, this is an opportunity of a lifetime. Because I am catholic, I can get us in and out of there. On your own, you would not know what to do. So, just shut up and come on a wonderful adventure."

He was right, of course. I packed my toothbrush and a change of clothes in a paper sack in preparation for the trip. I hoped that we would not have to dress like monks while we were there. I had lost too much of my hair for a tonsured hair style.

"Have you gotten permission from the college to leave campus, Josiah?"

"I don't need their permission. We are on a religious pilgrimage at Easter. They can't legally keep us from going," he assured me.

"Don't count on it, Josiah," I replied. "Mr. Rules and Regulations shows no mercy when you break Berea's rules. I'm already on his shit list and he would probably enjoy nailing me again on some infraction."

"Just relax and let's have some fun," Josiah urged.

I forgot to ask how we were to get to the monastery and Josiah did not volunteer any information. We just started out walking. When the three of us tired, Josiah produced a sign from a bag he was carrying. He had written on it the words, "Gethsemane." Josiah told us to kneel down on the roadside and clasp our hands beneath our chins as if we were praying. He remained standing, showing the sign to all cars passing along the highway.

"Now, don't either one of you say a damn word until we get to the monastery," he ordered us.

Several cars drove past. Josiah held up his sign and bowed slightly as each one passed. Finally a driver pulled his car over on the shoulder of the road and stopped.

"Need a ride to the monastery, brothers?" the driver asked him.

In silence, Josiah nodded his head in the affirmative as if we were monks at the monastery.

"Get in, brothers," the driver said. "I know that all of you are sworn to silence and can't talk out loud to me. But that is O.K. I will keep on talking and you can signal an answer as best you can. How long have you been a Cistercian monk?" the guy wanted to know.

Josiah looked at Melbert and me and grinned as he held up three fingers, pretending that we had been monks for three years. That little fake! That con artist! He was as slick as a possum's rear end in persimmon time.

"You have obviously been away from the monastery. What have you been doing and how did you communicate with people in the secular world?" the driver asked.

Melbert and I began to snicker. How would our friend get out of this one? Don't underestimate this little Josiah ability to sustain trickery.

Josiah formed a big circle with his arms. Then he walked his index and third finger across the palm of his hand. Next, he flipped his right palm over and back as if to indicate someone dying.

"I get it," the driver blurted out enthusiastically like someone who had just translated the Rosetta stone. "You all were riding in a wooden cart, the wheel broke, your horse died, and you were walking back to the monastery at Trappist."

Melbert and I could not contain our mirth. Both of us erupted in wails of loud laughter. I held my arms around my stomach to keep from throwing up.

"Oh, shit," Josiah muttered audibly.

"Yes," the driver interjected. "It must have been a bad experience."

Melbert and I laughed even harder. Josiah and this driver could not be for real. They fed off each other. Fortunately, the driver reached the monastery and set us out. As he drove back out the gravel driveway, I heard him mutter, "I thought those suckers were supposed to take a vow of silence. I suppose they can break it occasionally when they are away or if they have some emergency."

Now that he could speak, Josiah joined our howls of laughter. We had to sit down on a stone bench at the entrance to the monastery in order to regain our composure.

"You are such a lying con artist, Josiah," I admonished him. "You would sell your grandma for a moon pie."

"That fellow wanted to believe that we were monks and I let him believe it. It made his day to give us a ride. That was his good deed for the day. You two jackasses almost spoiled it for the three of us. I got you here, didn't I?" Josiah was a bit miffed.

I began to wonder at what point I had lost my sanity at Berea. I had started my college years quite rebelliously with Lettie and now I found myself willing to become one of Josiah's followers. I was getting involved with every hare-brained scheme that came along. The so-called normal students at the college avoided me, so I had no choice except to go with the fringe crowd. But I really loved Melbert and Josiah. Life was quite exciting with them.

When Josiah knocked on the door of the gift shop of the monastery, a monk dressed in a white robe with a black belt tied around the waist opened it and motioned for us to come inside. This monk's skin looked like yellow wax and he wore his hair cut in the traditional circle with a bald spot in the middle. I was quite surprised when I heard him speak.

"Welcome."

"We seek sanctuary for the Easter holidays," Josiah announced, "and perhaps beyond."

"Follow me," he said softly.

"I thought these monks could not talk," Melbert asked out loud.

"I have a dispensation to talk to visitors and those seeking sanctuary," he said warmly to Melbert.

He led us to a dormitory annex which had many rooms for visitors. As we walked down the hallway, we passed other men and boys who had come for their personal reasons to stay a while at the monastery. This monk put Josiah, Melbert, and me alone in single rooms. He handed us a paper with the weekend schedule written upon it. Placing his index finger across his lips in a sign of silence, he bowed to us and disappeared back into the gift shop. Josiah shook his head negatively reinforcing the rule that from now on until departing, we could not utter a word.

I quickly noted the meal times on the schedule and went in search of the dining hall. It had four very long, plain tables with plates and tin drinking cups already in their places. I also noted the official prayer times, not that I had any intention of going to pray with the monks. There was plenty of religious reading material in our cells, but little else. The monastery had a library and there would be a chance to do much reading. Wasn't that what I had been doing every day at Berea? I wanted a little bit more.

We were now on our own. I went down to the main church and studied the beautiful artwork on the walls and above the altar. Then I went to a small flower garden outside the church. It was peaceful here. Next, I went back to the gift shop where talking was allowed. I studied all the many different cheeses in the cooler and the preserves and canned goods offered for sale.

"Where and how do you make your cheese at this place?" I asked the monk.

He handed me a colorful brochure about the monastery and told me to go visit the dairy the following day.

I did not see Melbert or Josiah until supper time. Since it was holy days at the monastery, ringing bells was not allowed. A monk came down the hallway with a wooden clapper ringing it like a bell. The sound carried a great distance to all the rooms on the floor. I walked hastily to the dining hall and stood in the doorway in awe as I studied all the congregation of monks in their robes. It was a sea of black and white and it was a true picture right out of the Middle Ages. A reserved section at the end of the table served as eating space for visitors. I sat down next to Josiah and smiled. The monks served us a large bowl of soup and a huge hunk of homemade bread. I gobbled it down and waited for seconds. There would be no seconds. Josiah shook his head to warn me not to ask for seconds. Curbing one's appetite seemed to be part of monastic life. I would even have welcomed one of Berea's peanut butter and jelly sandwiches at this point.

After dinner, I went directly to bed. I slept soundly except for hearing the devotions played all night on the closed speaker in the dormitory.

At breakfast the following morning, I ate assorted homemade cheeses and bread with tea. Unlike the night before, I felt more gratitude toward the monks that were feeding me free of charge.

Josiah was not around to direct me. I wanted some adventure, so I walked outside the monastery walls toward the fields where I saw some monks busily cleaning some fields for planting. They were doing the work by hand. Without greeting any of them, I simply joined in their work. I carried limbs, dried broom sedge, stalks and other debris out of the field and piled it along the hedgerow imitating what they were doing. At one point, I dropped a log on my foot causing excruciating pain to shoot up my leg. I bit my fingers and ran several paces away to a huge oak tree where I concealed myself and yelled at the top of my lungs, "Oh, shit! That hurts!" The monks pretended not to hear me.

Two hours of hard work were good for me. It reminded me of how hard I had had to work in order to survive in Ottie's world. A smiling monk walked up to me and handed me a tin cup of cold milk and some cheese he had wrapped up in his pocket. Then he reached out and gave me a warm hug. He was thanking me for helping with the work. As he started to walk away, I went to him and hugged him back to let him know that I understood his meaning and that I was reciprocating.

On the return walk to my room, I began to realize that my adventure with the Cistercian monks could be extremely beneficial. Whereas I had started my journey as a joke, I began to see wonderful, beautiful people who had dedicated their lives in service to God and mankind. Their choice did not make sense to me, but I respected them.

The wooden clacker summoned us all to the church for evening vespers. Josiah, Melbert, and I had to sit in the balcony with the non-monks. It was an exhilarating experience hearing the monks sing Gregorian chants. A small part of the service was spoken out loud. By this time, I was so hungry to hear a person speak that I didn't particularly care if it was a religious text.

On Easter Sunday morning we three Berea students joined all the visitors and monks for a special mass performed by the bishop. Meeting the bishop was like you and me meeting our president. I walked down the main aisle of the church and the bishop blessed me with holy water. The water fell in cool droplets across my hair, face, and shoulder. I warmly accepted that blessing from a church I did not belong to and from a creed that was not my belief system. There are good people everywhere. I had agreed to go about doing good deeds among people.

Upon being released from my sanctuary request, I ran out the door of the gift shop and yelled "Ya-hoo" at the top of my lungs. Josiah and Melbert came running behind me. They were not as demonstrative as I chose to be.

"How are we getting home, Josiah?" I asked. "The monks won't feed us anymore."

"Let's just sit down on this stone bench and see what happens," he replied.

Near the wall of the monastery, three nuns and a brother walked back and forth speaking out loud. The monk had permission to talk out loud to them. When their conversation ended, the nuns walked past us toward a station wagon.

"Hey, sisters" Josiah yelled, "are you going anywhere near Louisville?"

"Yes, we are," one replied.

"May we three ride with you?" he asked.

"Come on," they waved to us.

The nuns set us off at the bus station in Louisville. There we sat with no money in our pockets and no tickets to get back to Berea.

"You two sit here and wait on me," Josiah requested.

He disappeared through the bus station door and was gone for a half hour. When he came back in, he handed me money to buy a ticket to Berea. Then he exited the station and disappeared around a line of taxis waiting for passengers. He returned shortly and handed Melbert enough money for a ticket back to Berea. Then he was off again.

Melbert and I went to the ticket counter and bought our tickets. Josiah flitted through the door, walked to the ticket window, and purchased his own ticket home.

"How did you get this money?" I wanted to know. "Are you out there turning tricks or something?"

"No. I just explained to passengers that three of us monks needed bus tickets to get back to the monastery. Would they like to make a donation?"

"You are going to Hell, Josiah," I advised him.

"Wherever I go, Fred, do come along. You are sure to have fun, aren't you?"

 I wouldn't exactly say that hanging out in a monastery (not speaking, praying all the time, eating a lot of cheese) constituted fun. But who could argue with Josiah? I adored him!

THE SIGN OF THE CROSS

And then I went away.

I just went away. I left with no warning. I left Berea with no farewell. My friends knocked on my door with the intent of inviting me to breakfast, but there was no answer. They repeated their knock and waited a few minutes in the event that I was sleeping soundly. Finally, my roommate opened the door and leered at them through half-awake, droopy eyes.

"What do you want?" he said harshly.

"I want to speak with Fred, please," Alfred said nicely, trying to disarm my roommate, David, whose displeasure at having been disturbed was evident.

"The bastard is not here. He is gone and he ain't ever coming back!"

He slammed the door abruptly in my face leaving me stunned and confused. He told me later, when I had returned to campus, that my friends had made their way across campus toward the dining hall. Wherever they had walked among the ancient oaks lining the sidewalks, they had thought that I was there. In his mind, Alfred had reviewed many of the comical episodes that I had shared with him.

He carefully crossed highway 25 and made his way to the dining hall where he, Melbert, and I always ate. He shaded his eyes with his right hand as he scanned the dining room looking for Melbert. He became angry when he could not find him. The little fellow was sacking out in bed right when someone needed to talk to him.

As Alfred sat down with his breakfast, he noticed that many students were staring intently at him. They seemed to know some things that he did not yet know. When he stared back, they dropped their heads toward their plates and dipped eggs with their forks into their waiting mouths. Their stares made him feel naked and guilty of something.

When he placed his tray in the dispensary, he could no longer hold his angst. Alfred rushed across campus to find Melbert. He knocked furiously on his door, but there was no immediate answer.

"Dang it!" he thought. "I've been given a mystery to solve and the whole darned world has shut down!"

He heard the slight turning of the lock to Melbert's door. The latches squeaked as he slowly opened the door and peeked out. He had been crying. He looked at Alfred with a most hurtful look that he had ever seen in his life. Melbert could not speak. He simply lowered his head and shook it in great sadness. Alfred followed him into the room, hoping that he would have some information about Fred.

"His roommate said that he was gone," Melbert began speaking softly. "What does he mean 'gone'?" he wanted to know. His roommate seemed to be glad about whatever has happened.

Melbert sat down on his bed. His little, rotund body sank back into the bed covers. He put on his glasses and Alfred could see that his eyes were blood shot. So he apparently knew what had happened with Fred, yet he was reluctant to share with me.

"The bullies drove him away," Melbert began to speak softly. "The same ones that harass us have been unmerciful with him. They made fun of his poverty. Because he was feminine and graceful, they inferred that he was gay. Some one of them called President Frances Hutchins and told him that Fred was gay, that all his friends were too, and that the fun name we used for our group, 'Fred's Witnesses', was a gay cult that preyed on students all over campus. The President referred the matter to Dean Orwig, who called him to his office to face the allegations. I'm afraid we are next."

"Surely the dean will not fall for anonymous telephone calls, accusing a person of something that is not anyone's business and is deeply personal. What has Fred done wrong? What is his crime? The crime is committed by the bullies. Where did Fred go?" Alfred was devastated.

"Fred went back to the Trappist monastery, to the monks where he feels he will be safe. They won't judge him there and they certainly can't talk about him, at least not out loud. The Cistercian monks have taken a vow of silence. It is too bad that individuals on the Berea campus have not taken the same vows. Melbert had not lost his sense of humor.

Later that day Melbert ran to Alfred's room to tell him that the Dean of Men had summoned him to his office in order to discuss this sordid affair. Was the dean trying to prove the allegations or was he seeking to exonerate the three of us of vicious gossip? I had never seen Melbert so morose.

The guillotine fell. Alfred could not believe the summons from the Dean. He was being summoned like a common criminal to answer for non-existent crimes. The accusers remained anonymous. The tormentors remained anonymous. Those sitting in judgment of us were very real and our college diplomas rested in the balance.

"The president received a phone call, anonymously, a few days ago from a person who identified himself as a former student. He made accusations against Fred, Melbert, and you of a sexual nature. He did not say that Fred had done anything to anyone. It was an accusation of sexual orientation, a state of being. He accused Fred of theft of some of his personal items. I have the campus security searching all your rooms at the present time for any evidence of a crime," the Dean said by way of explanation. "What is your side of the story? I have already discussed the situation with Fred. I understand that he has left campus."

"I don't have a side or story," Alfred replied. "I don't really know what you are talking about. Do I have to hear false accusations without your telling me who is making them?"

"This person is called 'Darbie' or that is what he said. That is all that I can tell you," Dean Orwig explained.

"I know this person," Alfred told the dean. "He is on leave this semester. We all knew that he was a sexual predator. Fred and I refused to participate in his liaisons on campus. He promised that he would get even with us. I guess this is it. Sir, are you charging us with a crime? With an indiscretion? With an assault? I don't even understand why you have called me to your office."

"It was by request of the president of the college because he received the call," the Dean explained. "I'm caught in the middle of a situation about which I know nothing. I cannot ascertain guilt or innocence without interviewing everyone implicated. Believe me, I am truly sympathetic."

"Fred told me that he had come to you and that he had asked for help when a group of students had been stalking him. You told him that you could take no action until they had done some physical harm. Sir, do you understand the damage that psychological abuse can do? This fellow Darbie has not attacked me physically, but he has inflicted emotional damage beyond repair. Neither you nor the president of the college should have even taken the call from a vengeful individual. Where do we go to get our dignity back?

"Do you think that this Darbie fellow should be allowed back into college?" the Dean asked Alfred. The question took him by surprise.

"No!" "Under no circumstances should he come back here."

The whole episode had backfired on the bully.

But the effects of this super bully episode had destroyed two fine people. Melbert transferred to a small school in New Hampshire. Fred hitched a ride to the monastery at Trappist. He had desperately wanted to get away, but he had had no money. The monks had given him temporary sanctuary.

"You are not becoming a monk, are you?" the bishop of the monastery had inquired. "This beautiful world needs you. It needs your joy, your intelligence, your humor. Young people need you as a friend. Look, these bullies have made your life miserable. I'm sorry that they made your daily life so unhappy and I'm even sorrier that your college didn't expel all of them."

Dean Orwig dropped the issue. "Tell Fred that it is fine if he comes on back to school," he told Alfred.

I did not return to the Berea campus until the end of summer. I never reconnected with it, the faculty, or students who were there at the time. My perception of everything and everyone had been broken by a shameful accusation from an anonymous bully and gossip. It is important to understand that an accusation of being gay in the 1960's was no laughing matter. Berea had already dismissed one student for being gay. That student had made a pass at the dorm president who had complained to the Dean. What humiliation to have a college president discussing your sexual orientation! My spirit had already embraced the silence of the monastery. I visited there often and took solace among a group of brothers who extended a life-long friendship. I would never feel the same again toward Berea.

Whenever I returned to visit Trappist Monastery, the monks greeted me with hugs and a sign of the cross. I felt safe in that holy place.

THE WAITRESS

The moon was full and the occupants of Pearsons Hall were restless. All of them should have been busy studying, for it was already seven-thirty pm. Female students had already signed into their dorms at seven o'clock. They could come back out at eight-thirty for a half-hour street break, but from that point on, they were locked in their dorms for the night. Berea guardians figured that if they locked all the girls up, the boys would go home. This concept was quite humorous, considering the fact that many of the Berea males were gay. Good Christian women were happy that someone was protecting the virtuous Berea women.

I was sitting in my room a bit homesick. I wanted one of Otties's dark-brown, buttermilk biscuits filled with Duke's mayonnaise and a thick slice of home-grown Cherokee black tomatoes. Far away from Carolina now, I was beginning to understand that Ottie had cared for all us children in her own peculiar way. I missed the farm. I missed my dad, Eli, although he had died four years previously in 1957. What would he think of me in college, sitting in a room at Berea, striving to release myself from his narrow world and an even more narrow-minded valley in which he lived? He would not approve of my African-American friend, Chloe, or my roommate, Bashir. He would disown me a second time for studying at a place so liberal, so diverse, and so accepting of all.

My stomach was growling because the evening meal at the Berea cafeteria had been so horrible. The meal had consisted of frozen fish sticks, thawed and fried in fat, corn taken from gallon cans and reheated in a serving pan, along with the ever-present mashed potatoes. The mashed-potato-making machine never stopped running. We could hear its beaters swirling the potatoes in a huge metal pot that attached to the apparatus. I wondered where Berea found its cooks until one of the student workers told me that the students themselves were the cooks. Oh, good grief! I should have known it. Right now my stomach wanted a hamburger with slaw and onion and an order of French fries dripping with grease. There was only one option in finding it at this hour. I would have to go to the All Night Restaurant.

Berea had four eating places in the years 1961-65---the cafeteria, the snack bar, Little Mama's Pizza, located on the back street near Boone Tavern Hotel, and the All Night Restaurant located west of campus. I rarely had spending money when I was at Berea. I could not afford a cup of coffee when it cost just a nickel. This night, however, some change jingled in my pockets because Gertie, my older sister, a hair stylist in Danville, Virginia, had sent me $5.00.

The air was crisp and a full moon hung low over Draper Hall. Ancient trees lining the walkways stood out as ghostly black against a lighter horizon. One lone light burned above the door to Draper Hall and some happy moths danced and flitted around it. Silhouettes of students entering and leaving the library cast a feeling of Halloween across the yard. I entered the main sidewalk of highway 25 at Phelps-Stokes Chapel, and then I walked west toward the Berea town theatre located to my left. Its marquee flashed like a lit-up carnival midway. At my distance, I could plainly read "Lilies of the Field" starring Sidney Poitier upon it. A smell of freshly-popped popcorn blew from inside the theatre on to the street ahead of me. I could literally taste the hot, melted butter covering the popcorn. It made my stomach even more ravenously hungry for a greasy-spoon hamburger.

The little greasy-spoon restaurant sign came into view. Unlike the garish movie marquee and Draper Hall moth light, the unpretentious sign stuck out over the street with no light at all above it. Uneven letters, daubed in cheap, red paint, spelled out "All Night Restaurant." This quaint place was famous to generations of Berea students prior to 1965. Each had paid homage to it, individually, in the waning hours of morning or in raucous groups that just wanted to get out of the dorm and off campus for a moment.

The restaurant had two rusty screen doors at the entrance. One door opened to the outside; the other opened to the inside. Patrons joked that the doors kept the flies in and out. When the weather turned cold, management placed a cheap, wooden door with glass panes in between the two screen doors. The restaurant building had originally been a shoe store that was thirty feet wide and a hundred feet long.

Several sets of booths that could seat four people lined the wall to the left. On the right, there was a counter running the length of the building. Built-in, swivel stools lined the counter. They were set at a height that allowed the rednecks to swirl around on them like children playing in a park. The counter was pockmarked with holes and cutout places from years of wear. People had used knives, forks, spoons, and coffee cups on its vinyl surface.

Behind the counter, there was just enough room for the cook to work the grill and for the lone waitress to pour drinks. There were three shelves above the cook's space where he stored spices, empty coffee cups, glasses, napkins, and other paraphernalia of his trade. Proudly displayed in a dusty frame above the short-order grill was a health certificate reading "Grade B."

The little greasy spoon had honestly earned its health rating of grade "B." One could swear that the cook and waitress worked diligently to obtain it. An odor of spoiling garbage cans permeated the place. The cook wore the same grease-stained apron and hat for a week at a time. Before pouring coffee, the waitress often swiped the inside of the cup with a dirty cloth that she used to clean the table and counter top. That is why I insisted that she pour me extra-hot coffee.

The cook used his naked hands to place hamburgers on the grill. With the same unwashed hands, he took a bun from a package, placed it in a steamer, and then he put the meat, onion, slaw, and mayonnaise on the bun. Students joked that the waitress probably formed the hamburger patties with her dirty hands, and then rolled them down the aisle to the cook.

There was a 1950's jukebox which lit up in a multitude of colors. Hanging at the end of the aisle was a sign reading "restroom." Among Berea students, the standing joke was, "make sure you empty your bladder and colon before coming to this regal establishment." Hank Williams and Elvis Presley records dominated the jukebox selections.

The only waitress for the greasy spoon was a forty-five year old woman who reminded me of Jethrene of the "Beverly Hillbillies." She dressed in ankle-length dresses emblazoned with flowers. Life had been harsh to her and she had wrinkles to prove it. She was a local product of Madison County where poverty was evident. She knew that Berea students were as poor as she was, but she was filled with jealousy, because the college students were finding a way out of their world of poverty. Time had passed her by. Therein lay a source of her extreme dislike of anyone who came in from the campus. She would serve you if she felt like it. If not, she would let you sit until you got tired of waiting and went home. Most college students bought a nickel cup of coffee, anyway, and then they left her no tip. She had the strength of a gorilla and she was known to throw troublemakers out of the restaurant by the scruff of the neck.

I sat down in an empty booth with the number "four" etched on the wall beside it. I liked sitting with my face toward the entrance door, so that I could study every person who came through it. Jethrene sensed that I had money in my pocket this night and she intuited that I might let go of a small tip for her. She had served me enough to remember that I usually drank coffee. She wiped the empty cup with her damp cloth, poured steaming hot coffee into it, and brought it to my table. She plopped the cup down in front of me. Some of the coffee spilled on to the table top and she wiped it up with the same cloth that she had used to clean my cup.

"Are you one of the cheap spenders tonight or do you want something else?" she mumbled gruffly as she placed her right hand on her hip to balance her rotund body.

"I want a well-done hamburger with onion, mustard, slaw, and French fries cooked dark brown," I said sweetly hoping to defang her attitude.

"Hey, Stu, she yelled at the cook. "Run one cow through the kitchen and nuke a set of fries."

This dame was so proud of the restaurant's "B" rating that she wore it like Hester Prynne's scarlet "A." She rarely emptied the garbage can or washed her dish cloth or mopped the floor for fear that the health department might actually raise the rating to "Grade A."

I sat waiting for my first-class snack to arrive as I studied from my French text. In my mind, I was in my mother Ottie's world now, except that I was in Kentucky. While waiting for my food, some redneck dropped some nickels in the jukebox and played Hank Williams', "Your Cheating Heart."

The nickels clinked as they fell through the slot down into the coin box. A magnetic hand searched through the collection of records in the jukebox, picked out one, and placed it on the turntable. Hank Williams' nasal voice crooned out, "Your cheatin' heart will tell on you, I cried and cried the whole night through...."

I was back in Ottie's world on a Saturday night, listening to the Grand Ole Opry on a battery-powered radio. Gertie, Justine, and I were gathered in the living room next to the fireplace with a kerosene lamp casting out a weak light. I was reading out loud to Gertie. Ottie was baking apple pies in the kitchen. She was singing along with Hank Williams in a slightly off-key voice. "You'll walk the floor the whole night through...." I could have sworn that Ottie was dancing, or at least, in my memory, I wanted her to dance.

Jetherene shook me from my reverie when she poured me a second cup of coffee. She held the coffee pot a foot above the cup. Some of the hot liquid splashed on my arm and textbook, but she did not care. The song on the jukebox had ended. I took a sip of the hot coffee and read from the French textbook.

The hamburger and fries were Hillbilly heaven. As I bit into the morsel from heaven, grease, mustard, and juices ran down my chin and fell on the table top. I let them lie there, because Jetherene would wipe it all up with her all-purpose cloth. At this moment, I did not care if Jethrene had rolled my hamburger patty down the aisle to Stu. I was back in the Carolina hills that had birthed me, and I loved it!

Jethrene poured me another cup of coffee. As she walked away from my booth, she turned and asked me a strange question.

"Are you gay? I heard some Berea students discussing you last night. They said you were queer."

"I'm happy most of the time. Why do you ask?" I replied curtly.

She had spoken her question quite loudly and others in the restaurant had heard what she had said. They stared at me disapprovingly.

"Well?" She insisted.

"The only way you will ever know, Jethrene, is to go to bed with me. You are not my type," I hissed.

"I don't sleep with queers," she said through clenched teeth.

"No one would sleep with you, Jethrene, queer or otherwise," I managed to cough out through my anger.

Jethrene's assumption about me was dangerous, because Berea had just expelled a student for acting on his sexual orientation. Town bullies sat listening to this conversation about me. They stared out under raised eyebrows letting me know that, if assumptions were true, that I deserved a severe beating.

I did not leave Jethrene a tip.

It was midnight when I polished off the rest of my hamburger and fries. I paid my bill and left. As I exited through the double screen doors, some of the rednecks stood up as if they were going to pursue me.

On my walk back to campus, I thought a lot about all the cliques that students had formed. I did not belong to any of them. They functioned like street gangs. They were blood tight. It would take a miracle to penetrate them. I wasn't doing well on the friend-ship front. Now I knew the answer. Fellow students thought that I was gay. How did that happen?

I was more sophisticated than many of them. They feared anyone different from them. Chloe was the only one that had my back. Wayne, Alfred, John, and Barbara were close enough, but they were members of other cliques.

I did not trust anyone. Already Vixen had reported me for plucking a flower. Mr. Rules and Regulations had me in his sights. Everyone seemed to be misreading me. I decided to accept everyone as they were, leave them alone, and get close to none of them.

A lone male figure walked past me, turned and stared strangely as I took the sidewalk toward my dorm. When I looked back, he was still there, standing like a statue. He seemed fixated on me. I felt threatened. Cold chills ran up my arms. I did not recognize the stranger as being a Berea College student.

JUMPING OUT OF
CLASSROOM WINDOWS

The door to the science classroom opened and a mole walked in. I'm not talking about a mole found in vegetable gardens or the one that burrows across lawns. This was a human that looked like a mole. He had a long snout with whiskers sticking out where his nose should have been. He wore dark-rimmed glasses with extremely thick lenses. He shuffled slowly across the room to a large desk at the front and laid his briefcase down, and then he turned to face our class.

From the front his body looked thin. He had wide, splayed feet similar to a circus clown. Big ears like dish antenna rode the side of his head. They had ceased to hear acutely long ago. Without clear vision and acute hearing, this mole floundered through life. Unbelievably, he was our substitute teacher for science for the semester.

I had looked forward to Dr. Strickland as my teacher because the catalogue listed him as an award-winning teacher. This mole was his replacement and he had to be between seventy-eight and eighty-five years old. How could Berea officials inflict this poor man on its students? How could they inflict Berea students on him? Before my studies were finished, I would experience six more teachers like him.

His name was Dr. Shortsight and I'm sure that at some point in his life he had been an excellent teacher. But there comes a time when a person should retire. He had a doctor-ate degree, so he had to have some talent. Berea had dragged him out of retirement, probably because he was willing to work for peanuts. It is often hard to rise above the ability of your teachers to teach you. I was growing weary of worn-out types being thrown at the front of the classroom to pinch hit for an absent professor. I was not alone in my feelings either.

Dr. Shortsight began calling the roll, because students were required to attend class. He would call a name, then walk up to the student and stare down into his face through super lenses, then walk back to his desk. He would call another student's name, and then repeat the action. It took him thirty minutes of a seventy-five minute class just to call the roll.

Next, he would lecture from behind his podium in a droning voice that lulled many of us to sleep. His voice sounded like an old truck trying to pull a heavy load up a mountain while stuck in second gear. His teeth clacked spasmodically in his mouth causing him to mispronounce words. He could not keep on his topic even using notes written on yellow, weather-worn paper lying in front of him.

Within three days, our entire class was bored to tears. Students tried to deal with the boredom by reading silently from the textbook, passing notes, studying for other classes, whispering to each other (he couldn't hear or see beyond the first two rows of seats), or napping. At the end of each class, students rushed out the door to get away from him. I told my roommate, Wayne, that I could not endure the semester with this horrible substitute.

One day during the second week in science class, Dr. Shortsight had taken his usual thirty minutes to call the roll. Students placed diversionary materials on their desks as he began to drone in a monotone voice, "Oceans once covered this part of Kentucky zzzzzzzzzz." In the midst of this boredom, I heard someone in the middle of the class get up, fold his desk handle, and walk to the left where six large windows lined the wall. He unlocked a window, raised the sash as far as it would go and stepped through the window out onto the lawn. He walked away in broad daylight in view of all of us.

Students gasped in disbelief. This brave soul had just walked through the window out of Dr. Shortsight's class and he didn't even notice it. The poor fellow kept droning like a broken record. Some students began to snicker out loud. Others joined in. Then the whole class roared with laughter.

"Uh what? What's that? Did something fall?? "Dr. Shortsight asked.

"I just dropped my books on the floor," one student explained covering for the brave soul that had just walked out through the window. More laughter ensued.

Word spread across campus like wildfire that someone had jumped out of a classroom window in the science building in order to get away from a boring teacher. Like gossip, the story was retold incorrectly until people were saying that a student had thrown Dr. Shortsight down the shaft outside the science classroom. No one wanted to divulge the name of the student who had accomplished his heroic deed.

All the class reported to the science building the following day and went through the routine of roll call. At the end of roll call, three students got up, folded their desk handles, walked in single file to the window, opened it, climbed through, and strolled away among the oak trees. Nothing could stifle the waves of laughter that rolled over the classroom. Poor Dr. Shortsight turned in circles trying to discern the source of the noise of windows opening, because he couldn't see but a few feet in front of him. The situation was so comical that students began to look forward to coming to class.

It got better. Some days later Dr. Shortsight called the roll and turned his back to pick up his lecture notes. Eleven students stood up, folded their desk handles, walked to the row of windows and lined up in a neat row. They opened the entire row of windows. Hearing the noise, Dr. Shortsight walked a few steps forward where he could make out the form of one of the standing students.

"May I help you, sir?" he asked in a most professorial way.

"Yes," the student replied. "Can you tell me what crinoids are and what is the nearest place that I can find one?"

(Shreiks of laughter from the class)

In his most helpful way, Dr. Shortsight walked back to his desk and referenced the class text, giving the eleven students time enough to walk through the windows and disperse across campus. In a comical turn of events, he stood directly in front of us and seriously read the following, "Crinoids are fossilized sea creatures millions of years old. They are found in abundance in Paint Lick, Kentucky."

(More waves of laughter)

I laughed so hard I could not breathe. One girl next to me threw up. Students literally rolled in the aisles of the classroom while heaving with laughter. Even the more studious Berea students broke through their stone faces and laughed uproariously. Dr. Shortsight went right back to his droning lecture, while his students practically lay prostrate on the floor.

By now, our class was famous all over campus. At the appointed time, students from everywhere came to the science building and lined up to watch the exodus from Dr. Shortsight's classroom. It was the best circus show on campus. He called the roll and turned for his lecture notes. Half the class rose simultaneously and marched toward the open windows. With applause from the audience outside and fits of laughter from those left inside, they made a triumphal exit from this ivy hall of non-learning and marched away amid peals of laughter.

Posters with the notice "come see the best show on earth" and "Jumping out the windows for science" as well as "Shortsight, Shortsight, he's my man; he lets me exit when I can" appeared all over campus.

There is no way that this side show could get any better, but it did.

Our classroom sat directly even with the lawn outside. However, there were two floors of the building located under us. Eight round shafts had been built down two floors to allow light and air to move to the lower floors. It was not intended that people walk over or around these shafts. It was dangerous. A fall down two floors could kill a person.

On this best of all days, Dr. Shortsight called roll. Half the students in the classroom rose and walked to the window. Unfortunately, they panicked and began pushing those in front. One student named Tex (wouldn't you know he was from Morganton, N.C. like me) stumbled and fell feet first down one of the shafts. People screamed and cried. Dr. Shortsight thought they were applauding his teaching and so he stopped lecturing and took a bow. People were afraid to look down the shaft fearing that Tex was dead.

Biology classes and labs were in progress on the lower floors. Hearing a thump and cries for help from above, students observed a pair of dangling legs, just visible at their windows. They flung open the windows in their lab room and attempted to pull the feet down, but without success. Many ran upstairs and joined the large group that had already assembled just outside Dr. Shortsight's classroom.

Some clever students ran to Seabury Gym next door and brought back long ropes used for athletic climbing. They lowered the end of one rope down the shaft so Tex could tie it around his waist. A long line of students grabbed the rope and hoisted Tex back into the light of day. By the grace of God, Tex had had the presence of mind to grasp one of the metal pipes crisscrossing the side of the building between the two lower floors as he was falling. Outside of a few cuts and bruises, he survived the ordeal intact. Looking back through the windows, we could see and hear Dr. Shortsight still droning on with his boring lecture about ancient seas covering the entire state of Kentucky.

Tex became a folk hero at Berea. Three days before the end of the semester, Dr. Shortsight called the roll. The entire class rose in unison and, with the precision of a drill team, marched through the open windows and walked away from the science building. Dr. Shortsight was oblivious. He continued to lecture about Paint Lick, crinoids, ancient seas, sugar plums and the Easter Bunny.

View of the center window (ground floor) used by students to exit the science building to escape Dr. Shortsight's boring lectures. There are two floors below the window.

FRIEND OF MINE

Wandering across campus to find Howard Hall, I wondered who my sophomore-year roommate would be. I hoped that it would be someone compatible, not a hillbilly redneck fresh from Ottie's world. Please, I don't want to room with jocks or music majors or someone with no class. I wanted someone that would be my friend or at least someone friendly. When I opened the door to room B6 and walked in, I saw a person with a regal demeanor.

He sat there grinning with a wicked smile on his face. "My name is Wayne Hambright," he told me. "I was just wondering who would walk through that door. I had prayed for someone compatible, no hillbillies, no jocks or music majors.

I burst out laughing. "I'm Fred. It is nice to meet you. We are roommates for this year." I shook his hand.

"I've got the top bunk," he told me.

"OK by me," I laughed. "I'm afraid of heights anyway."

We were off to a good start. Wayne had black hair that had already turned somewhat gray. He was taller than me by an inch. His skin was so lily white that he looked as if he had been born and raised in a cave. He had all his teeth, an unusual case at Berea, and they were pearly white. He hailed from Blacksburg, a small town in upper South Carolina. He pronounced it "Blatsburg."

That speech peculiarity was an enduring part of Wayne's persona. The sounds "ck" and "x" did not resonate in his brilliant mind or, perhaps, he felt no need to put forth the effort to say them. He pronounced them both as "its." He said "sits" for "six" and "Blatsburg" for Blacksburg. If anyone ever called me on the phone and pretended to be Wayne, I would ask them to pronounce the number six. I could find him in a crowd of thousands just by yelling, "Wayne, where are you from?" If someone answered "Blatsburg," I would run to embrace him.

Wayne gave me the stability of friendship that I needed to make it through Berea.

That friendship has lasted over fifty years. I hope it will last beyond eternity. During the school day, we went our separate ways and after supper we gathered to study in room B6. Wayne was spontaneous and bold. Day and night did not exist for him. There existed only time. He refused to recognize either clock or the sun and moon. He moved without borders among all three of them.

His happy nature changed one day. He came into the room and sat at his desk without greeting me or uttering a single word.

"Had a hard day, huh?" I mumbled. "Has Mrs. Van Cleaveron been on your case?"

"No, Prieto." He hissed the syllables of this name through his teeth.

"I thought that you liked calculus," I mentioned to him.

"I do. But I can't take Dr. Prieto. Fred, he is a refugee from Cuba and cannot speak adequate English yet. Nobody in the class can understand a word he says. He knows his subject matter, but he can't get it across to the students." Wayne was distraught.

"I can't stand Mr. Rules and Regulations, Mrs. Kerfluffle, or Mrs. Van Cleaveron either. Thank God I don't have them as teachers."

"When I complained to Dean Orwig, he told me to handle it," Wayne continued. "He would not let me drop the class, so I told him that I was going to fail it. Dr. Orwig did not care. Maintaining the honor of an ineffective teacher seemed more important than resolving the dilemma of twenty-two calculus students."

"Wayne, our foreign language department has only one French teacher. She is not native French. She was in the army and learned French after leaving it. She did study at the Sorbonne in Paris, but who hasn't? Her French is wretched. I'm stuck with that for four years. She will teach virtually every class in my major. That depresses me. With all their money, Berea could hire better than that. She probably works for peanuts. I'm depressed."

Wayne accepted his "F" in calculus with dignity and got on with his life. I, on the other hand, declared war on my own department.

"Fred, would you like to ride with me to Richmond?" Wayne asked me one day as he burst energetically into the room. Richmond was fifteen miles north of Berea.

"Yes, but how? We aren't allowed to have cars on campus," I reminded him.

Quoting an old song, he mocked, "I don't care what mama won't allow, I'm gonna do it anyhow." He pulled me out of my chair and out the door.

We walked down the hill behind Howard Hall, across the soccer field, by the college pond, beyond the wheat field where we crossed railroad tracks. A 1957 blue Chevy was parked on a side road. Wayne jingled the keys to it in the fingers of his right hand.

"We got wheels!" he sang out.

"What the heck are we going to do in Richmond?" I enquired.

"Liquor run," he said nonchalantly.

I went into an apocalyptic fit! No beer or alcohol is allowed on campus. This is a kiss-of-death ride if anyone finds out.

"Settle down. Sooner or later some silly event will get us expelled anyway," Wayne said philosophically.

"I'm already on everybody's list here now. If my name gets associated with booze, I'm toast," I whined.

"Enjoy the ride," Wayne said with assurance as he spun wheelies and threw gravel across the railroad track. He drove like a maniac toward Richmond. He pulled a roll of money out of his shirt pocket and explained that everyone in Howard Hall who wanted booze had given money and a list of what they wanted. He was the buyer. Ottie would be proud in this moment to know that I was following in her footsteps bootlegging liquor.

"Look at my hair, Fred," he said. "I look much older than twenty. The salesman never asks to see my I.D."

My grandfather's hair was not as white as his. We pulled up to a store with a flashing neon sign that read, "Richmond Liquor and Beer." Wayne disappeared inside and reemerged in a few minutes with his arms loaded with vodka, bourbon, and wine. The salesman carried several cases of beer for him. After loading the goods in the back of the car, we sped back to campus.

The hallway where we lived in room B6 ended at a single window that opened on the road that passed by Howard Hall. Dorm residents heard Wayne's car and ran out to form a gauntlet down the hall. They passed all the liquor and beer down to our room where Wayne divided it according to his list. He smiled and handed me a $5.00 bill.

"Partner in crime," he smiled.

In days to come, dozens of oranges appeared in the window sills all over Howard Hall. Using hypodermic needles, ingenious students had filled the oranges with vodka. Passing visitors marveled at how health conscious Berea students were to be eating oranges instead of potato chips. If they only knew!

Wayne came into the room one evening and told me to bring my bedding and pillow. We were going to camp out in the wheat field near the railroad track. By this time, I trusted him implicitly. Had he told me to shoot Mr. Rules and Regulations, I would surely have done it. I followed him out to the wheat field like a little puppy.

When my roommate needed a break from the stress of campus life, he always slept on a mountain top, in the wheat field, or on top of some farmer's haystack. We walked deep into the wheat, not knowing how near the railroad track we were. We settled down to sleep on the hard earth. It took me a long time to fall asleep, for I was mulling over the reason that I was sleeping on hard earth in the middle of a wheat field next to a railroad track. Wayne Hambright! I would have followed him into the jaws of Hell and back.

The wheat was golden brown and it threw out a fragrance from drying stems. Above us the Milky Way swirled the length of the vast sky. He pointed out Orion, the Big Dipper, the North Star, Pegasus, and the planet Venus. The lights of Berea campus lit the night in the distance and Draper Hall spire pointed majestically into the star-studded night. The acrid smell of burning garbage moved over us. The city was burning its garbage in an open pit nearby. A peace settled over the wheat field, and we two pioneers fell asleep.

The overwhelming blast of a diesel train engine split the night. Wayne and I sat bolt upright. The two a.m. train was approaching a crossing just above our bed in the wheat field. As we peered over our left shoulders, our sleepy eyes thought the train was bearing down upon us, not on its track, but right through the middle of the wheat field.

Wayne grabbed his bedding and fled across the wheat field away from the train. He ran in such a panic that I swear he walked on air through the wheat. The stalks of wheat lay flat where he trod over them. His white hair stood out on the sides of his head and he had a look of shear panic on his face. No amount of my calling could bring his blind flight to a halt. Grabbing my bedding, I pursued him. Though it was dark, I could see his path through the wheat field. The crop was laid waste. It looked like a herd of wild buffalo had passed through. When I got back to Howard Hall, Wayne was fast asleep in his bed.

Wayne Hambright and Fred E. Epeley at Wilson's Creek, North Carolina, 2015.

These two men were roommates at Howard Hall, Berea College, 1962.

The cupola of Howard Hall, the dorm in which Wayne and I spent our sophomore year.

It is located in the John G. Fee Glade.

MERRY CHRISTMAS TO YOU, TOO

Christmas season arrived and snow began to fall through the oak trees and barren redbuds. The flakes drifted softly as if the whole earth was a snow globe and a giant hand had shaken it, sending downy flakes across the sidewalks and paths. Calls came in to Howard Hall from Chloe, Cotwin, Evelyn, and John for me to join them in the snow to go caroling in the town of Berea and the countryside surrounding it.

We wrapped ourselves warmly in heavy coats and crunched through the glistening snow off campus into the countryside around Berea. We hiked in the direction of Indian Fort Theatre.

Chloe, Evelyn, and Cotwin were black students and the rest of us were white southerners. What an unlikely combination! We locked arms and skipped through the fresh snow singing "Jingle Bells."

On the outskirts of the town of Berea, we came to a neat-looking house where we stopped and sang, "We Wish You a Merry Christmas." An older man and woman opened their door with big, smiling faces. When they saw a group of white and black students together, they slammed the door shut in our faces and disappeared back into their house. Undeterred, we continued our caroling trek.

We chose another house that had an artificial snowman in the yard where the occupants had strung colored lights all over the roof. Our little choir belted out a terrible rendition of "Silent Night." Three kids bolted out of the house on to the lawn and their parents followed close behind. Upon seeing two black students and three white, they grabbed their kids and ran back into their house. They turned off the colored lights and pulled down the window shades right in our faces.

"They don't like the way we sing," I joked with John.

"It's worse than that," he replied. "They don't like us!"

"I wouldn't dare go Christmas caroling with a mixed racial group in my town in North Carolina. You are from Virginia. I bet that people feel the same way there," I asked John.

"We've gotten used to interracial friendships on campus, but the greater world outside doesn't agree with us," John mused.

"I think that we have hiked too far away from campus," I suggested. "Let's go back and sing to people in the dorms."

The five of us merry singers turned around and headed back. Our feet crunched on the light snow. In the distance, the spire of Draper Hall shone through the night. Flakes of snow swirled around the floodlights that made it visible against the night sky. Our spirits were still high with Christmas spirit.

In our innocent revelry, we had forgotten that possible conflict lurked beyond the campus limit. I gasped when I saw a group of people standing in the road ahead with huge snowballs packed in their hands. They had stacked snow in the form of a fort and they were waiting for us to come back their way.

"My God," I screamed out. "We've walked into a "skoad" trap!"

All five of us grabbed snow in our hands and packed it into heavy snowballs. Our adversaries let fly with a barrage of snowball missiles. They aimed the first volley at Chloe, Evelyn, and Cotwin and ignored the two of us whites.

"Lie down in the snow behind us!" John yelled out to Chloe and Cotwin. "Make snowballs for us to use!"

Heavy snowballs, some with a piece of rock or gravel in the middle, flew back and forth across the highway. We specifically aimed our snowballs at the "skoad's" heads. One took a direct hit and fell, moaning, to the ground. I got hit in the face with a well-thrown ball of snow. For a few seconds, I saw stars.

"There are too many of them," I screamed at John. "Let's run!"

I left the highway and ran through the snow along the edges of people's yards. My friends followed in quick pursuit.

"Merry Christmas you pussies!" someone yelled from the "skoad" group.

"Have a Merry Christmas, too, assholes!" I yelled back when I had gone far enough that they could not catch me.

That which we had intended to be a mission of fun, laughter, and good will, had turned into a racial and social conflict. As we retreated toward campus, there came the usual barrage of racial insults yelled after us. This was the third episode of racial hatred that I had experienced in a short period of time.

In this pathetic "skoad" attack, I saw a reflection of myself and the society from which I had come. My face hurt from the snowball hit and my heart hurt for Chloe, Evelyn, and Cotwin.

I sat down in the snow beside the old millstone next to Lincoln Hall and I wept.

"Merry Christmas to you all! Peace on earth, good will toward men," I managed to mutter sarcastically.

WE RESERVE THE RIGHT
TO REFUSE SERVICE

D r. Orwig congratulated me on the repayment of the freshman year loan and quickly wrote vouchers for fall semester and books. With said vouchers in hand, I ran to the phone and called each of the female dorms to see if I could locate where Chloe was living. I found her in Fairchild Hall. That building was the oldest dorm on campus and was reputed to have ghosts. The receptionist summoned Chloe to the phone and I greeted her with the state song of her native Tennessee.

"Oh, do stop this nonsense, Fred," she screamed over my off-key singing. "I'd sing your North Carolina song back at you, but I doubt you hillbillies have one."

"Carolina, Carolina, Heaven's blessings attend her, while we live we will cherish, protect and defend her...." I crooned making her more irritated. Meet me at the snack bar and I will sing you some real sad songs," I teased her. "If you are not there in ten minutes, I will serenade you in the front yard of Fairchild Hall."

"Oh, Lord, why do I put up with him? Help him, Lord, for he is a nutcase," she laughed as she placed the phone back on the receiver and rushed down the stairs toward the snack bar.

I gave her a welcome-back hug and bought her a cup of coffee with the money I had earned in Princeville. I gave her my dorm name, Howard Hall, my phone number, and the room where I would be living. She told me that she had worked all summer in Louisville serving tables in a restaurant. When I told her that I had worked as a wetback in Illinois, she could not contain her laughter.

"You are just one step from being black like me, and like me, you have to take any job that is out there," she chuckled.

"I had a good summer, Chloe, but the way people treated Mexican workers and black people in Illinois disturbed me greatly. Northern propaganda makes it always sound like white people up there treat minorities with love, respect, and kindness. That is baloney. I saw as much racism in the Midwest as I have ever seen in the South. Southerners don't hide their bigotry. They post it on signs such as "Whites only" and "colored water fountain." Whether above or below the Ohio River, racism is just wrong," I poured out to her how I felt.

"In Louisville, I felt like a hired hand. The fact that I was in college and above average in intelligence made no difference to the people I served. I was their little dog to fetch food and coffee and make their lives a little happier. Some even referred to my skin color and I was often referred to as N....," she shared with me sadly.

"A civil rights movement is beginning in this country. Maybe it won't be too late to benefit you and me," I explained. "Coming from a rigidly racist background, I have had a closed mind about minorities, but I am beginning to shift the way I see people. Berea brings a new perspective on respecting others. My friendship with you is helping to break my own shackles of misunderstanding."

"I have experienced as racism on this campus. It is more muted and subtle, but students take another sidewalk to avoid walking past me. Some refuse to speak even when I say 'hello.' Some mumble racist epithets under their breath when I walk by them. The more things seem to change, the more they stay the same."

She sipped coffee from her mug, which she held between both hands, and stared out the glass window at the pinnacles beyond the Student Union Building. I drank in silence with her. We came from such different backgrounds, yet here we sat as friends. What had transpired in us that society at large could not yet comprehend?

"Chloe, you and I have suffered for different reasons. You suffer because you are black. I suffer because people perceive me as different. 'Vincit Qui Patitur,' 'He Who Suffers Conquers,' goes one of Berea's mottos. I guess we will just have to endure it all."

"I'm getting a little homesick for my mountains, for the hills and "hollers "that nurtured me. My home life was wretched, but I miss it. Social workers don't understand mountain culture. What an outsider might see as abuse is not really abuse to us. The whole way of life in Appalachia is abusive. Poverty is abuse. Ignorance is abuse. Having too many children when one cannot care for them is abuse. But all of us belong to that culture. Despite the abuse, we all belong with our ignorant, poverty-stricken parents. And, in truth, we want to be with them. My family may not be much, but it is all I have."

She laughed when I paid for the coffee.

"You never have a damn nickel in your pocket, Fred. Where did you get the money? Have you been walking the streets? Stay off my street corner," she laughed uproariously.

"You don't have street corners in your part of Tennessee, you just strut up the valleys," I answered her bending over with laughter.

"You might make it through your sophomore year, if I don't kill you first," she teased me.

"Oh, take another basic math course," I yelled as I pushed through the exit doors to the Union Building. She waved warmly. I was looking forward to this sophomore year.

Berea students returned from their respective places of work, travel, and study. The campus came alive with energy and spirit. Wayne and I got settled in our room "B6" in the basement of Howard Hall. I loved living in the semi-subterranean atmosphere of this dorm. We had one window that opened below ground with a view upward to the lawn about three feet above. At the end of our hall was a window that opened to an asphalt road that circled the dorm and Pearsons Hall that stood nearby. We had to climb a set of ten stairs to get even with the sidewalk outside.

I resolved to do well academically this year. Humanities, a required course for second year, lasted all year long. It consisted of music, art, and literature. Reputed to be the hardest required course on campus, it forced students to spend hours and hours of study just to pass it. Other courses on my schedule demanded more study than last year. So I placed my study desk in a private corner, set up study materials, and disciplined myself for several hours of study per night.

It was late November of 1962. Everyone had long settled into their routines. I had studied all afternoon in my nook in room B6, and I wanted to take a break away from campus. I was feeling lonely and I wanted someone to talk to. I called Chloe to ask her if she would like to walk down to the All Night Restaurant for a hamburger and coffee. She told me she would meet me in front of President Frances Hutchins' house near Fairchild Dorm. The weather was cool and rainy. I walked by Seabury Gym directly to Highway 25 and the president's house. Chloe stood wrapped in a brown overcoat with a scarf tied around her head.

"Gosh, I need a short break," I said wearily.

"I have concentrated so hard that my mind hurts," Chloe said taking a deep breath.

We walked past the music building, past Knapp Hall, past the Berea movie house down to the All Night Restaurant. The town of Berea was just a few blocks long here. To the left stood some run-down buildings that used to house businesses, but now were empty. We crossed over Highway 25 to the restaurant. I opened the outside screen door. She opened the wooden door between, then the inner screen doors that kept the flies in. We sat down in the first booth on the left. I slid my feet under the table and removed my shoes because they had gotten wet on our walk from the campus. I sat facing the door and Chloe sat viewing the back of the restaurant.

"Damn, your feet stink!" Chloe teased me.

"I've been saving this smell for you for weeks. It goes with the restaurant," I laughed.

Half a dozen patrons sat on the swivel stools drinking coffee, eating pie, or greasy hamburgers and fries. The jukebox roared out again "Your Cheatin' Heart" as some patrons sang along and patted their feet on the floor. I saw Chloe's face freeze in place, no emotion showing. Her conversation with me had ceased.

"What's the matter," I asked, "don't you like Hank Williams?"

She did not respond. Chloe dropped her head in her hands and stared at the top of the table. Turning around in my booth, looking over my left shoulder, I saw every person in the restaurant staring at the two of us. Their faces were not blank, they were full of hatred. Jethrene, the waitress, and two patrons huddled, talking softly pointing in our direction. Someone unplugged the jukebox leaving the restaurant in silence. Boiling water hissed from a burner on the stove, where the cook was boiling eggs to make egg salad. One of the overhead lights hummed. Men sitting on the swivel stools had turned away from the counter so they could look directly at us.

"N-----alert!" an unidentified patron yelled across the restaurant.

"N-----lover alert!" another screamed as he hurled a rolled-up piece of paper at me.

"Queer alert," a third person yelled out.

Jethrene left her group and sauntered back to where we were seated. Having come here many times before I blurted out to Jethrene, "Could we please have a hamburger each, all the way and a cup of hot coffee?"

"No, you may not! We don't serve your type here," she said popping her chewing gum as she spoke.

"What do you mean? You have served me coffee many times here," I explained.

"Yes, I have served your sorry, little, poverty-stricken ass and you never leave me a tip," she said angrily. "But you did not have this Negro girl with you."

"I fail to see your argument," I fired back at her.

"We don't serve her kind and your kind in the All Night Restaurant. You can be an N.....lover and a queer on campus, but you can't drag it in here. Now, get out!"

"I don't know what you mean by 'her kind', Jethrene, but calling my friend a N.... is mean, harsh, rude, and uncalled for."

"Let it go, Fred," Chloe begged me, "I've been treated like this all my life. We can get a hamburger and coffee at the snack bar."

My roommate had come to this very restaurant with his black friend, Carolyn, and had been served without incident. The restaurant had served most blacks without incident. Chloe had been to this restaurant with other friends and the waitress had served them without comment. Jethrene seemed to dislike me intensely and she stirred the patrons to attack Chloe and me on this particular night.

Chloe stood up, put on her raincoat and scarf and moved toward the door. Patrons in the restaurant mumbled the N-word at her and "queer," "cracker" son-of-a-bitch at me. They threw paper napkins, straws, uneaten food and other objects past our heads. Some crashed against the inner screen door. I quickly ushered Chloe out the door and took the brunt of the debris against my back. My coat was covered with food as I walked back toward campus.

The two of us walked along in silence. I nervously looked back from time to time to see if anyone was following us. The soft rain pelted our coats and shoes. Raindrops fell from Chloe's nose and hair. My breath was shallow and I nearly hyperventilated from the stress of what had just happened.

My heart was broken. I had never experienced such a vile attack.

"Welcome back to the world from which you just escaped," I thought to myself. "That restaurant crowd managed to bundle the two aspects that they hated most about people into one diatribe, "queers" and "Negro lovers."

Chloe was crying softly. She attempted to conceal her deep hurt from me. I placed my arm around her elbow.

"Don't, Fred! If they see us walking arm in arm, they could kill us," Chloe warned.

The two of us sat down on the steps of Phelps-Stokes Chapel and listened to the wind and rain. There were no words to describe what had just happened to us. I felt safer back on campus and the ringing of the chimes comforted me. All the centuries of discrimination against black people and hatred toward people like me rode this moment on our shoulders. I had never been attacked before based on my choice of friends, but now I felt the sting of hatred and fear thrown out from ignorant, hateful Christian people who found justification for their actions in what their Bibles had taught them.

When the chimes tolled 6:00, Chloe rose silently and walked away in the fog toward Fairchild Hall. Her shoulders were bent, she held her hands beneath her chin, and she shuffled like an old woman who was dying from the sheer weight of life. I watched her in sorrow knowing that she was beyond my reach at this time. I stood up and walked briskly for a few steps in her direction.

I yelled out, "It is not the color of skin, Chloe, or sexual orientation that defines a person. It's the love in your heart!"

The wind moaned through the leafless trees, and the fog swirled like cotton candy. I sat back down on the concrete steps of Phelps-Stokes and did not move even when the rain began to pour in torrents. My world had just been shattered again, and I did not care if I drowned in my sorrow in the pouring rain. The words came back to me from the first day when they had taught us our alma mater: "when danger and storm clouds were threatening, and stouthearted trembled with fear, the strength of thy heroes implanted thy roots in the wilderness drear...."

If ever I needed the spirit of Berea to guide me, it was now.

BROWN BAGGING

I pulled out the following items from a brown, paper bag: a peanut butter and jelly sandwich, a small bag of potato chips, a pint of milk in a cardboard box and a medium-sized apple. It was my Sunday evening meal at Berea College. This brown-bag meal had been issued to students from time immemorial. On certain Sundays, there was a cheese sandwich on white bread slices (no mayonnaise) and a chocolate chip cookie. The meal rarely varied from those items.

In my time at the school (1961-65), when a student had finished eating Sunday lunch, he went upstairs where the Alumni Office is now located. He entered into a very large room filled with hundreds of brown paper sacks piled to the roof. He showed his meal ticket to the student checker and he was rewarded with his Sunday evening meal: a brown paper sack filled with all kinds of surprises.

There were no refrigerators in the dorms where one could store milk. Peanut butter and jelly did not spoil. No sandwiches ever had a smattering of mayonnaise. Dry, it was just plain dry. A student could eat his sack supper on the spot, or he could save it until six o'clock in the evening.

When I graduated from Berea, I made it a point to share the paper sack meal menu with some nutritionists at a local hospital. They analyzed the meal for nutritional content. They found that the two slices of white bread had no nutrition at all. As a matter of fact, white flour can hardly be digested by the human stomach. Worms will not even get in white flour because they know there is no nutrition in it. It has all been milled out.

Potato chips are dreadful for one's health. Potatoes turn to carbs which turn to sugar in the body, and the salt in the packages shrinks blood vessels, thereby making the heart work harder. Once again, it has little or no nutrition.

The apple could be nutritious, but it was probably covered in insect spray that could make the body sick.

Cow's milk is designed by nature for use by baby calves, not humans. Many people are lactose intolerant. Adult humans can have difficulty digesting cow's milk.

In my opinion, it would have been better had Berea informed its students that there would be no Sunday evening meal at all. Go practice fasting! It won't hurt you to go from Sunday lunch to Monday breakfast without eating. Go buy yourself a hamburger at the Snack Bar. There was a slight problem with such a philosophy. People like me never had any spending money while we were at Berea. I could not even afford a cup of coffee at five cents, because I did not have the five cents.

Adequate food had always been an issue in my family. There were times when we had little or none. I was always glad to see my mother creeping out of the woods loaded down with jugs of white lightning, because that vision assured us that she would have some money after she sold it to buy some groceries for the family.

I must admit that I always got up early on Monday mornings to walk to the cafeteria for breakfast. I asked for double portions of cream of wheat cereal, eggs, and toast. The serving staff did not object, because they knew that many students were hungry after the long fast on the weekend.

I have often pondered why Berea initiated their brown bag policy. The explanation given was that the college wanted to give the cafeteria workers some time off. Well, mister, I don't ever remember being given time off from my work in the library, public relations, Knapp Hall, and the foreign language department. No one came and told me that I could skip my labor assignment for a day just because I needed a rest. Are we dealing here, again, with a feeble attempt to save money??? Starve the masses! We'll save some money and they will work harder to get fed. They might even be grateful.

My first march at Berea against oppression was not to Frankfort or Montgomery for civil rights. It was a protest against sack suppers. Berea students love to gripe and complain about the college. My group was exceptionally good at it. The Student Government Association organized a demonstration and boycott in 1962-63 against the food services department. We gathered in front of the Student Union Building with our signs and our complaining tongues denouncing brown bag suppers and poor quality food. I'm sure there were a few other issues on the table, but it has been fifty years since the event. There is a picture of our protest gathering in the 1963 Chimes.

We paraded around with our homemade paper signs on sticks, hooted and jeered, clapped our hands and sat down on the ground to socialize with our friends. We didn't yet know any anti-food protest songs.

The lady in charge of food services paced back and forth behind the glass doors that opened into the Alumni Building. With consternation on her face, she wrung her hands nervously as if she were headed for her own execution. In a sense, she was.

Students had planned to boycott meals in the cafeteria. They had decided not to tell in advance which meals they had planned to boycott. Whichever meal they did not eat, the food would be wasted and sent down the garbage disposal. A lot of money would go down the disposal with the food.

The standoff lasted about an hour. We all got hungry and bored. We were ready to move on to something else. The head of food services got brave enough to walk out on the Alumni Building steps.

"What are you so upset about?" she asked sheepishly.

"Your food!" students yelled in unison.

"I didn't know that my food wasn't good enough," she uttered softly. "I will gladly talk to your leaders about your complaints. Send them on in."

The leaders of the Student Government Association walked toward the building and disappeared inside it with the food service director. The rest of us began milling around not knowing what to do.

The food service lady walked back outside and said, "Y'all come on in and eat your dinner."

There was a stampede down the stairs to both cafeterias to get at the food!

I don't know which year Berea did away with the infamous brown bag supper. Whoever instituted its demise should have a heroic statue on campus. I do know that we carried one of the infernal bags with us to Montgomery.

To this very day, I do not eat sandwiches of any kind. Hand me a baloney sandwich and I will probably hit you. Don't even connect the words "peanut butter" and "jelly" in the same sentence in my presence. I can't guarantee what my reaction might be. In present time, I can think of a brown bag supper and feel sick to my stomach.

Today, I do not eat sandwiches of any kind. I do not eat potato chips. I do not drink milk. I do not eat cookies or anything made with sugar. I eat several apples a day. I do not allow brown paper sacks in my home.

When Berea invited me to campus in October, 2017, the college provided a nice spread of food in the room where we were having a discussion. If anyone noticed that I did not partake of the food, it is because we were sitting in the very room of the Alumni Building where those infernal sack suppers were dispensed every Sunday for four years. Pizza could not even override my sack-supper memories!

A PHILOSOPHY OF MILKSHAKES

A tall, black lady walked along the sidewalk toward the snack bar. There was nothing unusual about her except that she balanced her textbooks in a woven grass basket which she carried on the top of her head. I followed behind her filled with curiosity. Somehow I wanted the basket to topple from her head and spill its contents on the sidewalk. When she stopped at the crosswalk at Highway 25, she noticed me staring at the basket on her head.

The lady crossed the highway and made a left turn toward Union Church. I followed along behind her. She walked directly up the steps of Union Church without spilling the basket. As I continued to stare, she made a graceful turn of her body and danced back down the church steps.

"Come along," she called to me.

She put on a delightful balancing show for my benefit. She bent to her knees and duck- walked between two bushes, then skipped along the sidewalk up to the door of the Student Union Building. I decided to leave her there. As I turned to walk away, she yelled in a deep voice, "You! Come here!" I did not have the wherewithal to disobey her.

She took the basket from her head and placed it securely on top of my cranium.

"Walk down the steps," she commanded.

A group of curious students gathered around waiting to see the outcome of my basket adventure.

I stretched my arms outright and lightly moved from one step to the next. The basket held. Fellow students applauded my efforts.

"Come with me to the snack bar. We will share a milkshake," she invited. "Keep the basket on your head."

I entered the snack bar to hoots and howls of laughter as other students saw the basket on my head. The lady went to the counter to get our milkshake as I continued to sit sheepishly in my chair with a basket of textbooks balanced on my head. When the lady came back to our table with the milkshake, she lifted the basket from my head and placed it on the floor next to her chair.

"I like you, young man" she said. "What is your name?"

"My name is Fred," I answered.

"Where do you come from?" she wanted to know.

"North Carolina," I told her.

"I don't know all the places in the United States yet. I'm from Kenya. Do you know where it is?" she tested my knowledge.

"It's in Africa," I replied. "Its capital city is Nairobi. The Mau-Mau drove the English colonizers out in the 1950's. I once saw a movie about the struggle called, 'Something of Value.' Sidney Poitier starred in it."

She removed the paper from two straws and handed me one. Putting one straw into the strawberry shake, she slurped loudly as she handed me the other straw.

"Drink!" she ordered.

"I don't know where to place the straw," I said in a confused voice.

"You are not afraid to drink with Salome Nogola, are you?" she asked with a puzzled look on her face.

"No, my half of the milkshake is on the bottom. I will have to drink your half in order to get to mine," I teased her.

I plunged the straw deep into the shake and, like her, slurped with a loud sucking noise.

"What would have happened if I had knocked the basket of books off of your head?"

"Then you would have had to marry Salome. That is how we propose marriage to each other in Kenya."

We both let out a hearty laugh.

"Say my name, please. Salome Nogola," she requested. "The accent is on the last letter "e."

"Salome Nogola," I carefully repeated.

"I am named after a woman in the Bible. Her name is Salome," she explained. "I was born in a grass hut in Kenya. My family still lives there. I wanted something more than raising cattle, carrying water and wood, and having babies. I walked barefoot to Nairobi and asked a Quaker school if I could study there. They took me in. I had no money or means, but I had a brilliant mind. That has always been my collateral. The people there helped me find my way to Berea. The basket on my head is a cultural reminder of my home. I must not forget where I came from."

Salome and I were very much alike. I, too, came from poverty. I did not want my life to be milking cows, chopping wood, and making moon shine. I found my way to Berea as she had. I did not carry my mountain culture on my head in a basket, but it oozed out of every pore of my skin and was evident in my speech. Berea was the common denominator for a decent life for us both. The desire for a better life drove the two of us from different continents.

We both slurped loudly through the straws as we consumed the remainder of the milkshake from the cup. Salome placed the cup on top of my head and told me to walk with it to the trashcan.

"Come drink with me another day," she invited as she returned the basket to her head. She yelled, "Watch out, everyone, I've got eggs in this basket." I could hear her sustained laughter as her form disappeared out of the Student Union Building. The last thing I could see was the African basket handle bobbing up and down on her head.

The day when the restaurant refused to serve Chloe and me, I found my way back to the snack bar. I sat with anger in my mind and a hurting in my heart. Why did I befriend students of color? It would have been so much easier to let my upbringing hide beneath the surface of my personality. I could have pretended to be tolerant as many of my fellow students did. By forming friendships with foreigners on campus and with students of other races, I had to confront racism on a personal basis. When I socialized with black friends, people treated me as if I were black or something even worse. My embracing all peoples threatened many students on campus who were not yet ready to relinquish old patterns of thinking and acting. Liberal arts education attacks narrow minded thinking and forces students to consider a broader world beyond their upbringing.

I often wondered why black students chose me as a friend. I had little to offer them. I suppose we saw goodness in each other and we enjoyed each other's company. I was not only seeing what racism was like, I was living it. I became painfully aware of what my previous personal actions had done to other people.

I saw the top of a basket appear above the snack bar door and I knew who it belonged to. It was Salome. She purchased a strawberry milkshake and made a beeline to my table. Producing two straws, she invited me to drink.

I burst out crying.

"You are treating me better than my own mother, Salome," I mumbled. "I am a white person and you pass no judgment on me. I have just been refused service in a restaurant in my own country and community and have been thrown out of a greasy-spoon restaurant because I went there with a black friend. Never before did I realize what our attitudes and actions can do to another human. Hating others for any reason is demeaning to us all."

"You were with Chloe, weren't you?" she asked in a gentle voice. "I just passed her walking to her dorm. She seemed dispirited." I nodded my head.

"Freddie," she said sweetly taking both my hands in hers, "my people and I struggled in Kenya against British Colonial Rule. The Mau-Mau spilled much white blood and the British took their revenge in kind. There came a point when my people realized that freedom would come through peaceful means, not through violence. And it did. When we removed hatred from our hearts, we could yell 'Uhuru' (freedom) and then proceed to live it.

"You are different. Be proud of your personal identity. You are the only person on earth who can destroy you. Be patient. Bide your time. Change will come. You have a warm, loving heart but it has been gravely wounded. Do not consider yourself to be ordinary. You have been chosen to awaken people and walk in harmony with peoples of this earth. Believe first of all in justice, and then may you have every right to believe in yourself."

It was as if Salome came from the Dreamtime. She represented Mother Africa from which her American children had come. Her lineage produced my black friends at Berea. She carried the flame of black culture in her heart and she presented it with great wisdom. She came into my life to encourage and guide me, to temper my impulsive nature, to teach me lessons that were unavailable in textbooks. She came to teach me self love.

When Salome chose to share her milkshake, she had a lesson to teach the recipient. In my situation, she saw a person struggling to belong, a person attempting to break with his past, a young man seeking a family of his own, one that would be universal in scope. In that separation from the past, all beliefs about and actions toward people had to change. One could not associate race or color with Salome. She epitomized all that was good about human beings. The milkshake was her way of communion. Sharing the same glass was her way of bonding. Letting you carry her basket on your head signified her personal acceptance of you. And so, this lovely person from Africa entered my life and changed it profoundly.

Once a week we shared a milkshake and she taught me about her life in Africa. She gave me hope. She calmed my fears and introduced me to her philosophy of milkshakes.

"Fred," she said, "people cannot hate each other when they have supped from the same chalice, eaten from the same plate, suffered the same pains of life, and drunk a milkshake from the same glass. Two people must trust each other to drink from the same glass. They can respectfully drink only their part of the contents. They have to drink courteously and with good manners. All of life exists in that act of sharing."

I often took shelter under Salome's wings.

Salome graduated from Berea and returned to her native Kenya where she founded a girls' school for poor, disadvantaged children. She structured its operation on Berea's model. She did not stay in America long enough to march with me in Montgomery.

Upon returning to Berea in the autumn after Salome graduated, I found a note in my Post Office box saying that I had a package waiting to be picked up. The post office worker handed me Salome's woven African basket. In it was a note that read:

"I want you to have this basket. You are the person I've met that deserves to wear it on your head and one whom I believe will be a keeper of the flame that I lit here. Don't be afraid to be a color in the rainbow. Continue to look at people's hearts, not at the color of their skin." She signed it: "With Love, Mother Salome."

Salome lived only nine years after she returned to Kenya. When she had successfully established her girls' school, it was time to go. Her work was finished. She died as she had lived-in peace. Her work was finished. My work was just beginning.

"I am your friend unconditionally."

Salome Nogola

(Photo: Chimes, 1963. Newman Printing Co.
Used by permission of Berea College Archives)

MOTHERLY ADVICE

Salome placed a straw into the paper cup which contained a thick, frothy strawberry milk shake and slurped some of the ice cream through her bulbous, black lips. She extracted the straw which held a glob of gooey cream on the end and licked it off with her pink tongue. She then let out a large sigh, an exhaling of breath indicating great satisfaction. She laughed raucously as she slapped me lovingly across my back.

"And, now, what are the continuing perils of Pauline in your life?" she asked with motherly concern. "You have more issues than Carters has little liver pills," she smiled.

"You are picking up bad Southern Appalachian English," I told her. "Where the heck did you learn about Carter's Little Liver Pills?" I teased her.

"I listen to students around me. I listen carefully to how they talk. It is an education within itself," she said astutely.

"Salome," I asked sheepishly, "why do people bully other people?"

"Your parents should have had this talk with you when you were little, just like they are supposed to have the talk with you about sex," she responded.

"What should happen and what does happen are not one and the same. My mother, Ottie, never uttered the word sex except in a vulgar context. She did defend me when my sisters and I beat up our neighbor, Rake, when he wouldn't stop bullying me," I said by way of explanation.

Salome paused and stared away across the distant mountains through the snack bar windows. It seemed as if she had gone back to another time in her life, a troubled time, for the experience left her face covered with a sad countenance. A thousand years of time rested on her dark face that was just beginning to show a few wrinkles and a strand or two of white in her hair. She was fifteen years older than me and I respected those years as ones filled with wisdom greater than mine.

"I think that bullies are people who have been hurt very badly in life. They do not get the love and attention which they so desperately crave and they take their anger out on those around them whom they perceive do get it. They are lonely people who have been abused, verbally and physically, themselves. They desperately want to be popular and don't know how. They have big egos that can't be stroked. They become mean and harsh, unable to reach out and get what they desperately desire."

Salome was a fountain of wisdom.

"I came to talk to you about the fact that I am being bullied constantly by a number of students on campus and there are a couple of teachers that participate as well. I want to understand why they resort to hostile treatment when I hardly know any of them."

"I am fully aware of the situation behind the scenes because I hear people talk. It seems that a few people are jealous of your popularity. You dance well; you are more sophisticated than they are; you have a great talent for languages which they can't match. They want to have what you already have, but they can't. Some of them intentionally set out to destroy you completely. Rumors and lies fly from lips to lips. Those who don't know you believe what these students are saying. Then they pass it on. The bullies de-cided to spread the rumor that you are gay. Truth here does not matter. Once a person is deemed to be a witch, he cannot convince the public otherwise. The only power the witch has is that everyone will then believe whatever she says. The ostracism then be-gins. There is no way to change minds."

"You make good sense, Salome," I replied, "because the bullying started with a group of boys pitching pennies at me on the dance floor. They were a group of misfits that couldn't dance, weren't popular, and they got no recognition for anything."

"When I walked to Nairobi as a young girl and sought an education at the girls' school, people in my village bullied me. They were jealous that I had made a way to get out of our village and make a better life for myself. When I tried to go back to visit my family, many of them struck me with their fists. They spread terrible rumors that I had become a whore in order to pay for my education. After that, no village man would look at me. They actually believed the lies because they wanted to. That is what is happening with you"

"What can a person do to counteract these bullies and their lies?" I asked hopefully.

"Live your life in such a way that whatever the bullies say is a lie even before it is uttered on their lips," she advised.

"It is impossible to live a quality life when one is constantly barraged with taunts, threats, physical shoving, and despicable jeers about perceived sexual orientation," I responded.

"Why not confront the bully and tell him in no uncertain terms that you are not going to tolerate his bullying?" I asked.

"Then what will you do with his friends and accomplices who will just make the situation worse?" she asked me. "It would be easier to empty the ocean with a bucket as to stop these vile people."

"Why are people so fearful of someone's sexual orientation or religion or race? Sexuality and races are determined by nature, but a person is taught the prejudices of religion."

"Yes, Fred," she reminded me, "Gandhi said that Christians were the most un-Christlike people that he had ever met. Isn't it interesting that all the students hurting and maligning you are Christian? They all come from Christian families. That is their religious background, their experience. Did they somehow miss the teachings of Jesus about love, forgiveness, tolerance, acceptance, and forbearance? Their personal experiences of abuse, of being left out, were so full of hurt that their feelings overrode their moral teachings. People who feel unimportant have to have something or someone to hate."

"What shall I do, Salome? There are twelve hundred students on this campus and many of them are misreading me. They are listening to lies and innuendo coming from a small group bent on destroying me."

"Nothing," she said. "Do nothing at all."

She said the word with a profound finality that it shocked me. It was not the answer that I had expected.

"This, too, shall pass. You will survive. You will be a stronger and greater man for the experience. Learn to forgive. Learn to love. I am your friend unconditionally as I hope you are mine. There is no black or white, gay or straight, bully or victim. There is only Salome and Fred sitting at a table in the snack bar at Berea College in the year of our lord 1963. We are drinking from the same cup, the same straw, and the same straw- berries. This is the lesson of life that I want to share with you. There is just the oneness. Don't let the bullying get to you. All the water in all the oceans of the world cannot sink the smallest ship, unless it gets inside. Take Salome's love inside you and let it be your beacon, your lighthouse, your torch to be a lamp unto your feet through dark night."

She had finished. She got up and placed the paper cup and straw in the garbage can. She hugged me warmly nuzzling her dark nose in the nape of my neck. "I am Mother Africa. I am Mother Salome. I am Fred's mother and friend," she had said. Then she was gone.

From a nearby table there rained down on me a shower of pennies thrown by bullies who would never know the wisdom and friendship that were now mine.

A SUMMER WITH THE
PEACE CORPS AT BEREA

Miss Louisda of the Foreign Language Department at Berea summoned me to her office to inform me that the college had contracted with the United States Government to sponsor a Peace Corps training center for the summer of 1963. The group was headed to Senegal, Africa, where French was the major language. Since I was majoring in French, the college wanted to hire me as an individual tutor for some of these volunteers. It was the opportunity of a lifetime and I quickly accepted the offer. The salary was $350 for the summer.

With the election of President Kennedy, there had come a new birth of excitement and youthful enthusiasm for serving our country. He had told the nation not to ask what the country could do for them, but to ask what they could do for their country. He had reminded the youth of my time that the torch had been passed to us and that we held the responsibility of carrying it forward to establish equality in our own country as well as to go forward to improve the entire world.

The nation came alive with youthful activity. The Kennedy administration formed the Peace Corps to counteract Communist activity in developing countries. Thousands of volunteers stepped forward to join the Peace Corps and to accept Kennedy's challenge to do something for their country. Berea administrators caught the vision of what was happening and they boldly moved to be a part of the new era.

President Frances Hutchins called Stan Meisler, author of the book, WHEN THE

WORLD CALLS: INSIDE STORY OF THE PEACE CORPS AND ITS FIRST FIFTY YEARS, to ask him if he would direct the Berea program. In an interview on Nov. 23, 2010, Mr. Meisler stated: "...When the Peace Corps was starting; I received a phone call from Berea College.

They were going to train PCVs to go to Senegal, and they asked me to run the program...I turned them down, explaining that I did not know much about Senegal; I had only spent three months there, mostly in Dakar...When I found some PVCs who had trained at Berea, I told them how I had almost run their training program but declined because of my limited experience in Senegal. They laughed at me. ' Your three months,' I was told, 'were three months more than anybody on the Berea training staff had ever spent in Senegal.'" (Meisler)

Bill Moyers of Washington, D.C., took the reins of the program. I had the pleasure of meeting him when he visited Berea.

The program opened with 35 volunteers-in-training. They came from all over the United States, filled with an unbelievable idealism, to participate in a summer program that was so tough that it would make a Marine Corps drill sergeant proud. I decided to participate in all the activities that the volunteers did, so that I would experience the full training.

I rose at 4:30 A.M. each morning and proceeded to awaken all the male volunteers. Training classes started at 6:00 and ended at 9:00 P.M. They ate breakfast between 5:00-6:00 A.M. Both males and females joined together on the athletic field to do calisthenics. It was a rigorous activity. Next, they went to French instruction taught by a native speaker. After two hours of instruction, each person came to a personal tutor for a further two hours of instruction and practice.

I worked with Grace Poe, a middle-aged, pleasant lady from North Carolina, and a delightful young man whose name I no longer remember. Grace was doggedly determined to master French. There were days when she struggled. She actually cried through the French lessons. But she made it to Senegal.

The young man became discouraged after the first week of training. He made a great effort to learn French, but he really had little linguistic ability. To lift his spirit, I taught him to say, "Je promis de ne pas quitter la programme. Je vais reussir. Je n'y manquerai pas." (I promise not to leave the program. I am going to succeed. I certainly will.)

He dropped out anyway. He came to say goodbye. Hugging me, he said," Fred, I will always remember you." Tears in his eyes, he added proudly, "Je n'y manquerai pas." This was not the only sad event that I would experience during the summer, nor would it be the only goodbye.

Most of the volunteers intended to teach English in Senegal. Others were going to work in construction, well-digging, coaching, and other useful trades. These individuals spent two hours of daily instruction in their respective skills.

The construction group built a prototype building on the Berea campus. It still stands near the new science building. There is an historical plaque telling the story of its origin.

Each day there was a two-hour lecture on Senegal. One of the principal lecturers was David Hapgood from the Institute of Current World Affairs. He was an expert on Senegal. He lectured for an entire week to the group.

 Mr. Hapgood addressed the issue as to why individuals would volunteer for a Peace Corps assignment. In a private letter to Mr. Richard H. Nolte at the Institute of Current World Affairs, he states: "Why do these young people - usually recent college graduates in the liberal arts - volunteer to go abroad? The question is being studied by the multitude of social scientists attracted by the Peace Corps...I will simply report a suggestion, made by the psychologist at Berea, that accorded with my fleeting impressions of the trainees. This is that they are attracted to the Peace Corps because it fits today's picture of the All-American Boy (or Girl). Not surprisingly, in view of the origin and leadership of the Peace Corps, the trainees seemed to reflect the 'image' projected by the Kennedys. 'Vigah,' but vigor more for its own sake than for any clear ideal; caution; group spirit - no rough edges or negative attitudes; the Peace Corps as a way to Get Ahead while Doing Good. A Peace Corps man at Berea said that volunteers whose stated motives are selfish usually do better than those who say they are going for altruistic reasons. I detected no missionary types - mercifully, for missionaries (by definition, I suppose) go to Africa to dictate not to discuss. Some go for compelling personal reasons: a Negro girl at Berea was clearly looking for the cultural home denied her in her own country. I could only suggest that she read the New Yorker article in which Harold Isaacs describes the disappointment of American negroes who have gone 'Back to Africa'." (Hapgood) (4)

The "selecting out" process was brutal. Dozens of observers followed the volunteers around and took notes on how they performed in all their activities. A psychologist was present for all activities and a psychiatrist met weekly in an interview with each participant. Teachers and administrators were required to make weekly reports on each volunteer. Since I interacted with the volunteers on a more personal basis than their teachers, officials often interviewed me in reference to some volunteers.

It was very difficult for me to report on the volunteers, because I came to view them more as my college classmates. One young man had been accepted to coach the sport of tennis. I often wondered how many ordinary people in Senegal played tennis. It was tragic that the committee selected him out after the fourth week of training. They told him the same thing I had been thinking. Why did they accept him into the program in the first place?

I made only one negative report against a volunteer. He was a very loud-mouth, obnoxious, New Yorker who was quite abrasive in his attitude toward everyone. He refused to accept me as a member of the staff. He criticized me with the usual stereotypes of Appalachian people (ignorant hillbilly, barefoot, cousin-marrying dolt). It occurred to me that if he would treat me in such a disrespectful manner, what would he do to poor peasants in Senegal?? I wrote the truth about him. The committee "selected him out" the following week.

A very shy, meek young lady had just received a visit from her whole family the previous week when the committee "selected her out." They thought that she was not strong enough to survive the rigors of twenty weeks in Senegal. The poor girl was distraught. I have never seen a sadder sight.

The Food Services Department at Berea did not escape the unhappiness of Peace Corps volunteers. Berea contracted with the U.S. government to carry out the training program. Whoever planned the menus thought that cold cereal and milk or two pieces of dry toast were sufficient to carry young men through the rigorous morning activities. Some of the men explained to officials that they needed eggs, meat, bagels, and unlimited milk in order to sustain them until lunch. Many volunteers enlisted me to speak on their behalf because they feared being "selected out" if they spoke too strongly on the issue. I obliged them. The menu changed overnight. There appeared a veritable breakfast buffet with unlimited trips for participants.

Some of the men told me to stop waking them up at 4:30 each morning. They were grouchy and sleep-deprived and they somehow resented my intrusion. I stopped knocking on their doors. One week later they came to me and begged me to resume the practice of waking them, because so many were oversleeping. I refused. Let the roosters wake you up when you get to Senegal.

My two favorite people who came to Berea to work with the program were Fontaine

Belford and Luis Zuck. Fontaine had graduated from Hollins College in Virginia with a specialty in French. Luis taught linguistics. My friendship with them made the summer pass quickly. We often drove to Richmond in Fontaine's yellow Volkswagen to have a beer, because Madison County was dry as a bone.

Though Senegal is a black country, there were few black people involved with the training. I remember only one black lady who came from Haiti to help teach French. I usually met her at the Student Union Building for breakfast. The grass where we walked was always wet and she would greet me daily with the words, "L'herbe, c'est trop mouillee. Les pieds vont se noyer." (The grass is so wet that my feet are going to drown.)

After breakfast each day, I had to go to the library and collect major news stories of the day. A group of French teachers and tutors translated the news into French. During lunch, one of us read the news over the intercom to the Peace Corps volunteers.

The team psychiatrist met weekly with each volunteer. Each had to answer his question, "What are you going to do about sex while you are in the Peace Corps in Senegal?" The expected answer was, "I will do without." Volunteer behavior had to be impeccable, because eyes would always be watching them in their new country. "Get with another Peace Corps volunteer," the psychiatrist advised. "Don't go to prostitutes."

The training at Berea lasted ten weeks and, then, the group left for a two-week experience in Puerto Rico. Puerto Rico had a climate and topography similar to Senegal. Bill Moyers came to Berea for the send-off. Mr. Moyers shared with us that one of the first groups to go to Senegal were not accepted, because the Senegalese did not want to speak with an American accent. In Africa people speak English with a British accent. The American accent is considered inferior. So the first Peace Corps group to Senegal ended up next door in the Ivory Coast.

The $350 I had earned during the Peace Corps summer paid for my 1963 fall semester. I had been on campus the previous year, all summer, and then I would be there the next year without a break. This long sojourn on campus was one reason that led me to leave Berea at the end of the junior year.

When the summer was over, I knew for sure that I would never volunteer to be in the Peace Corps. Berea had brought a vast, idealistic world to its doorstep and those of us who were privileged to be a part of it grew in understanding and compassion. I focused my compassion, not on far-away Africa, but on what was happening to African-American people across America and on the Berea campus.

This small, red building, with a white roof,was built by Peace Corps volunteers in the summer of 1963 as a prototype house for Senegal, West Africa where they were as-signed. It is located between the new science building and the Appalachian Center. There is an historical plaque identifying the structure. I express my gratitude to Berea College for leaving this historical building intact.

Part II

Journey To Selma/Montgomery

Three original participants in the Berea to Montgomery march: Dr. John Fleming, Fred E. Epeley, and Mike Clark. All three are originally from North Carolina. Dr. Fleming and Mr. Epeley are both from Morganton, North Carolina. Mike Clark made the historical photos of the march. Dr. Fleming wrote a book, A SUMMER REMEMBERED, portraying his youth in Morganton. Though writing separately, Dr. Fleming and Mr. Epeley discuss the same events and issues of race relations in their town in the 1950s.

MY CHANGE OF HEART

The time for a changing of the heart had come. The change had already been born in my heart long before I had left Ottie's world. I was seeking a very different life. There was uncertainty in what I might find in the uncharted regions of my heart and soul. Ottie's world had flattened my emotional life like a gigantic hammer and the accepting spirit of Berea was slowly restoring it. Chloe, with her warm support and loving friendship, was helping me to weave a new tapestry. Wayne, John, and Alfred were new versions of Willard Worth, Curtis, and June Jr. These three friends represented what my brothers could have been had they not grown up in Ottie's world.

My sophomore year had ended with me once more making the dean's list. That dreaded humanities course turned out to be one of the best I would experience. The professors gave one "A "out of five hundred students. A "B+" was my grade. The episode of jumping out of the windows in Dr. Hardley's class would fill my heart with laughter for the rest of my life. The college had just hired me to be a tutor for students in a Peace Corps Training Program that was coming to campus in the summer.

This campus was now my new home. Whatever life had thrown at me here, I had absorbed it, just like I had done in Ottie's world. I had enough food here. I had a purpose. I had enough people to consider as friends or at least friendly. I had begun to guard the sanctity of the campus like I would the sanctity of my home back in Carolina. Pick a flower and I will nab you. Vandalize anything on campus, I will rebuke you. Steal anything at all and I will probably hit you. Among ourselves, we may beat Berea like a dog, but should an outsider demean her, a hundred sharp tongues will come to her defense. Now my chest swelled with pride as the student body sang "Berea Beloved" in Phelps -Stokes Chapel.

Vixen continued to instruct me in life's truths. I was no longer afraid of people. I did whatever it took to get what I wanted.

It was the month of May when the Redbuds dot the landscape like a Monet canvas. I had survived a difficult, challenging year. Yet there is joy ahead. I had a scholarship to study Spanish in Guadalajara, Mexico, in a few weeks. I had begun learning Spanish in my sophomore year and had progressed rapidly. Chloe, John, Alfred, and I had decided to celebrate my good fortune by taking a swim in a public pool in a nearby town.

The sun felt hot and steamy as we walked down the sidewalk toward the pool. Alfred and John were popping each other with the ends of their towels, leaving red whelps on each other's legs. Chloe and I walked in front chatting softly. As we neared our destination, we could hear the joyful shouts of young people swimming and diving. The strong smell of chlorine broke the air, leaving our noses running from its powerful odor. We expected to see other Berea students relaxing in the pool, because we could not swim on campus at Seabury Gym pool without a lifeguard. None was available when classes were in session.

It cost fifty cents to swim in the pool. John was treating all of us, so he paid the cashier two dollars, and we entered the pool area, sat down, and dangled our feet into the blue water.

Every swimmer in the pool climbed out quickly and sat down on the edge of the pool, as if a shark had just entered it. Dozens of pairs of eyes stared holes through us. I stared back into the faces of stone. Eyes of hatred glared back.

"Get out of our pool," people were yelling. "Get out of our damn pool."

"Are they talking to us?" I asked Alfred. The four of us looked around to see who they were talking to.

"Get that girl out of this pool. We don't allow her kind in here," swimmers yelled.

"We've paid our fee to swim in this pool," John yelled back.

"There is not enough money in this whole world to pay me to swim with a damn N.....," one offensive redneck spat out.

"My friend is a black lady, not an N....., and she has class, smarts, and kindness which are obviously missing in you, Asshole," I cursed at him. It was a dangerous comment for me to make. I was on their turf, not back at the Berea campus where I would be safe.

Members of this group began hurling flip-flops, bottles of water, paper, spit, and soft drinks, anything they could get their hands on. A wet towel wound tight as a ball crashed into the side of my head. There was no cut on my head, but the wound that was opening in my heart was wider than the sea. People in my life had often attacked me based on the choice of my friends. The hatred generated by our presence could have frozen an ice cutter.

The manager of the pool walked up to us and said that he had called the police.

"Why is everyone so angry?" I asked. "We have broken no rules."

"Yes you have," he informed me strongly. "City Ordinance makes this pool for whites only. Laws of Kentucky prevent blacks and whites from fraternizing."

"That Kentucky Day Law was rescinded long ago," I let him know.

"City ordinance has not been rescinded. I want the four of you to get out of this pool area right now. I'm refunding your money." He gave John back his two dollars.

The crowd of swimmers formed a thick circle around us, and I could hear and feel their hot breath. I scanned the crowd with my eyes and was shocked to see some Berea students among them. They were not defending us; rather, they had joined the stone faces and eyes of hatred that bore down upon us in this most auspicious moment.

A police siren broke the silence of the afternoon. Two obese deputies, chomping on tobacco, sauntered through the entrance to the pool and demanded to know what was going on. Twiddle-Dee-Fat-Dee and Twiddle-Dee-Fat-Dumb took out their night sticks thinking that we might resist. They shook the batons above our heads.

"We ain't having no California-style hippies demonstrating and swimming in our pool," Fat-Dee said. It was obvious that he was a high school dropout.

"If God had wanted you to come swim in our pool, he would have made that girl white," Fat-Dumb added.

"If God had wanted you to be a cop, he would have made you out of bacon," John said angrily.

The cop came over and rubbed his nightstick across the nape of John's neck. He fingered his handcuffs that were hooked to the back of his belt. He wanted desperately to place them on one of us.

"The only thing that keeps me from busting your stupid head is that your uppity college might sue me. Don't push your luck, though. Get up, all of you. Let's vacate this pool," Fat-Dumb ordered.

We sat for a moment.

"Do you want to go to jail?" Fat-Dee asked us.

"This is not the right time, friends," Chloe advised us.

The police escorted us back to the edge of campus. They stopped short of actually coming on to the campus, because they had no authority there.

As we left the pool, I thought about the amassed crowd with their stone faces and eyes of hatred, "I don't ever want to swim in a pool with the likes of you," I said to myself. "You have probably already pissed in the water."

As we left, half a dozen middle fingers went up in the air indicating the crowd's collective I.Q. I remembered my friend Sara from the fourth grade and high school. Bullies and hatred had driven her to commit suicide.

This experience was the moment in my life when racism, injustice, prejudice, discrimination, and bullying got very personal with me! I would embrace any opportunity to fight back.

MARCH 5ᵗʰ ON FRANKFORT

A lively debate was already in progress when I entered the snack bar. Some dozen or more students were seated in a circle around one of the tables. Chairs had been borrowed from surrounding tables and haphazardly placed around the table where George and Raymond sat. A few students sat backward in their chairs with their hands resting on the back. Arms and hands gesticulated in the air as students pounded home the points they were making in the debate.

"Kentucky has laws restricting black people from voting. They allow establishments to refuse to serve anyone they wish. Restaurants, hotels, movies, stores regularly refuse service to blacks. And don't forget the Kentucky Day Law that once forbade black students to attend Berea. It wasn't too long ago that it was rescinded," George said emphatically.

"What do you hope to accomplish by tramping around in the streets in Frankfort?" one bystander asked.

"The legislature and governor pass laws in each state. They can undo restrictive laws that prevent people from voting. People should be able to eat or sleep anywhere they choose. When large numbers of people make their voices heard, legislators act. Otherwise, nothing will ever change," George explained.

I eased away from the group of students and went to Fairchild Hall to find Chloe. I told her that she should hear this debate going on next door in the snack bar. I returned to the room with her. In my absence, the number of participants had doubled. Verbal exchanges were getting more heated.

"Since you are not a resident of Kentucky, why are you so interested in changing our laws?" a student asked him.

"My interest in freedom and justice is universal," he explained. "People in my home state are prejudiced, too, and blacks are often mistreated there. Changes that we can make in Kentucky can also affect the situation in Michigan."

Chloe walked with courage into the middle of the group. The fact that a black woman rose to challenge them impressed the assembled students and her presence immediately changed the tone of the debate.

"I want to tell you a story," she began speaking softly. "My family lives in Tennessee. My mother's family is from Georgia. One summer we went to visit my mother's family. For all of you who are white, you would have no difficulty taking a trip anywhere across this country. My mother had to pack food for all of us for the entire journey because no restaurant along the way would serve us food. We had to sleep in the parking lot of a black church or pull off along the highway because no motel would let us in. If we need-ed to use the restroom, we pulled the car off along the highway and went into the woods being careful not to trespass on some racist person's land.

If the car had broken down, we could not go to any service station for help. We would hope that some other black family would come along and assist us. The kids of my family could not stop along the way and enjoy tourist attractions, because blacks were not allowed to visit them. Do you think that I am not ready to march to Frankfurt and tell the governor and legislature that it is time to lift laws that make my family suffer? What-ever all of you have suffered in your lives, my suffering has been much greater."

The group of students fell silent. In view of what Chloe had just explained, there was no more debate to be had. I wanted to pour out my soul to the group about how I had been bullied and was being bullied at this very time on this very campus. But I did not have Chloe's courage of the moment. My protest would take a different road. I decided then and there that I would go to the Frankfurt protest on my own behalf. I would protest the treatment of black people and I would also protest against mistreatment of any kind.

Many students pushed their chairs back under the table and quietly exited the snack bar. Those who remained sat in silence. In the few minutes that Chloe had spoken, stu-dents began to consider their own personal actions in their lives. George had laid on the table a stack of flyers that read, "March 5 on Frankfurt." Students took several to post all over the Berea campus. Chloe and I took several with us and posted them at the post of-fice, on our dorm door, on trees leading to the classroom building, and on the doors of students we knew to be racists.

Most students on campus were non-committal when it came to civil rights demonstrations. They just wanted to keep the status quo and complete requirements for their diplomas. I became active with the firebrands who advocated equal rights. My hurt from being thrown out of the All Night Restaurant, the swimming pool, and having doors slammed in my face when I attempted to go caroling in town and my experience with campus bullies was very raw. I could express my emotional anger through debate, demonstrations, and refusing to accept bigoted behavior toward anyone on campus. And I could march.

The activist group posted sign-up sheets for those students who wanted to go to Frankfort. Chloe and I proudly signed our names. Finally, we would have an opportunity to strike back symbolically at those who had mistreated us so terribly.

Berea College officials, Cabinet, President, deans and faculty, stepped forward in support of the march. They cancelled all classes. They provided free transportation by college buses for any students to Frankfurt and back. They gave permission for all students to leave campus because they served in loco parentis. No parental permission was required. Many students decided to make the trek to the state capital.

Frankfort was no more than an hour's drive from Berea. No danger to our students was perceived, for no violence had yet occurred in the state of Kentucky. The trip was like an outing to a county fair. It took two buses to carry Berea participants. I was overwhelmed to be in a group of ten thousand people marching down the main avenue of the capital toward the capitol building. It was a happy occasion. Few residents lined the streets to watch the parade. The governor did not attend the rally but he did meet with representatives. I don't know where the lawmakers were, but we supposed thatthey were somewhere in hiding. The crowd sang songs and Peter, Paul, and Mary entertained all of us. Just before Dr. Martin Luther King, Jr. spoke, the crowd broke into the rousing strands of "We Shall Overcome."

Chloe and I marched together. I looked over at her to see a smiling face singing joyfully.

"Let's see how many more places we can get thrown out of, Fred," she teased me.

"I'm not taking any more snowballs for you, lady," I informed her. "If any violence breaks out here today, I'm going to be the biggest coward in the county. I'll be yelling, 'move over rabbit and let someone in front who can run fast.'"

"Why don't we sing them all a Christmas carol?" I asked her.

We joyfully broke into the happy strands of "We Wish You a Merry Christmas."

People around us thought that we were nuts, or even worse, drunk.

The crowd listened in awe as Dr. King spoke. Everyone knew that we were making history today. I surveyed the crowds around me so that I could remember. I smelled the air to remember it. I observed the helicopters hovering above, and I studied the hundreds of police patrolling the capitol and moving among the crowd. I looked at people in the crowd, mostly black. Most were poor. Their faces were etched with pain and suffering. Their eyes darted to and fro not trusting anyone. While there was great joy in the crowd, there was also fear. Whatever the results of the march might be, these people still had to live in Frankfurt after we had gone home.

Berea students carried themselves with great dignity. Not one person misbehaved. They mixed warmly with the crowd and listened quietly to all the speeches. These Berea students had come from the segregated South. Most had not associated with black people until they had come to the college. The diversified, tolerant life on campus was taking root in their lives. They were willing to give each his due, and the idea of injustice toward any people was becoming anathema among them.

After the experience in Frankfort, I began to pay careful attention to national events. I also moved closer to those students on campus who were advocating civil rights for people everywhere. I found myself clashing with Berea students who were not yet ready to let go of their upbringing. Custom was too strong and ingrained behavior was like stone. The more I advocated for justice and human rights, the more students disliked me.

Then the unthinkable happened. I opened my door one morning to find a note nailed to it: "N.....lover, get off the Berea campus!" Some racist hand had scribbled this note.

"You'll have to come and throw me off campus," I muttered out loud.

TROUBLE IN THE TRENCHES

The conference room was cold as ice when I entered and sat down in front of three ladies who made up the foreign language department in 1964. The three of them--one who taught Spanish, one who taught Latin, and one who taught French--sat with their arms crossed. Their faces were stone and their eyes exuded hatred, just like I would experience in Montgomery.

"You are summoned here because of an incident that happened with Miss Laverne. (Miss Laverne just happened to be sixty-eight years old and unmarried.) I am unhappy with your disrespectful conduct toward her," Dr. Erica's words opened the meeting. "You are here to give account of yourself, sir." She was filled with fire and offended to the core.

"I am here to give account of myself," I replied, "but in a manner that may surprise you. I simply told Miss Laverne that I was tired of her as my professor, and I felt that she had nothing more to offer me as a teacher in my major."

"Who are you to question what a certified professor can and cannot offer you?" she fired back at me.

"I am not stupid, Dr. Erica, and I am not a fool. This woman has been my teacher for every course in French since I arrived on campus with the exception of Madame Hurston and Miss Grackle. Miss Laverne has certain ability in French, but she is not native French speaker. She speaks and uses the French language like an American and her accent is atrocious."

"This lady has a certificate from the Sorbonne in Paris," she informed me.

"Yes, that is true. But I also know that anyone can go to the Sorbonne and get a certificate during the summer. It means very little to me. It has not given her an ability to speak native French and that is what I am protesting," I countered. "I protest the fact that her manner of teaching consists of going over exercises in the book, assigning more exercises in the book, and reading over them once we return to class. It has been this way in every course in my major. I am now at the end of my third year. What do I have to look forward to next year?"

"What do you know about teaching?" she challenged me.

"I know quite a lot, actually. As a student, I am exposed to all kinds of different teachers on a daily basis. Most at Berea use lecture methods. I have researched learning styles and have come to realize that the lecture method is the least effective way of teaching anything. Besides, French is a discipline that one uses in front of people. Unlike physics and math, when one engages someone in the French language, he will know immediately whether that person is proficient or not.

And, Dr. Erica, I teach myself all the time. I read, I do hands on work, I debate with other students at Berea, I explore. I seek to improve my weaknesses, and I never pretend to be better in a discipline than I actually am," I spoke strongly to her.

"That may be," she replied, "but I will not tolerate disrespect to my faculty."

"What is more disrespectful than what you have done to me for three years? Don't you remember that when we were studying "Modern French Novel" last semester, that you brought in another teacher, worse than Miss Laverne, to teach that? She was so old that it was difficult for her to get up the stairs to the classroom. She could hardly see at all and we had to repeat every question. She taught that course in English! If she had ever been able to speak French, it had left her. Furthermore, in my Spanish class, you hired Mrs. Leighton for one semester. She had had a stroke. She attempted to write on the board and couldn't. A high school student could speak Spanish better than she could. Are you hiring on the cheap side? You certainly are not hiring on the high academic side," I protested.

"If you are unhappy, you don't have to go to school here," the department chairman let me know.

"Oh, yes I do have to go to school here. I am poor. I have little means. But it seems that my standards and expectations are much higher than yours. If I had the money, I would be sitting in Paris at an outdoor cafe sipping wine and speaking with real people who actually know the French language. It is surprising to me that you three professors are not willing to listen to criticism of you and your program. Berea College teaches dialogue and debate and challenging issues that don't seem right to us. That is what I am doing. If you find it disrespectful, ask the college to stop doing such a good job of encouraging intellectual exchange on this campus." I was finished with them.

I got up and walked away. Looking back at Miss Laverne I said, "J'en ai mare," (I've had it up to here.) I doubt that she understood what I said.

At the end of the third year, I withdrew from Berea and went to New York to live with my sister.

New York was not where I wanted to be. I realized that I had made a mistake in leaving Berea. I could have my diploma in one more year. I called Dr. Morreim, Admissions Officer, and asked if I could return to Berea in the fall.

"Yes, Fred," he told me. "You left of your own accord. Berea did not expel you. You will have to apply anew to get accepted. The only housing available will be Pearsons Hall which is a freshman dorm."

"I accept these conditions," I told Mr. Morreim.

Dr. Erica had been awaiting my return. When I went to register for my senior year, she came running to the registration line and yelled, "Stop him! Don't let him register!"

I only needed two classes to complete my major in French. But I had to take them in Dr. Erica's Foreign Language Department. Dr. Erica had the upper hand and she was ready to slap me down.

"You can't come back into my department until you do some apologizing, Mister," she yelled at me.

"What makes you think that I have any intention of returning to your department?" I asked.

"There's nowhere else that you can take the French classes you need to complete a major," she smirked.

"Dr. Erica, I have decided to change my major to Hotel Management. Then I can travel and work in a French-speaking country where I can learn the language in a natural way. I will learn from people who are masters of French. You see, I will not be returning to your department," I said with finality.

With great agitation and frustration, she screamed, "You can't do that!"

"Just watch me!" I screamed back.

Dr. Erica paced up and down the registration line. She huffed and puffed as she stared at me contemptuously. Other Berea students watched her antics with interest.

"Don't act with such haste," she finally spoke these words to me. "I want to meet with you this afternoon and discuss the situation more."

"I'm not coming back to your department," I said forcefully.

"We can meet in the library."

When I entered the library later that same day, Dr. Erica was seated at a table with a lady that I had never seen before. "This is Mme Bouleau. She is from Paris. I have engaged her to teach you the two remaining French course as Independent Study. You will not have to ever return to the Foreign Language Department."

"You are giving me all I ever wanted, Dr. Erica. She is not make-believe French. I guess I should thank you."

I was sitting on the porch of Boone Tavern Hotel waiting for my ride to graduation ceremonies at Indian Fort Theatre, when Dr. Erica suddenly bounded up the stairs nearby.

"I see you finally made it," she laughed derisively.

"I do acknowledge the gift you gave me in Mme Bouleau and the Independent Studies. However, my opinion that you direct a very average foreign language department remains. I don't intend to do anything with my French major."

I finished a Master of Arts in French at Appalachian State University in Boone, North Carolina. Unfortunately, I had lost my enthusiasm for French.

My entire focus of study changed. I enrolled at UNC-Asheville and completed a major in German with Dr. Henry Stern, visiting professor from Duke University. I never taught French again.

When I was at Berea in October, I learned that the Foreign Language Department had been restructured. Along with French, Spanish, German, and Latin, students can now learn Chinese and Japanese. The college pays for majors to study for a semester in a country where the language is spoken. I congratulate the present faculty for the changes.

I don't know what brought about the changes in the Foreign Language Department, but they came too late to benefit me. It did not matter, thought. At home in Morganton, I was already taking my high school students to live during the summer in various German cities. The Goethe Institute in Atlanta, Georgia, paid for me to study in Heidelberg and Berlin.

Einsprachigkeit ist heilbar!

PASSAGE

Shortly after midnight, the fire siren on campus began a mournful wail. It started slowly, and then rose to a crescendo. It awakened many on campus. There was a fire raging in McKee, a small town outside of Berea, and the wailing summoned the students who were trained as firefighters to their respective pick-up spots on campus. Firefighting was the labor assignment for some students.

The siren from the fire engine began its mournful droning. Leaving the firehouse, the truck made its way across campus to pre-arranged points to pick up firefighters before racing toward the actual fire.

I sat bolt upright when the first blast of the siren occurred. I could hear students in my dorm scrambling to put on clothes and grab their fire gear. Some were already hustling down the stairway two steps at a time.

The fire truck circled the campus and then disappeared into the darkness toward McKee. I listened to the siren as its blaring horn grew dimmer and finally disappeared, leaving the campus once more in silence. Sleepy students fell back on their soft pillows craving more hours of sleep. Little did they know that they would awaken on the morrow to bad news.

Only the firefighters knew that an unauthorized student rode the fire truck with them. His roommate was a fireman who did not have the courage to tell him he could not get on the truck with the regular firefighters. It was an impetuous act of youth. It was a decision made in a moment of excitement in the middle of the night. These were a band of brothers whose love for their comrade clouded their common sense and reason.

The fire truck sped south eastward out the road where the Piggs lived, the same road that students walked to Mountain Day and to climb the East Pinnacle. It led to Indian Fort Theater where my class would hold graduation.

Red and yellow lights flashed, the siren wailed, and the student firefighters held tightly to the side rails, their jackets blowing in the wind, as the truck sped toward its destination. As the truck rounded a sharp curve, it turned over. It is impossible to know what happened. Maybe it was the speed of the truck. Maybe the water tank was only half full and became unbalanced. Maybe it was destiny being fulfilled.

The back part of the fire truck twisted, flipping the entire rig over. It landed on the new student visitor to the truck and killed him instantly. Firefighter students were thrown like bowling pins in all directions across the road and into an adjoining field. Some sustained serious injuries. The cab of the fire truck was demolished.

Neighbors who heard the crash flew from their beds and summoned police. Cars, following along on the highway pursuing the truck to its destination, ran to render aid. The acrid smell of diesel oil, of skidded rubber on the pavement, of bits of dry grass burning along the roadside rode the night air. These heartbroken Berea student firemen, realizing they had lost a friend, sat stunned in the field, on the asphalt, under trees, or stretched out upon the ground, their hands covering weeping faces. They prayed for daylight not to come.

Back on campus, daylight broke over a peaceful morning. As I was walking to breakfast at the Student Union Building, I noticed groups of students huddled together talking in hushed tones. Passing a student coming in my direction, I asked what was going on.

"Haven't you heard? A student was killed in an accident on the fire truck last night," he muttered through tears.

My legs grew weak and I sat down on the grass beside the sidewalk. A group of students walking behind me approached and asked if I was sick, if I were alright.

"A student was killed last night in a terrible accident," I managed to utter.

All of us remained there for a moment. I sat weakly on the ground, while the other students stood frozen like statues on the sidewalk. One student pulled me back on my feet and we walked in utter silence to the cafeteria. As I went through the cafeteria line, I noticed that the dining room was dead silent. Ordinarily it was alive with laughter, talking, students enjoying their meal. Today, however, students took their meal as if in a tomb.

In hushed tones, some students asked questions about the accident, trying to understand the immensity of what had just occurred. Some did not want to believe what they were hearing. Many did not eat the food on their plates, for the emotion in their stomachs would not allow it.

A soft voice came over the loud speaker in the cafeteria announcing to everyone that classes were cancelled for the next two days. Counselors were available for any student who needed their services. A prayer service was scheduled in the Union Church at 10:00 that morning.

I called Wayne, Chloe, John, and Alfred and asked them to go with me to the service. In our short lives, we had not yet developed the emotional strength to deal with the death of a classmate. I was overcome with a feeling of fear. Though I wanted to cry, tears would not come. Disbelief pushed away our tears, so we sat listening to the speaker hoping that he would impart some eternal wisdom that would ease our hearts.

The following day, hundreds of Berea students lined both sides of Highway 25 that ran through the campus, in order to view the wrecker pulling the remains of the smashed fire truck toward a junkyard on the west side of town. Six of the student's best friends walked mournfully behind the wrecker. Arms around shoulders, they supported each other as they honored their friend by following behind the ruins of the wreck. Along the roadside, students wept openly. Some waved white handkerchiefs, others stood with bowed heads.

The next day a massive army of Berea students walked along the sidewalks that paralleled Highway 25 toward the funeral home where he lay in state. A line snaked for hours from the sidewalk into the funeral home. As I walked past the coffin, I remembered the time when he was on a team from his dorm when the school had a Quiz Bowl contest. He was so brilliant. They won the tournament. Now he was in that closed coffin and I was saying a final goodbye.

His funeral was held at church and, once again, students massed along Highway 25. Those too far away to hear the service watched the students in front of them and bowed their heads in unison with those in front.

Berea College held a memorial service.

How does a young college student get beyond the death of a classmate? He doesn't. It has been fifty years since his death and I still remember the event. I lost my innocence during those three days and I grew to recognize my own mortality. The sadness of the experience drew the students of 1961-1965 closely together for we had experienced a tragic loss.

Chloe and I blew up a white balloon, tied it with a blue string, and released it into the air in front of Phelps Stokes Chapel.

THE STALKER

My walk from the Snack Bar back to my dorm room on this particular evening was an unnerving experience. The streetlamps that lit the sidewalks between Highway 25 and Pearsons Hall cast shallow lighting, just enough that a person could barely see his way. Although I was a senior, I was living in Pearsons Hall for a second time. The huge, centuries-old oak trees that grew beside Draper Hall, the science building, and Lincoln Hall stood out starkly in the meager light, thrusting their bare limbs skyward like ghostly arms reaching out to grab any passerby. I had often walked this route after nightfall, because it was my pattern to spend a couple of hours socializing and dancing on the dance floor in the Snack Bar nightly. Never before had I felt any fear or threat on this homeward walk to my dorm. This particular night was different.

I had danced with Carol, Barbara, Sonja, and Candy for two hours after dinner. We loved dancing. It was one of the physical, social, and emotional releases we had because ours was a closed campus and we were stuck here until Christmas and Easter vacations. My grades would have been better had I studied after dinner, but I chose to dance. The girls had to go to their dorms by 9:00 so my dance partners all went home. I had no other choice but to return to my own room too.

The lights outside the Student Union Building next to Fairchild Hall were bright as midday. Lighting at the crosswalk at Highway 25 was equally strong. But the pathway along Lincoln Hall grew progressively darker as it led into the quadrangle. I skipped merrily across the main highway and hummed Peter, Paul, and Mary's new hit, "If I Had a Hammer," in a low voice. A movement to my right near the millstone next to the Home Economics building caught my attention. As I walked my path, a shadow figure walked parallel to me. I noticed that the shadow figure darted from tree to tree trying to conceal itself from my view. A few steps beyond Lincoln Hall I stopped walking and stared into the trees where I had seen the shadow figure. The figure had stopped as well. An uneasy feeling washed over me and I walked briskly forward. So did the shadow figure. I began to trot and then I broke into a full run. The figure did the same.

A feeling of abject terror overcame me. I could hear someone's footsteps pursuing me, but I did not look back to see who or what it was. I ran up the front steps to Pearsons Hall, pushed through the front door, ran to my room, and locked the door behind me. I ran to the window and pulled the blinds shut. I was sweating and breathing hard as I listened intently for footsteps out in the hallway. There was just a heavy silence. I picked up a science textbook and sat down on my bunk to read.

"It was just my imagination," I consoled myself. "Some other student was returning to his dorm, too."

Little by little, I slid deeper into the subject material in the book I was reading. I began to write notes from the reading assignment and I slowly fell asleep.

Click. Click. Someone was tossing small pebbles against the window panes in the huge window that stretched from the floor of the room almost to the ceiling. I ran over and locked the window. I peeked through one of the blinds out into the darkness. No one was visible. I propped one of my chairs under my doorknob hoping that the door could not be forced open. I turned out the lights and slid under the bedcovers. As I lay there struggling to breathe, pebbles continued to strike against the window panes.

In the ensuing days, I did not mention my experience to anyone. On Saturday, the Snack Bar was packed with a crowd of students, all dancing and enjoying the weekend. Barbara and I were dancing "the pony" on the fringes of the crowd of undulating students. When the music ended, a shower of pennies, nickels, and dimes fell at our feet. We both laughed at the joke. I picked up the coins and stuffed them into my pockets. Each time that I enjoyed a dance with someone, culprits seated at nearby tables hurled coins at my feet. I good-naturedly picked them up and stuffed them into my pockets.

The coin-tossing escalated. Sonja and I were gliding across the dance floor to a calypso tune. From somewhere in the middle of the room, handfuls of coins flew through the air. Someone aimed them at us. Most fell harmlessly on the floor, but several struck Sonja and me in the head and on our shoulders. When the dance was over, Sonja waded into the crowd and yelled, "This shit has got to stop. Someone could get hurt." It did not stop. I figured out that the coins were aimed at me, not my dance partner.

Carol and I talked softly to each other as we danced to "Unchained Melody." Our waltz steps had pulled my back toward the tables filled with students smoking, drinking coke, and talking. Coins flung from somewhere in the crowd hit me hard in the back, on my neck, and in the back of the head. I spun around and extended my middle finger at the crowd. Hisses and boos swept back at me from the students. I did not dance any more that night, so the coin-tossing stopped.

A male yelled out derisively, "Where's the dancing monkey? We want our dancing monkey back on the floor!"

"Go to Hell!" I shouted back.

When Candy asked me to dance with her, I returned to the dance floor where I placed the two of us as far away from the tables as we could go. No coins came this time.

For my own safety, I found Wayne and John and walked with them back to Pearsons Hall when the dancing was over.

All of the Berea students in the Snack Bar had seen the episode of coin tossing. Not one came to my defense. Not one stepped forward to identify the perpetrators of the harassment. No one asked them to stop. I tried to figure out why some individuals began to call me a monkey and toss coins at me when I danced. It dawned on me that these students could not dance. They were obviously very bright or they would not be Berea students. However, it seemed as if they were deficient in social graces as well as tolerance for others. It was the best they could do. While I danced and had a good time, they had relegated themselves to sit in a chair and get their enjoyment from harassing others. All they had to do was learn to dance. I would have gladly taught them.

Rex, Don, and Phil were sitting at a table in the Snack Bar drinking coffee. It was two o'clock in the afternoon and most students were still in class. Sonja and I were waiting for the three-thirty classes to begin. A student put some coins in the jukebox and selected calypso music. It was a setup. Upon hearing the music, Sonja and I got up and began dancing smoothly, gracefully, and quite professionally to the music. As we glided across the floor, I distinctly saw Rex, Don, and Phil reach in their pockets for coins which they blatantly hurled at us on the dance floor. Sonja left me and directly confronted the three boys.

"Why are you throwing coins at us?" she asked.

"We are just paying the monkeys for entertainment," Rex answered.

"You are not even at the level of a monkey, Rex. Why don't you just grow up! That is high school behavior. It has no place on this campus," Sonja said.

"Oh, suck a pig!" Don said to her smartly.

"I had rather suck a pig as you, you piece of shit," Sonja replied.

Sonja picked up her books and headed for the Draper Building. I gathered my books together and followed after her.

It was some weeks later when the Snack Bar was packed with students gyrating, shaking, twisting, and jumping up and down. The very floor vibrated from the mass of people dancing to the jukebox music. I was there with the usual girls. We had all decided that when we danced, we would disappear among the crowd. That way it was hard for coins to reach us without hitting everyone on the dance floor. A chant of "monkey dance, we want monkey dance" rang out across the din of voices from the unusually large crowd gathered in the Snack Bar. The girls and I ignored the taunts.

Around eleven o'clock the crowd of students began to disperse. I put on my coat and headed back toward Pearsons Hall. At the tree line near Lincoln Hall, three male figures stepped out of the shadows and blocked my passage. It was Rex, Don, and Phil. A fourth figure remained standing indistinctly in the shadows. I did not know who he was. But I discovered this night that he was working alone in taunting me. He was not with the three boys. The three formed a circle around me and stood staring with hate-filled eyes.

Don spoke first. "Why did you give me the finger the other night? I don't take that off anyone."

"I aimed my insult to whomever was harassing me," I said to him. "So it was you. Why are you harassing me? I do not even know you. What is your point?"

"I don't like men who dance and socialize with black people. You are an embarrassment to most of us men on campus. Some of us intend to put a stop to you," he replied. He reached out and gently smacked my left cheek with his hand.

They slowly disappeared into the trees in the direction opposite the unidentified figure still standing in the shadows. As I walked forward toward the dorm, these guys yelled out "Monkey meat, you are going to be monkey meat, you N.......-loving son-of-a-bitch!"

So there was my answer! I could dance and I had black friends. I was a threat to many students. My behavior was the antithesis of how they had been brought up. Men don't dance, certainly they don't enjoy dancing. White students don't associate with dark-skinned people. They were the cowboy type. l was not playing their game. I did not fit. They did not want me on their campus or in their world and they had decided to do something about it. The narrow world from which they had come dictated that when you hate a person you bully him. To bully is to show power. As individuals, they would not have the courage to act on their feelings. It took a group of three or four to screw up their courage to act.

It was my senior year in college and I still could not shake free from Ottie's world. I had experienced the same type of bullies in high school. It was as if I had brought them along with me or, perhaps, bullying was an ever present trait of low-level human beings. When someone or something threatens the human species, their first reaction is to destroy it. I refused to capitulate to this group of goons. I knew who three of them were. It was the fourth one that presented the greatest danger.

In the next few weeks, I began to notice that wherever I went, a certain person seemed to be always present. He was over six feet tall, had black hair, wore glasses, and looked out on the world with beady eyes that resembled search beams. I first noticed him in midday, sitting two tables away from me in the dining room. During the meal, he constantly stared in my direction as if he were reconnoitering my situation. As I walked to and fro from classes, I saw him sauntering along behind me. When I went to the Snack Bar to relax, he always seemed to be there, sitting two tables away. He never drank coffee or danced or socialized with anyone. He just sat there, staring in my direction.

Rex, Don, and Phil did not overtly annoy me all the time. However, when I walked across campus after dark, there was always a shadow lurking among the trees. Then, someone threw pebbles once again against my dorm window. There came a pounding on my door at three in the morning. Notes appeared on my dorm door. Sometimes, notes appeared or were left secretly in my textbooks which I left in the bookroom when I was eating in the dining room. One note carried the cryptic message "If you meet the Buddha on the highway, kill him." I knew that the sentence meant that a real Buddha would not be on a highway in the first place. Yet, there seemed to be an undercurrent of a threat of bodily harm. I had had enough. I went to talk to the Dean of Men.

He listened sympathetically, wrote some notes in a folder, and dismissed me with the explanation that no one had actually harmed me, so there was little he could do. These student actions constituted silent warfare. My whole life was being interrupted. I decided to flush out this sly fox that lurked in the shadows.

On a Saturday afternoon, I hiked out alone to the college pond approximately a mile from campus. It was not a developed pond, just a sinkhole that had filled with water. It was located next to railroad tracks in the middle of a wheat field. Shrubs and trees grew around the edges of the pond. I knew that my stalker would know I was there and maybe he would reveal himself. I sat down against a tree and fell asleep.

"You should not have gone to the Dean," I heard a voice yelling at me from across the pond.

Shaking awake from my slumber I replied, "You should not be hiding in the bushes and harassing me. I do not know who you are. What have I done to you?"

"I know who you are," he said.

"What do you want from me?" I asked him.

"You," he said sarcastically. "I want to crawl inside your skin and be you."

That was all. He was gone. I ran from my tree and looked out across the wheat field toward campus. A lone figure walked from the field back up the small hill where the Draper Building stood. It was a lonely figure, human yet not quite human. There was something simian about him. This dark figure had decided to make my life miserable or had he? I could not impute a motive to his actions. He had said, "I want you. I want to crawl inside your skin and be you." It would be folly on my part to ignore this bizarre person, yet I could not live my life in fear.

Two days later when I opened my door to go to class, this figure stood across the hall leaning against the wall. We stared at each other. "Hello," I said impulsively. He did not answer. Before leaving the hall, I turned and asked him, "Are you interested in me sexually?" He did not reply.

Two hours later when I returned from class, he was still loitering in the hallway. He made no effort to harm me physically, but he was a master at intimidation. I decided that he would be in my life vicariously and that there was nothing I could do about it. When I asked other students if they knew who he was, none knew. They had seen him on campus but not in classes.

At graduation in June, I walked in line with others in my class at Indian Fort Theater.

As I approached my seat, I happened to glance two rows behind me and there he sat. This figure was stalking me even at my graduation ceremony. A few minutes into the graduation service, a storm broke and everyone ran for cover. I did not see him again.

What was this man trying to do? Did he hate me? Did he secretly admire me? What did he mean by saying that he wanted to get inside my skin, to be me? He never attacked me physically. In a strange sense, he seemed to be gentle. Maybe he wanted to be my friend and did not know how. It is possible that he wanted to possess me like a farmer owns a dog. Could he have been in love with me??? Was this individual disturbed mentally? I knew that I was leaving Berea permanently. Graduation would be my solution to this problem and possibly my salvation.

Two years later in 1967 I was teaching French at Meade County High School in Brandenburg, Kentucky. Joe, my roommate, and I went to buy antiques on a Saturday. At lunchtime, we sought out a bohemian restaurant in the countryside south of Louisville.

"What's on the menu today, Fred?" my roommate, Joe, asked as we sat down at a table facing the entrance to the restaurant.

"Well, if you had asked me that question two years ago at Berea College, I would have said that it is a brown paper sack supper. On the menu would be a peanut butter sandwich, an apple, potato chips, and a carton of milk about to go sour." We both laughed at the joke.

But I ceased laughing very quickly when the door to the restaurant opened and four people walked in. They wore police badges on their belts. Among them was the stalker from my college days. I heard one of the men in the group address him as "Bill."

ACTIVISM

Wayne and I were sitting in the snack bar one day in March of our senior year when George and Raymond came in. We greeted them and spoke pleasantries for a few minutes and then the two of them bought coffee and sat at a nearby table. We overheard them talking about just getting back from Selma, Alabama.

"What were you doing down there?" Wayne enquired.

George told us that he and five others had gone down to Selma to participate in a march across the Pettus Bridge with Dr. Martin Luther King, Jr. and a group of political activists. They were asking for voting rights for black people. He also informed us that he hoped to generate interest on campus to get a group of students together to march with the group from Selma when they reached Montgomery. We thanked George for the information and asked him to keep us posted.

"Many students on campus don't like what George is doing politically. I've heard students in my classes make disparaging remarks about a 'Yankee from Michigan' stirring up dissent," I told Wayne. "I like the guy, personally, and I really admire his courage and ability to organize. Had it not been for his efforts, there would not have been Berea participation on the March 5th gathering in Frankfort. George and his group of six or seven people did everything to make that march happen for us. I went. It was a life-changing experience," I said in a soft voice to Wayne.

"People outside Berea think that it is a bastion of radicalism. It is liberal, but most students on campus right now do not openly support civil rights demonstrations. Opposition to George and his group is building. I hear grumblings from every quarter of campus," Wayne interjected.

I got George's attention by waving my hand in the air. I wanted to ask him a couple of questions about Selma.

"George, I saw on the news a few days ago that a lot of violence occurred at a bridge in Selma. Were you mixed up in that?" I wanted to know.

"My friends and I were at the bridge as Dr. King and his group attempted to cross it and move toward Montgomery. However, police prevented anyone crossing the bridge. The leaders said a prayer and directed us to return to our assembly point at one of the churches. I'm glad it didn't get violent for us," George told me.

"So your proposed participation in a Montgomery demonstration does not go to Selma, is that correct?" I wanted to know.

"No," he replied. "If I can organize a group to go, we will not go to Selma. A group of three hundred marchers will come from Selma and we will meet them in Montgomery and finish the last four miles to the capitol building. Our group will definitely not march from Selma."

"George, I really like what you are doing. My interest is growing and I might want to take part in the march. I respect your courage to put yourself on the firing line and stand proudly for what you believe," I told him.

"Thanks," he said. Raymond and he excused themselves to go to class. "See you guys."

I did not realize that several Berea students sitting at tables nearby were listening intently to my conversation with Wayne, George, and Raymond.

"Why can't you guys just mind your own business?" a student seated nearby asked..

"What might my business be?" I responded forcing the voice to be more specific.

"Your business is to go to class, learn all you can, get your diploma, and let the people of Alabama resolve their own conflicts," the voice informed me. Other students chimed in agreement, "That's right, uh-huh, correct, and get your diploma."

"Perhaps you have a narrow perspective of life, "I responded. "Maybe you are focused on going to class, getting a diploma, and minding your own business, but my perspective of life is more encompassing. Alabama is not capable of resolving its conflict with black people. Nothing will change without outside encouragement. If your education is limited to the Berea campus, then you will have a very narrow education, indeed. Most of us come from segregated states, schools, communities, and lives. It is uncomfortable to break away from that. But winds of change are sweeping across our land. We can hold to the old, or we can open our minds to voting rights for everyone."

"We don't like radicals like you and George disturbing the peace of people on this campus. Transfer to UCLA or Oberlin where dirty, long-haired hippies like you will be at home," the insult came.

"I stand with George and what he is doing," I shot back. "Furthermore, I will receive a diploma from Berea in one month because I have finished all of my requirements. I will not allow you to define Berea for me. I come from the same background as most of you, but, thank God, these four years here have opened my heart and head more than it has yours. You will have to live in this new world that George is helping to build or maybe you want to return to the backward hollows of Appalachia. I really don't care. I stand on my own two feet."

"If you go to Montgomery and march with that group of misfits, I hope that someone shoots you," one young man said to my face.

"If I get shot, it will be because I'm acting on personal principle, not sitting on my lazy ass in the snack bar criticizing someone else's view of life. Your conduct in these last few minutes proves the necessity of demonstrations to change the bigoted minds of not just the uneducated, but also the cream of the crop on college campuses.

Furthermore, I have experienced bullying and harassment from students on this campus. The harassment is very much akin to how black people have been treated for four hundred years. I'm tired of all of it. This march will be my act of defiance against bullies, black or white.

"Let's go, Fred," Wayne urged.

As we exited the snack bar, this enlightened group of valedictorians of their high school classes, these outstanding academics of the campus, these pseudo-educated fellow students threw paper cups and napkins at me. In the days to come, they and their cronies bullied and harassed me, referring to me as an "Activist."

A few days later George and his group plastered informational papers all over campus asking for students to sign up for the march to Montgomery. I tore off the bottom application of one paper, wrote my name, (Fred Epeley, P.O. Box 704), and proudly dropped it into George's post office box.

I remembered how Chloe and I had been thrown out of the all night restaurant, out of the public swimming pool, had doors slammed in our faces when we went caroling and the ostracism I had endured for having a black girl as a friend. I remembered harsh treatment when people perceived me as "different." I remembered Sara and her suicide because of bullies. I remembered David hitting me in the face at school at the end of the eighth grade. These issues had now become very personal for me. The actions of these Berea students in the snack bar were the final straw. I would become an activist for real.

A COMING STORM

I burst into Wayne's room holding a copy of a letter from Dean Thompson telling us we could not go to Montgomery.

"They won't let us go!" I yelled at the top of my lungs. "The bastards have denied us permission to go!"

"What are you talking about?" Wayne wanted to know.

"Look at what it says here. President Francis Hutchins and the cabinet have said "no" to the petition for us to march in Montgomery. We are not approved," I said angrily. "Theirs is a specious argument. They say they are concerned about our safety, but their real reason for refusing is liability. They don't want to be held liable in the event that someone gets hurt."

"Remember, Fred, that a student was killed not long ago. That must be fresh in the president's mind. We do not know if the college was held liable in his death or not. They are afraid," Wayne reminded me.

"They have no courage," I rebutted. "We can't use the Berea activity bus either. And look at the other restrictions they have imposed. They will not excuse us from classes nor labor assignments either. The axe of denial has fallen on us. The college denies us this historical opportunity, because they are afraid they might have to shell out a few dollars in the event that someone might get hurt."

"In all fairness, think back a year ago when the college, this president, this cabinet, and dean supported students in the march on Frankfort. They dismissed classes, they provided free transportation, many faculty went along, and Berea fulfilled its historic duty to support civil rights for black people," Wayne reminded me.

"The hypocrites did that because it was easy. Frankfort presented no danger. It is only an hour away from campus. No violence had occurred there previously. They could remain in control of the situation. And, just maybe, they let us go to Frankfort because they knew they would deny permission to go to Montgomery if the idea came up," I countered.

"The world is not ending, Fred," Wayne cautioned me. "Remember that Berea is a private institution and can do whatever it pleases. These officials don't really owe you or anyone else an explanation for their decisions. Settle down. Let this idea go. Get involved in something else."

Wayne was a wise man and I was a firebrand.

I went to Fairchild Hall and asked for Chloe to join me in the snack bar. As we walked in, dozens of students stared at the two of us. We would come to recognize these stone faces everywhere. Usually eyes of hatred stared from behind them. These students obviously had heard that we activists, we radicals, had been cut off at the pass with the administration's decision.

"Chloe, have you read this letter from the Dean?" I asked.

"Yes, I have," she responded.

"What do you think of it?" I wanted to know.

"Nothing new for me," she laughed. "White bosses have been telling me and my people what to do for centuries. Now you are feeling the impact of what it is like to be denied. As long as you are my friend, Fred, you will be treated as if you were a black person."

"So be it, Chloe. You've always had my back at Berea and I'm going to stand behind you, too," I reassured her.

"Did you know that George has already scheduled the issue to be discussed by the Student Government Association tomorrow night?" she asked.

"No, I didn't," I said.

"Why don't we go sit in on the discussion and see where the campus stands on the issue of our marching in Montgomery?" she suggested.

"Yes, I want to go hear the debate," I said.

"Did you see the argument the Dean used for refusing us the Berea activity bus?" I asked her.

"No, may I look at the paper again?" she requested. "He argues that liability insurance covers the bus only if it is used in an activity that is college approved. How silly! All they have to do is approve the use of the bus and the insurance will cover the trip. There is a Catch-22 here," she laughed.

"Do you think George will accept this denial and give up on the march?" I asked her.

"Heck, no," she responded. "That fellow is a pit bull. When he sinks his teeth into an idea or if he has a goal to achieve, nothing can derail him. I like him a lot. He is a good example for us to follow. I'm going to find him and tell him we support him all the way."

At that moment, Rod, a student that was strongly opposed to Chloe and me, sauntered up to the table and hissed, "I see you and your hippie group have been cut off at the pass. You don't represent the majority of students at Berea anyway. Do whatever you want to, but don't put the name of Berea College in front of it."

Turning to all the students seated in the snack bar, he shouted in a loud voice, "Do these people represent us? Do we care what is going on in Montgomery?"

"No!" came a resounding, hostile chorus of responses.

One could surmise that the administration had already brain-washed this group. Once again, crushed up paper cups came flying our way. We let them fall where they may without reaction.

"I'll meet you at the SGA meeting tomorrow night at 7:00," Chloe said as she left.

She walked through the crowd of seated students who jeered at her under their breath. Chloe walked with her head held high. She turned and waved at me. I knew what she was doing. She used her warm gesture toward me as a means of flipping off the whole damn crowd.

There was standing room only when the SGA met at 7:00. Representatives got right to the issue of Montgomery and use of the activity bus. George and our group felt that the Student Government Association could override the president's refusal to use the activity bus. We felt strongly that our fellow students would support our efforts.

What a surprise! The SGA overwhelmingly voted to deny us use of the bus. However, they did endorse the trip. Their arguments centered, just like the administration, on liability. They warned of personal danger. There was a possibility that the Klan would kill us. (We were more likely to be killed by the Klan on campus than in Alabama.) We were warned that people had already been killed in Alabama. Instead, they wanted us to write our congressmen, the President, the NAACP, or Santa Claus. What a bunch of softies! They voted lock-step with the decision of the college. They even told us not to go as representatives of Berea College. We had to go as individuals representing ourselves.

We were the spirit of Berea College. Perhaps we were a higher moral version of Berea College than those fellow students who were adversaries!

WHEN MEN LOSE THEIR WAY

Student leaders distributed the letter from Dean Thompson to all of us who were interested in going to Montgomery. It stated that the college would not approve the trip and that the college activity bus was not available for the group to use. Furthermore, the college would only excuse us from classes and labor if teachers gave their permission. In addition, those under twenty-one years of age had to have a written permission from their parents to leave campus. Marchers got busy forging parental signatures. That is the only bad act that I ever saw any of the marchers commit. (Rev. Mother, we have sinned, because we had to.)

The letter was much more than a statement of denial of permission to go to Montgomery. The college threw every obstacle it could think up in our way. I was shocked, because just a year earlier, we were allowed to go to the march on Frankfort. The school had cancelled classes. It had provided transportation and had supported that group in every possible way.

I wondered what had changed in the year since the march on Frankfort. For one thing, a student had lost his life in an accident involving the Berea fire truck. He boarded the fire truck in the middle of the night. It was unfortunate. I cannot say for sure, but Berea was probably held liable in that event. Frankfort was about an hour's drive away and it was easier for the college to maintain control of the students and situation. No violence had occurred in Frankfort before or after the march. We had spoken to a local situation where we lived in Kentucky, so college officials probably had felt more attuned to it. The college had not had to shell out much money for gasoline and expenses for the activity bus to Frankfort and back.

Montgomery was different. It was at least six hour's drive away. It would cost the college a lot of money. Violence had occurred in Selma and other towns in the Deep South. People had already died. The Klan had firebombed buses with freedom riders.

We would be considered freedom riders and they could attack us as well. However, President Johnson had announced that National Guard troops would we stationed in Montgomery to protect marchers.

I have wondered what went through the minds of the men who denied us permission to go to Montgomery. I know that the decision came through the college president. But did he consult with the Board of Directors? Did they advise him to deny permission or was it a personal decision on his part? The college lawyer probably advised against it. Dean Thompson wrote the official letter to the prospective marchers. It is doubtful that he played any role in making the official decision. He probably carried out what he was told to do.

It is my opinion that the college cared about our safety. It is also my opinion that they cared about their own liability and image. So did the decision boil down to a question of money? They did not want to pay for the activity bus and gasoline for such a long trip.

The risk of injury to any one of us was too high. Such injury would decimate the reputation of the college, not to mention the fact that Berea could be struck with multiple lawsuits. Otherwise, why did the official letter inform the group that we could not go as representatives of Berea College? We were to go as individuals. If you go as perfume, folks, don't take your fragrance with you.

The actions of President Hutchins perplexed me. On the one hand, he met with student leaders and listened to their entreaties respectfully. On the other hand, he stood stoically in his refusal to grant official permission for the trip. He came to see us off on the trip when we were leaving for Montgomery. He even donated his personal vehicle for us to use. Yet, he was hard core in his refusal to endorse the trip.

I want to suggest my own theory as to why President Hutchins refused to let our group go to Montgomery. It goes back to the previous year when Berea and President Hutchins had withdrawn permission for the National Council of Churches and the NAACP to hold a training program on campus. Originally, Berea had approved the program, but then they had withdrawn their permission. In a letter from President Hutchens to Mrs. R. W. Rueter of Washington, D.C., the President says,

..."The program of the National Council was not a Berea program. We did not plan it. Our personnel were not sharing in it. Primarily, we were to provide housing and dining facilities for it...Newspaper publicity which accompanied the planning of this program unfortunately led people in Mississippi to view it as a danger. Preparations were under way to meet it with violence. Berea College was looked upon as a training ground, a launching pad, and as a dispersal area for an invasion of Mississippi...." (Hutchins)

The President did not fully trust the people working with the National Council of Churches. This same organization was sponsoring the march to Montgomery. Berea's relationship with it had soured. Having already denied them once, President Hutchins could not now send a group from the college to march with them in far-away Alabama. He could not risk retaliation against a Berea group for his former decision. There was a possibility that opposing forces would attack Berea College or any group representing it.

President Hutchins had information that the rest of us did not have. He knew that a possible threat existed, but he could not share that information with the students. He had to walk a fine line so that violent groups would not attack the college. He actually supported our group, but he could not officially authorize our participation. The reader might wish to inspect correspondence between President Hutchins and many concerned alumni and others who supported the college. The letters are found in the Berea Archives of the Hutchins Library on campus.

Our group of marchers did not buy into the arguments about safety. We were more focused on human rights and the plight of those who had no equality in our society. My personal decision to go to Montgomery came from the mistreatment I had endured throughout my entire life. I had seen firsthand what it was like to be black or even to associate with a black person. My decision was very personal. I had experienced bullies in Ottie's world and on the Berea campus. I would march in Montgomery for myself and on behalf of my black friends. It would be a platform for me to say to all my tormentors, "I've had enough! You cannot mistreat any of us anymore."

Berea touts its historical commitment to black people and I don't doubt that. However, at this one point in its history, its moral compass was not clear. It seemed to turn its back on a group of students (who defied their rules anyway) and who acted with the highest courage, morality, and in keeping with the moral commitment to the ideals of the school itself.

So, who made the decision to deny our group permission to be a part of history? Was it the president's decision alone? Did it come from the Board of Directors through him? Did it come from their insurance company? Why did the college go to such lengths to stop us? What was their ultimate fear? I personally believe that President Hutchins made the decision. In view of what he knew on a greater national scale, he was justified.

One of my professors treated me harshly because of the trip. She would not excuse my absence from class and she did not allow me to make up my work. She gave me zeros. Another had even scheduled a test for that day and had assigned written papers. My senior grades reflected the punishment.

I reiterate that our group went without official permission, a fact that could have led to our expulsion from the college. It could have cost me my diploma. If I had not gone, it would have cost me my integrity.

SEND FORTH THY SPIRIT

It was early March and my two favorite trees, Breath-of-Spring and Redbud, were blooming. I went to the sidewalk beside Fairchild Hall and broke a blossom of the breath-of-spring bush and inhaled its sweet aroma. Then I walked under the ancient oak trees on campus to Phelps- Stokes to where my tulip magnolia was just budding. I didn't care if anyone saw me break a bloom.

I crossed Highway 25 and sauntered down to the music building, a place I rarely went. Something was drawing me here this chilly night. I sat down on one of the concrete slabs in front of the building and stared at the Doric columns, holding up a Greek-style porch that rested even with the second floor of the building. Pulling my jacket more securely around my shoulders, I looked up at the night sky. During my four years at Berea, I had stared many times into this magnificent sky filled with twinkling stars. I breathed deeply of the cool air.

I was sad and confused at the actions of the college president, the cabinet, and the dean. In just two months I would receive my diploma. I would be a graduate of Berea. What was happening flew in the face of all that the college had taught me since my freshman year. Were the leaders hypocrites? Had I been deceived?

At orientation four years earlier, the college had taught us about the founding of Berea. The early abolitionist founders had risked their lives to establish a school for black and white students, one that would give a strong Christian foundation to all. They had never been concerned about liability. Their contemporaries had beaten them physically, had burned their buildings, and had driven them back across the Ohio River. And, now, these modern-day keepers of Berea's flame were showing a lack of courage.

Why was I taking this march and the events swirling around it so seriously? There were those who argued, "It's just a march like any other. Calm down."

"If you have not walked in my shoes or shared my life experiences, how can you suggest that I calm down? Perhaps you do not yet grasp the vision of what this march will hold historically for Berea College and the nation."

From inside the music building, there arose a humming of a beautiful song that had been emblazoned on my heart in the last four years. On Wednesdays and Sundays, at the end of each service at Phelps Stokes, our choir always ended the service with the song, "Send Forth Thy Spirit." This song never failed to lift my spirit, and the rendition by the choir was memorable. Something had sent me to this music building tonight for a renewing of my spirit. I listened intently as the choir began to rehearse the song.

"We ask thy blessings O Heavenly Father..."

The first few words touched my heart, opening a dam of pent-up emotion, not only for the trip to Montgomery, but also for my last four years. My mind moved into a reverie.

"And may the faith of earth be renewed..."

My prayer: I send my spirit to all the peoples of the earth tonight who know suffering as I have known.

The song mentioned an act of renewal.

"May the earth be renewed..."

My prayer: I want to renew myself. May I understand the suffering of the people of Selma and Montgomery! Fill my heart with compassion. Let me lift my face toward the rising sun and stand with the oppressed of the earth.

My prayer: May I love all peoples and claim a part of God's glory!

Berea, you have become my home, you have filled my heart with your love, as Divine Love flows from spirit. I am now saddened, and I am feeling that your love has left me. Return to me a state of peace. Restore my faith in you. Do not bring me thus far and leave me broken and abandoned. That which you have taught me, that which you have been to me, will be everlasting, Berea, and, through me, it will pass to those whose lives I touch. What you do with us, your children, will be everlasting. You have the power to bring great understanding.

The notes of the song faded upon the night wind. But the power of its meaning continued to move my heart and soul. I was weeping. I wanted to hug someone. I wanted to hug my mother Ottie, but one cannot hug an idea. Berea stood not only as an idea, but as an ideal. It held a special place in the hearts of the students who had just been denied permission to go to Montgomery. But they would not relinquish that love at any cost.

I realized in that priceless moment that I could share my own spirit. I could choose to overcome the bullies, the racists, and my tormentors. My fear of who I was had drawn them to me. I would have to be at peace with myself. Then, my calm, peaceful spirit could go forth to renew my own life and then to help renew the face of the entire earth.

At that moment, I came of age.

"I will no longer allow Berea College to serve 'in loco parentis' for me," I said out loud. "I will attend the march in Montgomery, even if I must hitch-hike. If they expel me, I will start over. Hundreds of schools all over this nation grant diplomas. What difference if I get a diploma at age 22, 30, or 60---or never?"

The spirit now moving within me was greater than any student, any president, dean, SGA, or event. The religion and faith pounded into me in my youth had taken root and now they were emerging as a driving force in my decisions.

I breathed the night air deeply into my lungs and exhaled the words, "SEND FORTH FRED'S SPIRIT!"

The author walks across the grassy triangle near Boone Tavern Hotel where the

bus and cars departed and returned to Berea. (Photo July, 1965)

ACROSS THE GREAT DIVIDE

George and his dauntless little group did not fold in face of denials from the administration. Permission to go to Montgomery had been denied. The group could not use the activity bus. The college left it up to professors and labor supervisors to excuse participants from classes and labor. Marchers had to get signed parental permission in order to leave campus. Berea College was not trying to punish us in any way. They were serving as our parents (in loco parentis) during this era of the sixties. The institution took its responsibility seriously to make us safe and to care for us as our parents would. Marchers and administration stared at each other across a great divide.

Our leaders called for a march to the president's house in an attempt to change his mind in the decisions against us. Approximately one hundred marchers, faculty, and clergy met in the Danforth Chapel located behind the Draper classroom building. As I sat waiting for the meeting to begin, I carefully watched the myriad of colors cast by light shining through the stained glass windows of the chapel. Multicolored designs cast blues, pinks, reds, and yellows in a kaleidoscope across the rustic chairs made of wood and cane. Flying buttresses arched upward making room for God and his angels to occupy the space above us. A gigantic organ sat in its loft behind us looking like a huge gargoyle protecting our gathering.

Students talked in low, hushed tones respecting the place of our gathering. The six student leaders huddled behind the pulpit discussing important issues and tactics. The mood was quiet, respectful and hopeful.

I do not remember who spoke that evening, but the words they spoke were burned in my memory and heart.

First speaker (clergy): "We ask divine guidance upon this group assembled, on their mission, and in their personal lives. We ask for guidance to act with respect, humility, and dignity in all that we do here. Amen."

Second speaker: "When this meeting is over, we will march to the home of Dr. Francis Hutchens, our college president, to ask him to meet with our representatives. Please remember, students, that we have no personal quarrel with our president. He is a great man, educator, and leader. Let us treat him with the utmost respect which he deserves. Refrain from shouting, chanting, slurs, or any show of disrespect. When our journey is finished, we have to return to Berea to live among our community of students, faculty, and administration. Do not destroy the good will we have already established."

Third speaker: "I remind all of you that we practice non-violence. Obey police and persons of authority. Should you be attacked, lie down on the ground and do not resist. Carry nothing on your person that could be construed as a weapon. We are a mighty army of peace and love and we have the power of the moral high ground riding with us."

Fourth speaker: "Our campus is sadly divided. The majority of students seem to think differently than we do. It is not our purpose to change anyone's mind about civil rights for such would be a deeply personal decision. We do not wish to engage in internecine warfare. Please remember that the Bible says that a house divided cannot stand. Allow others space to think differently and summon the courage to love them as they are."

We stood and sang the alma mater.

Berea, Berea beloved, where friendships are formed fast and true,

And all men stand shoulder to shoulder as brothers beneath white and blue.

Thy memory be enshrined in every heart, thy spirit be of us a part,

And though we wander far away, thy chimes will ring for us each day.

A flower nurtured by the plain, and watered by the mountain rain,

May you ever flourish there, O Berea, the beautiful, the fair.

(Cable and Johnston, '29)

(Used by permission of Berea College Archives)

Then the group of marchers set out for the president's home.

A cool, spring rain was falling outside the chapel. It seemed to me that the very skies were weeping for our cause. Drops of rain fell in the gnarled branches of the ancient oak trees near the entrance of the Draper building. Water ran in small rivulets down the tree bark and soaked gently into the Berea soil. Skies were gray and there was no thunder. Our group was providing the lightening and, in honor of our purpose, the thunder held its voice.

Ladies in our group bound their heads with white scarves and wrapped knee-length raincoats around their shoulders. The men pulled their short jackets tighter to keep out the rain. The wind blew at times sending a chill across the sidewalks, the trees, and through our assembled group, forcing people to huddle together for warmth.

It was a short walk from the Danforth Chapel to the president's home. His home was visible the minute one walked out the door of the Draper building. It sat across the rectangle of buildings, beyond the old library, across Highway 25. It was an imposing brick edifice with white door jam and windows. A circular driveway arched in front of the building like a rainbow.

Our group of one hundred walked in silence under the ancient trees that had looked down on generations of students like us. These trees had seen all kinds of protests, debates, and disappointments. In their wisdom, they knew that we, too, would pass away into the corridors of time, leaving just the sound of our footsteps on the sidewalks. The first marchers in the line carried a seven-foot canvas sign with the college motto written neatly on it:

"God hath made of one blood all nations of men."

Upon arriving at the president's home, the group sang "We Shall Overcome" with dignity. President Hutchins immediately opened the door to his house and greeted us as a gentleman of his quality would do. His image is burned into my mind. He stood in the doorway, his dark glasses dripping with the falling rain. His face was serious for he knew that this was no social call. Realizing that the day was raw and, that those of us, who were his charges, were suffering in the cold and rain, he quickly agreed to speak with six of our representatives. That was it. It was so simple. Two dignified groups were reaching out across a great divide to compromise, to hear grievances, to act as most highly civilized people.

There was, however, an ugly side. As we dispersed to return to our dorms, some of our dissenting fellow students stood among the oak trees with white pillow cases over their heads, reminiscent of the Ku Klux Klan. They booed as we walked past. We knew who they were for we were all classmates.

If our small group had never boarded a bus or had never walked a single step in Montgomery, we had already learned lessons of a lifetime. We held the moral high ground. I had great confidence in our student leaders who were now sipping tea with the college president, both extending their hearts and hands across an issue that did not have to be a great divide.

A FAMILY DIVIDED

There would be no official permission for a group of Berea students to march in Montgomery. President Frances Hutchins had denied permission and the Student Government Association had declined permission for the group to use the Berea activity bus. Furthermore, tensions on campus between activists and those opposed to a march in Montgomery had grown. Students with ugly, racist attitudes attacked Gorge Giffin and his supporters by nailing unsigned posters on various trees across campus. These Berea racists chose to remain anonymous, fearing to challenge Montgomery supporters in open debate.

These racist students drew strength from the college decision to decline official permission for a march.

The "debate of posters on oak trees" got nasty. The following poster appeared one morning on one of the oak trees in mid campus. (I have quoted exactly from their posters. I did not correct grammatical errors.)

"To Whom It May Concern:

We object to being degraded by a handful of ill informed, Qualified Marchers (see other poster) Using the name of Berea College; and pretending to represent the college community when only a small portion of Berea College is actually participating!!! We hope that the dignity and reputation will be upheld, and not scarred by this minority!! If you march, do so as individuals as you do not have the sanction of a majority of the college community.

Signed: Interested students for racial integration, but not forced integration." (Poster I)

Frank Corbett responded to this racist group hiding behind their unsigned posters: "...Secrecy is antithetical to the principles of a free, open society that most of us as Americans and Bereans cherish. Therefore, will the persons responsible for these signs please identify themselves." (Poster II)

The response to Frank was swift and brutal. The anonymous group (or person) disparaged all of us who wanted to go to Montgomery. The attitudes expressed on the posters represented the feelings of many Berea students in 1965. Reason seemed to have taken a back row seat to emotion. Though bright and talented, many students had not yet come to terms with their own racist backgrounds. Their college experience had not yet expunged what their society had taught them.

"Dear Mr. Corbett (Marcher and Berean):

We are sick at the stomach to learn that you are sick at heart to learn that (you know what) exists at Berea (namely clear thinking intelligent people). We think that you, Mr. Corbett, represent that group of starry-eyed, quasi-intellectuals and one-worlders who are currently trying to socialize America, make it a police state. Thank God good ole U.S.A. isn't run like Berea College.

In other words, go to Hell Mr. Corbett (or to California)

Signed: the NAAWP"

"(My note (Mr. Corbett): evidently they mean to imply that the NAAWP stands for the National Association for the Advancement of White People - this group has been legally incorporated in at least one state and it sounds as if we have a Berea chapter!)"   (Poster III)

Opposition students never revealed who they were, yet it wasn't difficult to figure out their identities. They were the same students who had bullied and had abused me on a daily basis. When the Montgomery supporters marched to the President's House to protest his decision not to give permission for the trip, several students with white pillow cases over their heads, lurked among the oak trees near Lincoln Hall as the marchers dispersed. We recognized them. Berea was a small campus where everyone knew everyone else by first name. Voices, body builds, and body language gave away their identities. A house divided cannot stand. Many of us did reap the whirlwind for our choices to support the civil rights struggle.

George Giffin, Danny Daniels, and Roy Birchard, who formed part of the Berea College Committee for the March to Montgomery, decided to raise money to charter their own bus for the trip to Montgomery. Money poured in from Berea faculty members and those who chose to remain non-vocal, yet evidently supported our move toward civil rights. The committee raised $750. The bus rental came to $680.40. Those numbers were a large sum of money in 1965.

The anonymous NAAWP members did not engage in open debate, using facts to argue their case. As racists and race baiters generally do, they launched personal attacks. In reading their postings, I found myself accused of being a starry-eyed, quasi-intellectual, one-worlder who wants to socialize America as a police state. They forgot to mention that, for black people, America was already a police state. They told us to go to Hell or California. I guess they thought that the two places were synonymous.

I'm sure the opposition was irate when they learned that our group of marchers had represented ourselves and Berea College in Montgomery. I wore a Berea sweatshirt underneath my sweater. We carried a huge sign reading," God Hath Made of One Blood All Nations of Men." We marched with dignity and pride, knowing that the eyes of the nation were upon us. And if these campus racists could have seen members of our Berea group openly weeping as we approached the Capitol Building in Montgomery, our hearts overflowing with emotion from having won the victory to be in Montgomery, maybe they could have understood that we were worthy members of the Berea family. On that day, we knew that the right for everyone in America to vote would come. I felt pity for those racists then. I still feel pity for them today.

NO TRUMPETS BLOWING

Word spread quickly across campus that President Hutchins did not lift the refusal to go to the march nor to use the school activity bus. The intrepid little activist group moved into the next phase. They began a fund drive to raise money to rent a private Greyhound bus to take students to Montgomery. Collections of donations came so fast that none of us participants had to do any work. Faculty members privately opened their purses and generously poured out money to fund the Montgomery project. Clergymen around Berea passed collection plates to their congregations who responded generously. In two days over seven hundred dollars poured into our coffers, enough to rent a bus and some left over to help with other expenses. I cannot prove it, but I just bet that Dr. Hutchins quietly made a contribution behind the scenes. He was not against us. As president, he had to follow instructions from the trustees of the college. He volunteered his own personal car for us to transport students to Montgomery.

A message went out to the participants that we were going to Montgomery. With no time to spare, girls forged their parents' signatures. Those boys under age twenty-one did the same. With the attitude of "Reverend Father we have sinned, but everybody will get over it in time," we joyfully prepared for our journey.

We were instructed to take very little with us. Boys should shave close to departure time. Dress as if you are going to church. Bring toothbrush, comb, and an extra shirt. Bring money if you have any. Most participants had no spending money. We would do without food except for the cafeteria brown bag supper consisting of a peanut-butter sandwich, milk, potato chips and an apple. There would be no other food for many hours for me. Travel light. That advice made sense for that is exactly how I had come to Berea in the first place.

I ran to talk with Chloe. We both responded joyfully. We now had our chance to respond to the groups of people who had mistreated us. Soon, maybe, we would be able to sit at any lunch counter, restaurant, sleep in any motel, or get service in any store... and vote.

Our joy turned to fear when we realized that people could be waiting in Alabama to kill us. Both of us had seen the police brutality at the bridge in Selma. On television we had seen the water hoses, dogs, and troopers smashing bully clubs against demonstrator's heads. If the Klan wanted to burn our bus, it could. If a sniper wanted to strike at a group of white college students supporting civil rights, it could. We would be helpless as we marched in Montgomery.

"Are you ready to die for this, Chloe?" I asked her somberly.

"No, Fred, I am not," she replied.

"I'm not either," I admitted. "I had rather be a live coward as a dead hero any day."

"I'm not doing this to be a hero," she explained. "I've been wounded all my life because of my treatment as black person. This is the first step upward to equality. I'll focus on that and, if I die, I'll let God sort it out."

"I had to ask my question. I have felt no fear up to the present because the trip was not real. The march was an idealistic goal that seemed far away in another dimension. Now that we are actually going, reality is setting in. I'm just admitting that we could all get badly hurt in Alabama if things go awry." I was having a conversation with myself, attempting to bolster my courage.

"Fred, we are like Caesar at the Rubicon; the Greeks at Thermopile; David facing Goliath; Napoleon at Waterloo; the French when they swore the oath,'ils ne passeront pas!'" she waxed loud and profane. "Our little corner of the world is changing the whole world, moving it to a better place."

"Well, I have certainly grown in tolerance and understanding by having you as my friend," I told her. "We are about to grab the groundswell of an historical event, a moment that will be etched in time. Fifty years hence, I hope that I can rise proudly to tell people, 'I marched in Montgomery.'"

"And I will proudly tell people that Fred Epeley was my friend, that he always had my back in all situations, and that he restored my faith in people. He walked with me and took the slurs, the hits and the abuse. And he stood up to bigots on the Berea campus who, pathetically, had not yet heard Berea's message," her voice trailed off into silence. No words would form in my mind. I simply hugged her.

The Montgomery group gathered on the steps of Union Church around five-thirty p.m. on Wednesday, March 24, 1965, for a short departure service. Dr. Francis Hutchins was there to see the group off. Clergy said prayers. Our Greyhound bus rested proudly across the road from Boone Tavern Hotel. Outside of our small group and several well-wishers, few of our fellow students came. There were one thousand two hundred students attending Berea in 1965, so it is evident what a miniscule number of us cared about Montgomery. No bands played. No one sang. There were no trumpets blowing, heralding our departure to go to war against bigotry and hatred.

All the girls rode on the bus as did many of the men. There were four cars driven by faculty members or clergy. I rode in a car. It was our plan to have two cars in front of the bus and two behind to prevent vehicles from ramming the bus or being able to fire-bomb it. Those of us riding in cars knew that we would sacrifice our own safety to protect people on the bus. We had a better chance of getting out of a car in case it was fire-bombed. With five people riding together, we had little leg room. It did not matter. By the end of the journey, we were sleeping all over each other. All the stories told of singing freedom songs on the bus, chanting, playing games did not happen with me. The men in our car discussed politics, debated the pros and cons of our struggle to go to Montgomery, and told personal stories of our own private lives.

The four cars changed places frequently. I was riding behind the bus at departure and, in Knoxville, our car moved in front of the bus. We passengers had agreed not to bring class materials with us. All of us wanted to be focused on each other and our purpose.

When the Greyhound bus and our car engines cranked with a roar, my heart leapt in my chest. All my life long it was the Greyhound bus that had transported me to new adventures and new worlds. Curtis took me to Forest City at Christmas on a Greyhound; I rode a Greyhound to Berea; a Greyhound took me to Princeville and back; and now a Greyhound was leading me to a new world of political activism. A few supporters waved white handkerchiefs while others stood with worried faces hoping that we would return safely.

The bus made a right turn around the triangle in front of Boone Tavern, stopped at the light and crosswalk where Berea students crossing the roadway stared strangely at us. Then it pulled on to Highway 25 and slowly droned forward past Fairchild Hall, the president's house, between the art and music buildings, and into the town of Berea.

As we passed Phelps Stokes Chapel, I saw two of my friends, Wayne and John, holding a home-made sign which read, "Good luck, Fred." They were my heralds. They were my guardian angels. They were my trumpeters. They were true friends!

On a larger scale, however, there were no trumpets blowing for us. We were not Aida making her triumphal entrance into Egypt. We were gliding away into the Kentucky night. We would return proudly, like Roman soldiers of old, wielding our shields or we would lie prostrate in failure upon them.

QUIT DAT TICKLIN' ME

Our little convoy of five vehicles made its way down Highway 25 toward Corbin and Knoxville. We were facing a thirty-six hour ride cramped in four cars and a Greyhound bus. I rode in the back seat of a station wagon, just behind the driver, and was lucky to have a window to lean against and a view other than the four men in the car.

In the coming twilight, I could see a few low-lying knobs and pinnacles stretching out ahead of us. We were on a two-lane highway that curved like an angry snake through hills composed of shale whose broken pieces lay intermittently along the roadside. In the far distance toward Knoxville, a tall metal tower with a flashing red light on top broke the monotony of the gray sky. We made a rest stop at a Stuart family's house and then sped onward toward Chattanooga. From Chattanooga to Birmingham the road ran through the black delta flatlands and disappeared into the night.

I opened my brown paper sack supper and munched on the infernal peanut butter and jelly sandwich which the Berea cafeteria always insisted on serving us. I drank the milk, too. Thomas took my potato chips and swallowed them in a gulp. I stuck the apple in my pocket for breakfast. Then I rolled my jacket into a ball and used it as a pillow against the car window. There would be no deep sleep, however.

My thoughts passed into a reverie which took me back to Golden Valley where I was born and had lived until age 9. I remembered my mother Ottie telling us to lock our doors tightly at night because a "Negro" was wandering through the valley breaking into houses. Not only did I lock the kitchen door, but I also propped one of the chairs from the kitchen table against it in the event that said "Negro" would be very strong. Two days later, something tried to break through the kitchen door and Curtis shot the door with his shotgun. We all assumed that we had attempted to kill this wandering, phantom "Negro."

I remembered Rufus and the event at Stan's store when he gave me candy. Not even as a child could I believe that this man was bad. But the adults set the rules and they dictated that I was supposed to hate "Negroes."

When my sister and I were in high school, a hurtful event took place. The school librarian assigned my sister and a friend the task of performing a song for the library association meeting in Raleigh. She insisted that they perform it for the entire student body as an assembly program. The skit was a song called, "Quit Dat Ticklin' Me." It was written in black dialect and had to be performed with the two girls dressed in blackface. It happened in 1959.

The morning of the performance, my sister put on her makeup at home before we left and then she got on the bus with her face painted black. Her lips were outlined in red and her eyes were circled with white paint. Her hair was braided so tightly that it stood out all over her head. She had tied white bows at the end of each braid. She wore a cotton dress with an apron and big, white bloomers that went to her ankles.

In a terrible act of fate, when our bus stopped at a four-way intersection, it just happened that the bus carrying black students to their elementary school passed by us. All of the black students saw my sister sitting there dressed like a stereotype, staring out the window at them. My sister plopped her head in her hands and cried. But how does a child tell an adult that they don't want do a skit?

When my sister and friend came on stage later in the morning, their hands were covered with white gloves and they made gestures from the old vaudeville minstrel shows. During the chorus, "Quit Dat, Quit Dat, Quit Dat Tickling Me," they tickled each other, jumped to the side, and then leapt into the air shaking their heads and pulling their hair. They were pseudo, black, stereotype people.

Of course the students loved it. The librarian who accompanied the song on a piano, loved it too because it made her look important.

Watching this little spectacle, I hung my head, feeling great hurt for my sister. Afterwards, she expressed remorse for having conducted herself in such a hurtful manner.

Bullies picked on my sister and me after that performance. They tried to tickle us, punched us, and threw paper at us. Wherever we went, students yelled at us, "Quit Dat

Ticklin' Me."

When I was returning from Morganton one Saturday, I arrived at the 6:00 p.m. bus just as it was ready to leave. Upon entering the bus, I saw that the only empty seat was located behind a black woman who had already sat down. The driver ordered her to get up and give me the seat. There was no other place to sit, so this older lady, who had probably worked hard all day, had to stand in the aisle until she reached her destination. The seat beside me remained empty. After leaving the bus, I felt bad about what had happened, but I could not undo this error.

In my own way, I had been as terrible as the bullies who had taunted me. Color had its privilege then. I now felt remorse for my childish transgressions based on ignorance and cultural upbringing.

Our car hit a pot hole in the road and shook me slightly awake. I mumbled something and went back to sleep.

In my life from birth to coming to Berea, I had had no interactions with black people. Blacks had always been on the periphery of my life. I had lived in a totally segregated, white world where we called them N... and treated people of color with disdain. Deep in my heart I knew that what society was doing was wrong. But I was a product of my upbringing and I had been taught successfully to view black people as inferior.

Then why was I sitting in this car headed for what would be one of the most important events of the Twentieth Century? Why was I willingly going to mingle with thirty thousand black people? My very life was on the line. As a white person, I was a target for people who had been brought up like me, if they wished to do me harm. What had happened in the four years since I had arrived on the Berea campus?

I had come into a moral awareness that had always lain dormant in my soul. I had awakened from a slumber of discrimination because bullies had attacked me all my life. I had been picked on because I was poor. I had been called a sissy. I had been viewed as different. The only group I could feel superior to had been black people. Upon arriving at Berea and discovering that my first roommate was black, then having formed a beautiful friendship with Chloe (who was riding the bus), and then having embraced Berea's commitment that "God hath made of one blood all nations of men," my moral compass had been moved and I now made choices to stop discriminating against people.

The acts against Chloe and me, when we were thrown out of the restaurant and swimming pool as well as other incidents on campus, made mistreatment against anyone a personal issue for me. People had treated me just like they had treated black people and I did not like it one bit.

This march in Montgomery was my atonement, not only for my own personal sins, but also for my family up and down the genealogical line.

The car hit another pot hole jolting me out of my reverie. Then I got a real dose of reality. I did not know whether to laugh or cry, when I looked out the window and saw a huge, smiling statue of Aunt Jemima outlined in neon, shining against the dark sky, announcing the "best darn pancakes in all of Alabama."

THE PRICE OF A MOVIE TICKET

The station wagon in which I was riding bounced along Highway 80 toward Montgomery. I was desperately trying to sleep, but the crowded conditions of the station wagon wouldn't allow it. I leaned my head against the shoulder of the student next to me. My mind floated in and out of consciousness. At one point, I returned in my memory to my home town in the 1950s.

Morganton, North Carolina, located in the piedmont of the state, had produced two students on their way to Montgomery- John Fleming, a black man, and me, a white man. We two had grown up on different sides of town in separate, segregated communities. My school, Glen Alpine High School, had provided new books that I had needed for a decent education. Old, used, cast-off, discarded books had been sent to Olive Hill School, where John had studied in grades 1-12. All these students had been crammed into basement facilities together. These black students had had to make do with a teacher, a blackboard, and a piece of chalk. Discarded, worn-out books from the Morganton and Glen Alpine libraries had made their way to Olive Hill as well.

An elementary school for black students had been set up in the western part of Burke County, not far from where I had lived. On a daily basis my bus, filled with all white students, had passed a bus filled with all black children, as we had gone to our respective schools. Both groups had stared out the bus windows at each other in silence. Sadly, it had been a world that our parents had created, one that we had been destined to change.

The main square in downtown Morganton held a magnificent court house which had been built around 1835. Two water fountains had flanked both sides of the building. Above one fountain had stood the words "whites only" and above the other "colored only." Directly across the street there had stood the Mimosa Theater, a somewhat upscale theater that had shown the latest movies. In keeping with the rules of the segregated society of the time, whites and blacks both had attended the showing of movies. Whites had sat downstairs in the main auditorium, and blacks had sat in the balcony above the whites. There had been a spiral staircase inside the theater lobby that had led to the balcony. Blacks had bought their tickets and had climbed the staircase directly to the balcony, without being able to interact with whites. Both groups had left each other alone, until the incident of the coke bottle.

My family had lived in the western part of Burke County which had been made up of small, subsistent farms. A substantial community of blacks had been located nearby, just off Highway 70. The bus stop for the Suburban Coach Bus Company had been located on the edge of the black community. Most people had had to use bus transportation at this time because few people had owned cars. Blacks would not wait for the bus at the bus stop. They had gathered at the Jamboogie, a social club about one-fourth mile from the regular bus stop. Our parents had warned us not to walk past the Jamboogie. An uneasy peace had existed in our part of Burke County.

My half-brothers, June Jr. and Willard Worth, along with their friends, Bud and Mack, had a great antipathy toward black people. Their attitudes had been ingrained since birth. If one had asked them why they hated black people, they would not have been able to explain it. They had just been taught to hate by those around them.

June Jr., Willard, Bud and Mack bought their movie tickets along with popcorn and cokes in bottles. They chose seats in the middle of the theater. June Jr. poured peanuts from a pack into each person's bottle of coke. They settled in for an afternoon filled with Hoppalong Cassidy westerns.

Some unthinking individual in the balcony (it could have come from the white section, since the balcony was divided into "black and white" sections) tossed a green, glass coke bottle high into the air. It spun as it hurled toward the floor below, toward the worst target that the Devil, himself, could have chosen.

Whoever threw that coke bottle from the balcony probably had his reasons. Yet it had been an act of foolishness that would have far-reaching consequences. It had glazed June Jr.'s knee as it had broken into pieces at his feet. That bottle could have hit anyone in the theater without severe consequences, but it had seemed to single out the person with one of the most racially hateful attitudes in the county. June Jr. leapt to his feet and yelled, "Who threw that damn bottle at me? Some N.... is going to get his ass whipped!" He sat back down and fumed through the remainder of the film.

When the movie ended, June Jr., his three friends, and a group of white boys ran to the spiral staircase, where they knew that the blacks would be exiting the theater. They attacked the first black person that came down the stairs. Blacks poured down the staircase, whites poured out of the theater, and a melee broke out in the lobby. The manager called the Morganton police quickly. When the police arrived, without any explanation, they began to club any black person they could get their hands on. They did nothing to the whites who had started the fight.

From that day onward, at every Saturday afternoon matinee, a gang of white youths waited for the film to end and then they went to the stairs to attack any black who dared walk down the stairs. The manager had to call the police in order to let the blacks leave the theater.

Black people who wanted to enjoy a movie knew that the price of a movie ticket would be a fist fight. Black attendance at the theater dwindled. The manager finally banned June Jr. from coming to the Mimosa, because his loss of income had became too high.

I shuffled my feet around under the front seat of the station wagon and let out a half-snore as the memory of the theater filled my mind. The actions of my half-brother and the gang of whites at the matinee had made a deep impression on me, and what they had done was pushing me to advocate for civil rights in a march on Montgomery.

John Fleming grew up in Morganton. He and I became friends at Berea and we both marched in Montgomery. We joined together to advocate for the right to vote for all people. We two men, black and white, walked together in a common purpose so there would be no more coke bottle incidents in our town. In his book, A SUMMER RE-MEMBERED, John writes of his life growing up in Morganton. It is the beautiful story of a loving black family struggling to live a normal life in the midst of Jim Crow and apartheid.

There are no more fights at the Mimosa Theater. The price of a movie ticket is paid in cash now, not in conflict.

BIRMINGHAM TO MONTGOMERY

Our little convoy made a rest stop at the Greyhound bus station in Birmingham around 5:30 a.m. Car riders and bus riders mingled together talking and stretching their legs and drinking water from the "white only" fountain. Some of us were startled when we inadvertently heard an exchange between our new driver who was supposed to drive the last leg of the trip to Montgomery and the dispatcher.

Driver: "I ain't driving this damn bus to Montgomery. No one told me in advance who would be on the bus assigned to me. No way. I ain't going near Montgomery today."

Dispatcher: "You have to drive to Montgomery. We don't have a substitute for you."

Driver: "I done told you, I ain't driving a bunch of freedom riders to Montgomery. I could get killed for doing it."

Dispatcher: "Outsiders don't know who is riding the bus. You will look like an ordinary Greyhound bus making its run. Hang on! Let me see what I can do."

None of our group moved away from earshot of the dispatcher because we really wanted to see what would transpire. The bus driver waited and stared nervously at our college group milling about the station. He moved as far away from us as he could. The voice of the dispatcher came back on the microphone:

"The boss says there will be extra pay for you for making the Montgomery run today."

The driver reluctantly agreed to go, but he was not at all happy about it.

This exchange between driver and dispatcher unnerved me. I was observing local Alabamians discussing the march themselves. They were showing consternation, a deep-seated fear for their own safety if they participated in any way in this demonstration. What was I supposed to feel? Did they know, perhaps, that something was supposed to happen to marchers along the way? I became uneasy, but I tried not to show any fear to my friends in the car.

The route to the southeast through the Black Delta toward the capital of Montgomery led through fields being plowed in preparation for cotton planting in the spring. The flat, black, Alabama earth spread endlessly toward a horizon that was beginning to show the first light of day. We were crossing farmland where slaves had labored in the hot sun since the beginning of our country. I could imagine black bodies stumbling behind horses and plows cutting rows for the cotton seed. My mind imagined acres of white cotton covering the flat land like windswept snow. Alabama rarely had snow. Having seen the cotton, they would know what a white-out blizzard would look like.

Our driver called out, "We are in Elmore."

All the passengers in our car sat up and stretched as much as they could. Daylight was breaking over the landscape. Our car followed the bus through twisting roads into the city of Montgomery. We finally pulled into a school complex where a big sign read "St. Jude." We had arrived at our assembly point.

Students poured off the bus and out of the four cars into the fresh Alabama morning. This was as far south as most of us had ever been. Spring was already in full swing here and strange and different fragrances greeted our noses. Thousands of people lay sleeping everywhere-on the ground, on car hoods, in vehicles, on open cots, anywhere a space was available. Just about everyone in our group had a dire need to urinate, but the school was locked and no Porta-Johns were visible. There is no question that a group as smart as ours could solve this problem.

Some students used the facilities on the bus before it left for its parking place. Many of us who had ridden in cars could not wait in a long line to use the bus restroom.

Some of us men took the seven-foot long canvas sign with the school motto written on it down to a secluded section on the St. Jude football field. We held it in a circle, turned our backs, and allowed individuals to go inside the circle and relieve themselves. Our group lightened into laughter thinking that we had just peed behind the school motto. Payback, maybe, for all the obstructions they had thrown in our path to get here.

Reality set in. Police helicopters buzzed above us. Crowds of police wandered around the school and through the crowd. People woke up from their night's sleep and a beehive of activity swept across the schoolyard. I was disappointed when word passed through the crowd that the march would not get underway until around noon. Once again we had a few hours to wait.

I found Chloe and we sat down on the grass in front of the Berea sign.

"How do you like Montgomery, Alabama?" I asked her.

"I've not seen any of it yet," she said wryly. "We rode all night in the dark and now we are sitting on some grass with a view of a Catholic school and a few run-down houses. Not much to write home about, yet," she complained.

"What are you thinking right now, Chloe?" I wanted to know.

"It's like waiting all year for Christmas, Fred, and when it finally comes, you've waited so long that it doesn't matter. I had hoped to be filled with pride and joy, yet I'm now just a tired woman whose feet hurt and I want to lie down and sleep. My exhaustion has deprived my body of emotion."

"I see all these hundreds of strangers milling about around the schoolyard. They aren't even talking to each other. Maybe they are saving their voices for yelling and singing later in the day. Nothing has happened yet. I'm feeling the vastness of the world right now and realizing how small we are at Berea. We think that we are important; however, in the greater scheme of world events, we are but small sands on the ocean floor. It could be that fighting to get here was the important part of the journey," I said.

"It will get more exciting, I'm sure," Chloe expressed her optimism.

She leaned back against my knees and fell asleep.

"Line up! Line up!" a voice shouted out, "the march is starting!"

I shook Chloe awake, put on my coat and lined up behind the seven-foot long canvas sign bearing our motto "God hath made of one blood all nations of men." Other Berea students carried placards with the same motto written on them as well as "Vincit Qui Patitur (He who suffers conquers)" on others. Mike Clark snapped a photo of our group that would travel around the world. I'm standing on the right side. My coat is tan and my glasses are black-rimmed. There is a part in my hair.

Berea students talked excitedly among themselves. Anyone back in Kentucky, who thought that they had cowed us into just representing our "individual" selves here, would be sadly mistaken. I felt more a part of Berea College at this proud moment than any other moment in my life.

The line began to move forward and fifty-eight Berea College students and adults, I among them, marched proudly into history.

THE PHOTO

Lights were still burning in the basement of Fairchild Hall where the office of the school newspaper, The Pinnacle, was located. It was getting late. A solitary male figure sat hunched over a worn wooden table that showed years of wear. Four well-used chairs sat haphazardly around the table and room. Coffee stains and black ink streaked the table top and ran down the chair legs. Some bored or deeply-thinking writer had carved his initials with a pen knife into the soft wood.

The figure wrote furiously in a lined composition book. He periodically erased what he had written and started the line again. He occasionally eyed a cheap battery-operated clock on the wall in which the big hand clicked away the hour.

Mike Clark rushed to meet his deadline. He was a sports writer. He was going on the march to Montgomery. He knew that many students on campus were angry about the march and many did not care about it at all. Mike wanted to be a haven of intelligence and reason in a sea of angry voices.

He had just finished the rough draft of his article on sports, when a fellow student, who worked with him on the newspaper, burst through the door. The fellow reporter was flushed red in the face, his breathing was short and deep, and he seemed greatly agitated.

"You look like you just saw a ghost," Mike teased him good naturedly.

"I might turn into a ghost if I go on that damn march with you," his friend replied.

The student thrust the school camera into Mike's hands and said, "You take pictures of the event, Mike, I'm not risking my life in this adventure, school photographer or not."

"Wait, wait!" Mike yelled as the guy opened the door and stepped out into the hallway. "I've never made pictures for a newspaper in my life. I don't know how to do this. I write articles about sports and athletes. Suppose the pictures don't turn out?"

"This fool demonstrating and marching has caused nothing but trouble and bad feelings since it began. I will not risk my life at the hands of some KKK person's hatred just to make The Pinnacle look good. You want pictures, you go make them."

The outside door of the basement of Fairchild Hall slammed shut as the ex-photographer's footsteps echoed down the empty hallway. Mike stood sheepishly in the hallway looking after him, feeling as if he had just been asked to paint the "Mona Lisa" or carve the "Pieta."

He examined the camera. It was a single lens Reflex with two lenses. There was a photo button, a focus lens, strap and lens cover. It did not look so terribly complicated. He held the camera up to his right eye, looked through the view finder, and symbolically snapped his first vacant picture. His historical fate had just been sealed.

Mike felt a sense of destiny as he became a photographer in spite of himself. He had little film to work with and he could not waste it practicing. He eagerly snapped photos of the march on the president's home and the bus in front of Boone Tavern Hotel as it was loading for the trip. He saved most of his film for the big day in Montgomery.

It did not matter what Mike Clark had decided to become in his life. The Universe overrode his plans and made him a man of destiny. It chose him to record one of the most momentous events in the history of Berea College. It did not call him, it chose him. Though he did not fancy himself a photographer, the Universe proved otherwise. A spirit of greatness moved though him. He caught the spirit of his time. Spiritual hands gently placed his camera in the right place at the right time to capture the emotion of an era, of a people, of a place. And he created a photo that has been seen around the world!

The four cars carrying the male students pulled in to the parking lot of St. Jude's School ahead of the bus bearing the female Berea students. It had been a tiring, overnight ride where no one of us had really slept. Students poured out of the cars and off the bus to stretch their legs and breathe fresh air. The area around St. Jude was filled with hundreds of people sleeping in bags, on blankets, or simply in their clothes on the wet ground. It was misting rain. The rain felt good as it fell against our droopy eyes and washed over our faces and hands. A few people were wandering around not knowing where to go or what to do. There was no place to get breakfast or coffee. No shelter stood to protect us from the elements. There was the school, the earth, and the open sky. There was no one present to instruct us what to do. We stood like the children of Israel, poised to enter the Promised Land, but Moses was still sleeping on a mountain top and he had not left us his map.

I sauntered around talking to students that I knew. Tom McClure had been my friend since we had entered Berea. We had lived in Pearsons Hall and then in Howard Hall the second year. I felt comfortable with him.

I periodically eyed George Giffen, who had arranged the trip, to see if he had information or instructions for us. I remember seeing Raymond Howard who had helped George with the organization of the trip. We were acquaintances. Barbara Cranford was standing in a group with George. She and I were both majoring in French and had been good friends for four years. She hailed from Marion, North Carolina, just twenty miles west of Morganton where I lived. I had first met Barbara when our respective schools debated each other at Cool Springs High School in Forest City, North Carolina. I represented the affirmative side of our team and she represented the negative side from hers. The topic we debated was, "Resolved that the United Nations should be significantly strengthened." The outcome of the debate is unimportant. A warm friendship formed there and has lasted a very long time.

John Fleming, an African-American student from my hometown of Morganton, was quietly talking with his friend Audrey nearby. I heard Tom McClure's loud voice wafting across the area. His laugh was infectious. Dr. Drake, history professor, stood regally nearby. Dr. Kreider, English professor, spoke warmly with other students.

St. Jude, our assembly point, stood at the south end of the black neighborhood of Montgomery. As far as my eye could see, white clapboard houses lined the street. Many of them were in disrepair, a fact reflecting the great disparity of wealth between black and white. There was a semblance of sidewalks joining the houses. Many segments of cement of the sidewalks were missing from years of neglect and ignoring. Children were already playing happily among the broken-down steps of houses and the non-existent sidewalk.

I could smell bacon fat frying in hot, black, iron pans and the aroma of hand-made biscuits. I was hungry from the long ride from Kentucky. If I had gone into one of the houses, the people would have shared their meal with me. But I saw myself as a stranger there and fear still filled my heart. I had the courage to ride hundreds of miles to march for rights, but I did not have the courage of my convictions to walk a few hundred feet and ask for a cup of coffee. That act would have had more meaning than all the marching I would do the rest of the day.

Some Berea students carried signs off the bus. A dozen read, "Vincit Qui Patitur" which means "He Who Suffers, Conquers." And then there was the canvas sign bearing the school motto: "God Hath Made of One Blood All Nations of Men." Several students stretched the sign out about seven feet. Berea students automatically gathered behind the sign. Mike Clark began snapping pictures. His camera clicked and clacked like crickets as he deftly moved around us capturing our faces, emotions, and discomfort as we waited for our march to begin.

Other noises drowned out the sound of Mike's camera. In the sky above us, there appeared several helicopters swirling over the swarm of people that were now gathering. Their rotors sounded more like a train chug-chugging along. It was a hateful sound, almost as if someone were waiting to kill us. Along with the sound of the helicopters, there came the cadence of soldiers marching. The Alabama State Guard, which had just been nationalized by Lyndon Johnson to keep order in Montgomery, methodically marched to take up positions at every intersection and roadway along our route. My fervent hope was that they were there to protect us.

I saw an army of men and women dressed in orange vests moving slowly toward us. A great shout of triumph and jubilation rose above the treetops and roofs. The marchers from Selma were arriving. They were a rag-tag army of tired people whose feet hurt. Three hundred in number, they sloughed off their weariness, hunger, and pain and breathed a new breath of strength and courage as they joined the thousands waiting to escort them to their victory. I felt a sense of awe. A lump formed in my throat as I was privileged to witness, to be a part of this moment.

George quickly assembled our group behind the Berea banner. Mike then snapped the photo seen around the world. It can be seen on the internet. Study our faces. Read our hearts. Honor us. The hope and idealism of the 1960's is there. The changing of American society can be anticipated there. Black and white people were living the motto written on the banner behind which we marched. And our love and pride in Berea College travelled the journey with us.

Mike scurried away making photos of people and places along the parade route. He periodically resurfaced to make other photos of our group as we meandered through the black section of Montgomery, then into the downtown business area. I will never forget the blank stares of people lining the sidewalks. They set their faces in stone and pushed their hatred of us outward with crossed arms and extended elbows. No event in my life could cause me to ever hate with the intensity I felt from these strangers on this day. Were they not good Christians? Well, yes, they were. But the love of the Master escaped them all on this momentous day. If their feelings this day determined their destiny, there would be a lot of people with Alabama addresses shoveling coal in Hell.

Mike rushed ahead and photographed Dr. Martin Luther King and other leaders who were going to speak that day. He took pictures of Peter, Paul, and Mary as well as Harry Belafonte. He captured unnamed people watching from the sidelines and those marching in the demonstration. He photographed the menagerie of state troopers and other police that guarded the entrance to the capitol building. Some of our group hoped that he could have gotten a photo of George Wallace peeking out of one of the windows of the Capitol Building.

Mike Clark was a man of destiny. He immortalized our group with his photo. His experience helped to mould the rest of his life, one of service to others.

I was just two months from graduating from Berea when the Montgomery trip happened. Mike was two years behind me. I regret that I never got to know him well. But, today, I proudly sing his praises and thank him for his epic work. Montgomery was one of my proudest moments. I stand behind the sign, "God Hath Made of One Blood All Nations of Men," as testimony to my own philosophy of life: "The world is my country. It is broad and lovely. And all men and women are my brothers and sisters."

Aim camera! Focus! Snap!

Result: An immortal photo of the spirit of Berea in action.

Thank you, Mike!

Mike Clark snapped this photo of the Berea Group as they waited at St. Jude Catholic School for the march to start.

(photo by courtesy of Mike Clark and used by permission of Berea College Archives)

OH, MARY, DON'T YOU WEEP

A great wave of humanity moved forward through the black section of Montgomery. I walked in the middle of the street directly behind the Berea sign in the midst of my group of classmates. Fear gripped me. I began watching every house and vehicle along both sides of the street, fearing that some Klansman was sitting there with his rifle ready to fire a bullet with my name on it. The entire group of marchers seemed uneasy, too. No one was singing yet.

I looked around until I located Chloe stepping smartly to my left. I moved to her side and said loudly, "Chloe, I promised you that I would walk beside you. Now is the time." We walked together. She held her head up proudly and I noticed that she was crying.

"Lord, it's been a long time coming," she whispered. "I have walked a thousand miles in suffering and pain. But these last four miles are the hardest. I don't know if I can make it," she lamented.

"You will make it, Chloe, if I have to carry you. We are walking the last miles to our destination and you mustn't give up," I encouraged her.

She nodded her head affirming what I had just said to her.

The cadence of thousands of feet smacked the poorly poured asphalt in this black section of town. We were a mighty army sustained with the faith that each person carried in his heart. We carried no weapons with which to protect ourselves. A sense of Divine Protection hovering over us permeated the crowd.

Lines of black people formed along the sidewalk. People waved from windows and doors. I remember a group of children dressed in their best Sunday clothes waving to us from the yard of a run-down house. Groups of people applauded us. Many shouts came from all directions: "Gawd bless you," "Thank you peoples," "May the Lawd keep you in his hands," and "Keep marching right into Canaan's land."

A little black girl ran up to me and handed me a home-baked chocolate cookie. As I bit into it, I began to cry. I was so hungry, for none of us had eaten for many hours. From somewhere in the Bible I remembered the line, "Blessed are those who hunger after righteousness, for they shall be fed." "Ye shall be led by little children." I ate the cookie with reverence as one would consume a communion wafer, because I really was here having Holy Communion with myself.

I waved to the crowd and they applauded me in turn.

"Come walk with us," I yelled randomly.

A voice came back, "We have to live here when you go back home."

Parents had brought their small children out to the street to experience this historical moment. Many of them waved to the crowd. I saw one little boy saluting as if we were soldiers in a military parade. My eyes focused on the older men and women who had known only segregation. They had never been able to vote. They seemed to exude a sense of satisfaction that someone had finally come to support them, to take up their cause.

I will never forget the sound of tramping feet. Thousands of feet clacked out rhythmical patterns. It was a threatening sound as of the rush of a mighty river. I looked ahead and could not see the beginning of the line. I looked behind me and could not see the end of the line. Our Berea group was absorbed in the moment. They waved, sang, cheered, and exuded a sense of satisfaction in their decision to be here at this moment of time.

One elderly woman, standing on the porch of her house, waved her handkerchief. Tears ran down her face. I ran over to the side of the street and yelled to her, "Don't give up hope. There is always a light shining through the darkness." The crowd of marchers swept me along and I lost her. Her lips were moving, returning a message to me that I would never know. I had so much wanted to run out in the crowd and hug that lady.

Some of the soldiers guarding the parade route were unhappy. Many turned their backs on us while others mumbled words of derision with their lips. I came close enough to one of them to say, "Thank you, sir, for protecting us."

"Go to Hell," was his reply.

My feet hurt from pounding the hard pavement. I looked down at the meager canvas shoes that I was wearing. One of them had a big hole torn out on top. My socks kept the rain from the pavement from wetting my feet. I studied the clothes people around me were wearing. Women wore cotton skirts or dresses and a scarf over their heads. Men wore overalls, jeans, or cotton pants. Everyone had on regular work shoes and socks.

I had a sudden urge to empty my bladder. Where? Would I have to ask to go into someone's house to use their bathroom? I shouted out to Berea kids around me, "Where's the toilet?"

"Go in your pants," someone off to my right responded.

Four black strangers who were marching behind me heard my desperate call. They moved up close to me, took off their raincoats, and formed a wall around me so that no one could see. One of them handed me an empty coke cup and said, "Do it." Then he took the cup of urine and poured it down the sewer. I expressed my undying gratitude to all four of them. They had come prepared for any eventuality.

Like an undulating snake, the long black line of marchers turned right toward the white section of town. The shouts of approval and recognition that we had been experiencing changed to a somber mood of defiance. It seemed as if there were more white women lining the streets than white men. Many of them were waving confederate flags as a reminder that their attitudes had not yet changed. Shouts of "N..... Go home!" and "Segregation forever," began ringing out from the crowd. People in the upper floors of buildings threw paper and garbage down on the crowd. A reign of spittle shot across some marchers ahead of me. It was no ticker-tape parade. It was a gauntlet of expressed hatred through which we were marching.

Chloe began humming softly under her breath. The song was one that my mother Ottie used to sing during those rare times when she drew her family close around her. White churches in Carolina sang the song. Often in Sunday school, we kids would stand and belt out the song at the top of our lungs.

"O Mary, don't you weep, don't you mourn..."

These words poured forth from Chloe's throat like a magnificent anthem. She sang them in a rhythm with her feet pounding the pavement. The words calmed my fears a bit.

"O, Mary-don't-you-weep-don't-you-mourn..."

"Pharaoh's army got drowned, O Mary don't you weep."

I began to sing the words with her.

"One of these days about twelve o'clock, this old world's gonna reel and rock,

"Pharaoh's army got drowned, O Mary don't you weep."

It is ironic that as we sang the words "twelve o'clock," I looked down at my watch to see that it was almost twelve o'clock on this day, March 25th, in the Year of our Lord, 1965. Our world had really begun to reel and rock. We hoped that the attitudes and laws against black people were crumbling with each tramping footstep. I was uncertain if what I was helping to tear down this day would ultimately be good for me personally.

In their earlier lives in the mountains of Appalachia, Berea students could not have imagined such a day as this. Those of us marching had seized the new idealism sweeping our nation. The conflict with our college now seemed far behind us. I let go of Chloe's hand, stepped forward, and placed my hands on the large sign our group was carrying. We fell silent for a brief moment and let the words on our banner speak for us. Taunts from the crowd rose to a crescendo.

STONE FACES, EYES OF HATRED

The huge line of humanity moved out of the black section of Montgomery and made its way into the white housing district and the downtown business area. Whereas the black people had welcomed us with joyful celebration and jubilation, the whites greeted us in silence. Just imagine that, silence! People stood five rows deep along the sidewalks. Many looked out upstairs windows or sat erect in chairs on second-floor balconies. Businessmen came out of their offices with smirks on their faces. Female office workers and secretaries stood in front of their places of work, their arms crossed in front of them as if they were holding back an urge to attack us. No heckling, no jeers, no insults, no curses, just silence at this juncture.

The overwhelming silence unnerved me. This enormous crowd of onlookers was crouched on the sidewalk, in windows, on balconies, and packed along side streets, ready to pounce on us if someone had given the signal. They engaged in psychological warfare with their stone faces and eyes of hatred. Few spoke any words at all.

One woman did walk parallel to our group shouting, "You sons-of-bitches have more than we do already!" That is all I remember hearing anyone say. Angry men flicked their lighted cigarettes into the crowd hoping to burn someone or set their clothes on fire.

There was a feeling of murder in the air. One businessman, standing on the balcony of his second-floor office, turned his stone face to me seeming to say, "You are white. Why are you betraying your own people? What does this have to do with you? Why are you in Alabama? If the police and National Guard were not here, I would kill you with my bare hands."

I answered him in my mind: "I have suffered at the hands of people like you. You use your religious beliefs, your Bible, and your god to condemn people who are different. Because of my friendship with Chloe, you have subjected me to what black people endure every minute of their lives. You threw me out of a restaurant; you threw me out of a swimming pool; you jeered at me, spat at me, called me names, and destroyed my proper-ty. That is exactly what you do to people of color all the time. I know what it feels like to be a second-class person."

A little lady sat on the sidewalk in a wheelchair. She, too, put on her stone face. If she could rise from that wheelchair and walk to me in the street, what would she do to me? Her eyes told me.

"I would stone you like the Bible says to do to adulterers, because you are an adulterer to your white race."

A burning cigarette flew out of the crowd and landed on my shoulder. A student marching beside me grabbed it and smashed it with his foot on the pavement. Looking in the direction from which the cigarette came, I saw a young man about my age pointing to himself letting me know that he had thrown it. He motioned for me to come into the crowd and fight him. I blew him a kiss! That act infuriated him. Were it possible, this young man would have taken my life.

A minister, wearing his white collar, stood with his congregation of old ladies in front of a church. They, too, stared with their arms crossed in front of them. "Would they in-vite me to a church social?" I wondered, "Or would they serve me for dinner." I was trampling on their ensconced belief system that black people were cursed, and their Bible gave them permission to discriminate.

Our whole line of marchers broke into the song, "This Little Light of Mine," and we clapped in rhythm to the tune. I felt better that this silence of a tomb had been broken. I sang out loudly to assuage my fear of being killed.

The marching line passed through an intersection where national guardsmen had been placed to protect the marchers. These guardsmen faced away from the line of demonstra-tors. They carefully screened all movement of people and vehicles following orders to keep us safe. One of them looked in my direction as I passed by and I said to him, "Thank you." He half-smiled and returned to his task.

For the remainder of the time that I walked through downtown Montgomery, I per-ceived everyone and everything as made of stone. The buildings were stone. The people were stone with their eyes of hatred focused upon us. The cars were stone. The trees were stone. The very air itself had turned to stone. Even my tired, aching feet felt as if they were made of stone and were walking in wet concrete. People's hearts had long ago turned to stone. These thousands of marchers dressed in overalls, plough shoes, plain cotton dresses and aprons were all here trying to make this stone world understand that those they hated were also God's children, warm, alive, feeling and worthy.

I did not hate these people. I hated what they had done to others all their lives. I understood how the white people of Montgomery felt, for I was a masterwork from their world. My experiences in the last four years had melted much of my stone heart. My presence here was an act of love for myself as well as for both black and white. It would take fifty years to see the results of what was happening on this day.

Mercifully, the line of marchers left downtown and turned on to Jefferson Davis Avenue. Standing in front of me was the majestic Alabama capitol with its two flags flying in the morning air: one of Alabama, the other Confederate. I was not offended because this was my heritage too. Hundreds of Alabama state troopers lined the steps in front of the capitol. I knew for sure, that with provocation, any one of them would have splayed my skull with his baton.

Ten thousand voices broke into the strands of "We Shall Overcome."

The majesty of the words and music filled my heart to overflowing, and tears began to form in my heart and eyes. Unlike so many people I had seen here, I was not made of stone. Chloe sought me out in the crowd and said, "Walk with me the rest of the way." I could not utter a word, because the dam of emotion in my heart had broken and I walked sobbing audibly beside her. We were experiencing atonement for the times we had not had strength to fight back against the bigots and tormentors we had encountered in our lives. This moment gave us power and hope.

The words of the song continued: "...Oh, deep in my heart, I do believe, we shall overcome...."

Chloe was crying too. As I looked out across our delegation which had struggled so hard to experience this magnificent moment, I saw that many of the Berea students were wiping tears from their eyes.

"Black and white together we shall overcome." "...We are not afraid...." "...Just walk hands in hand...." (Deep in my heart, oh so deep in my heart, I do believe that we and Berea College shall overcome.)

We group of poor kids out of the hills and hollows of Appalachia were experiencing a metamorphosis of our old lives. Some spark had awakened our hearts to mercy and compassion because we, ourselves, had known so much suffering. We were able to feel emotions with kindred souls who lived apart from the rest of America.

Chloe and I sat down on the hard pavement in front of the speaker platform and heard the speech "How Long, Oh Lord" delivered by Dr. Martin Luther King, Jr. I remember hearing the words "...freedom will flow down like water" and that the universe will bend toward justice.

When the rally was over, city buses took us back to St. Jude School, where we had started our march. I looked out the bus window into the faces of the people we were passing. I was desperately searching for some evidence that my presence today had made a difference. Only time would tell. The morning sun would shine on the black section of Montgomery tomorrow. Blacks would still ride in the back of the bus. No one would step forward to vote, yet. Stone faces cannot change their expression and eyes of hatred can only stare outward.

"Stone faces cannot change their expression and

eyes of hatred can only stare outward"

FIVE LOAVES, THREE FISHES, AND LOTS OF FRIED CHICKEN AND COLLARD GREENS

The march was over. Montgomery city buses had transported our group back to St. Jude's school for our return trip. Berea students quickly had boarded the bus and cars and our caravan had headed northward to the town of Collinsville, Alabama, to the home of one of our black students.

I had not eaten anything in thirty hours except an apple and a chocolate cookie a little girl had given me in the black section of town. I had carried no money with me. Faith had carried me on this trip.

Dr. Kreider told those of us in his Rambler that we were headed for Mrs. Vaughn's house. She was the mother of one of our Berea students. Though I had just walked with thousands of black people, and Chloe and I were close friends, I felt uncomfortable about visiting in a black woman's home in Alabama. I had not yet conquered my fears from the past.

"Be careful how you conduct yourself," Dr. Kreider warned us. "We are four cars of white men entering a black section of town after dark. People could easily misconstrue our intentions. Mrs. Vaughn knows that we are coming."

We pulled up in front of a modest, white plank house in the black neighborhood of Collinsville. A rather plump black lady with a huge smile on her face greeted everyone.

Standing on the porch behind her was a group of eight or ten other ladies who were assisting her in effecting the biblical feeding of five thousand. Though we amounted to only fifty-nine people, when counting the bus driver, it took the effort of feeding five thousand to accomplish what Mrs. Vaughn did.

She warmly invited us all into her home where a feast of fried chicken, collard greens, mashed potatoes, and home baked biscuits awaited us. This Berea group had little money to buy food, so it was magic when we packed into her kitchen and loaded our plates with chicken, collards, and biscuits. I was so hungry that my stomach ached. The first bite of her biscuits tasted just like the ones my mother, Ottie, used to bake when I was at home in Carolina. Looking at Mrs. Vaughn, I realized that she was my mother. She was mother to all of us. Providing us with food was the ultimate act of love for her and we returned that love tenfold by eating it with abandon. I sat down on the floor of the living room and began eating the greatest meal of my life.

"Children, children," Mrs. Vaughn chimed, "go back for more. We'll cook more if we run out."

I did go back for more. And I wrapped a biscuit in a piece of napkin to carry with me on the return journey.

My fear of being in a black person's home had completely vanished. I watched Mrs. Vaughn's helpers busily scurrying around the kitchen refilling drinks and stacking the plates high with more chicken. How could anyone hate these women? They did not know any of us. They did know that we were friends with Mrs. Vaughn's son at Berea. Yet, they were pouring out their love to us in providing what we needed most---something to eat.

Mrs. Vaughn stared around with a puzzled look on her face.

"Where is your bus driver?" she asked all of us.

"He is still on the bus. He would not come into the house," one student answered.

I watched Mrs. Vaughn exit to the kitchen where she took an empty plate from a stack on the table. She filled it with the best of chicken breast, collards, a heaping of mashed potatoes, and two brown biscuits. She poured a large glass of tea and topped it with a slice of lemon. Without fanfare, she exited through the front door and disappeared into the dark. In about ten minutes, she opened the front door and walked in with the Greyhound bus driver in tow. He was chewing on the chicken breast and sipping tea. Mrs.

Vaughn was serving love this night, and she would not allow anyone to excuse himself from it.

When I saw what she had done, I had to stop eating because I couldn't swallow. I motioned for her to come speak with me.

"Mrs. Vaughn, this is the first time I have ever been inside the home of a black person. Like the driver, I really didn't want to come in. But I'm glad I did. Being in your home without prejudice and hatred is what this march was all about today. Thank you for this wonderful meal. It took the spirit of Jesus feeding the five thousand with three fishes and five loaves of bread for you to take away our hunger tonight," I said. "Thank you."

She bent down on her knees and hugged me. "Yes, honey, but I don't think Jesus had collard greens. You have travelled a mighty long highway for people everywhere today. These biscuits and chicken are the least I can give back to you. I will remember you, young man, when I can go to vote. And I will know that a little white fellow from Kentucky walked his legs off and risked his life for my right to do that. And you may eat chicken and collard greens with me at my house any time."

That was one of the most beautiful moments of my life and I have carried it reverently in my heart for fifty years. Whenever I eat chicken or collard greens, I remember Mrs. Vaughn's promise and her smiling face.

As our group pulled away in the vehicles from Collinsville, Alabama, I looked back at the Vaughn house. She stood there waving a white handkerchief, smiling warmly. I felt as if I had just been touched by the hand of God.

UNSUNG HEROES

Our group returned to the Berea campus at around 7:00 a.m. on March 26, 1965, to a place where no one waited to greet us. The bus and four cars set us off in front of Boone Tavern Hotel at the same spot where we had departed. The campus was deserted except for some early risers headed toward the cafeteria for breakfast.

I walked to the cafeteria for breakfast and coffee myself. No one spoke to me. When I sat down at a table with some fellow students (thinking that they would be excited to hear about the march), they all got up and moved to another table, leaving me to have breakfast alone. For the first time in four years, the cafeteria food tasted good.

And so it would go for those of us who had defied the college, the Student Government, and the popular wishes of most of the students in the school. One friend who met me on campus was my roommate who, ironically, was from the state of Alabama. Barry did not care that I had gone on a civil rights march in his state. He told me that his state would change when it got ready to and we could not hurry the point. I really liked him. He warned me not to go back to the dorm and go to bed. He told me that if I had scheduled classes, go to them. Word had spread that all of the participants to Montgomery would be punished. (Barry died in Viet Nam).

In two of the classes I had that day, the professors gave a short exam. A two-page paper was also due. These assignments had been made while I was away. Since my absence was not excused, I received a failing grade for both. I was not allowed to make up the work. A hit on my grades would be part of my punishment for insubordination. These professors could not know that I had learned infinitely more on this trip than they could ever have taught me in their pathetic classes.

No students on campus ever asked me about the trip to Montgomery. When I chose to bring it up, they either walked away or quickly changed the subject. Discussing the march became anathema. Those of us who had made the trip did not discuss it either. Our group never got together again. It was only on the fortieth and fiftieth reunions that some returned, not to Montgomery, but to Selma.

The march occurred on March 25, 1965, and I received my diploma, by the grace of God, on June 6, 1965. I actually did graduate from Berea. Barely.

Berea College never approved nor gave permission for our group to go to Montgomery.

I cannot speak for others, but in my personal case, someone took retribution against me. One of the deans called me into his office and laid under my nose a folder with a list of infractions that I had committed all four years that I had been a student at the college. The last infraction, written in red ink read, "Student left college without permission on an unapproved trip." Among others, there was a verbal fight that I had had with professors in my department which had led me to withdraw from Berea for the summer. I did return. The department chairman would not allow me to return to the department; however, she did let me finish two French courses on independent study. Although I had finished all my course work in good standing, the Dean informed me that the board had taken under advisement whether I should be granted a diploma from Berea College. Granted?? I had worked diligently to finish all requirements. I was in limbo.

One week before June 6th graduation, the Dean summoned me to his office again. With a smirk on his face, he said that the board had recommended mercy in my case and that I could receive my diploma. It was May 29, 1965, and there was no time to do any preparations. During baccalaureate service, I picked a white snowball flower and wore it on my mortarboard hat as the line of students entered Phelps- Stokes Chapel. That was my protest. I expected Mr. Rules and Regulations to pounce on me and levy a fine of $5.00.

Graduation was held at Indian Fort Theater. Our line of graduates, dressed in gowns and mortarboards, marched in procession down the concrete steps and sat in metal chairs at the front of the theater. Just as President Hutchins began to address the crowd, a terrible flash of lightening split the sky and thunder roared across East Pinnacle. A deluge of rain followed. In a fast cadence President Hutchins announced, "By power invested in me, I now declare you all graduates of Berea." Everybody ran for cover. The Berea leaders on stage ran for cover, just as they had done when we had petitioned to go to Montgomery. I got soaked.

I stood under a shelter with my white shirt drenched and stained from the dirty gown I had worn. My class never had a proper graduation. I would like to do that graduation over.

But the surprise of a lifetime came. I felt someone tap me on the shoulder and I turned to look into the eyes of my mother Ottie. My younger sister, Lorene, was standing beside her. I broke into tears.

"How did you know? How did you two get here?" I mumbled through my sobbing.

"Somebody from the college, I don't remember who, called and left a message saying that you were graduating today. (Is it possible that one of the deans felt sorry for me?) Lorene's friend Elaine Collett brought us in her car. We drove all night from North Carolina to Kentucky. We made it. Too bad about the rain," she explained.

I hugged them both and stood as frozen in stone as the people of Montgomery did when we had marched by.

"I've got to get my diploma from the registrar," I told them.

I walked away in disbelief. Good had rarely come to me from Ottie's world, but it was there today.

I said goodbye to no one. I left as I had arrived in Berea, like a thief in the night.

My sister pulled the car around to the shelter and I got in the back seat. My mother held my diploma.

"You rode the Greyhound bus to Kentucky when you came to Berea; but today I'm driving you home in style," my sister laughed.

Thunder and lightning and torrential rain continued to swirl around Indian Fort Theater as my little group pulled away homeward toward North Carolina.

The dream of finding a family at Berea was just that, a dream. Chloe went away with no word of farewell. I never saw or heard from her again. The others whom I considered family faded away into oblivion. I only found out about them again whenever I read their obituaries in the Berea Alumni magazine.

I had been attacked, bullied, and mistreated on this campus by students and faculty alike. I had had moments of hilarity. Four long years had passed slowly, each helping to expand my knowledge and maturity. Today, even the rain had denied me a decent graduation ceremony. The most incomprehensible experience had been the struggle to go to Montgomery on behalf of civil rights. One part of me wanted to yell out, "Damn you all!" Another part of me felt sadness in departing.

There was too much I wanted to express at this moment. I stared at my diploma that my mother held lovingly in her hands. Remembering the awesome task of achieving it, I uttered these words of wisdom out loud, "Thank you, Berea College. You have taught me more than you will ever know!"

HANG THAT BANNER HIGH!

(I respectfully dedicate this chapter to four students who went to Selma, Alabama, and saw first-hand the struggle to cross the Pettus Bridge in an early attempt to march to Montgomery. They returned to Berea and laid the foundation for a group to march in Montgomery: George Giffin, Frank Corbett, Henry Thompson, and Raymond Howard. I thank you. I salute you. You are true, unsung heroes. It was an honor for me to walk along beside you through the streets of Montgomery.)

He came from the far north, from a land of snows, forests, and placid lakes. I came from the misty hills of an ancient land called Appalachia. His people did not practice discrimination nor had anyone there owned slaves. Mine was a land of pain and sorrow, where whites had owned Negro slaves. Since the Great War, black people and white people had been estranged, and the society had become segregated. The two races lived side by side, but unequal.

He came south to Berea, speaking his Michigan accent. I came north to Berea speaking English akin to that of Shakespeare. Our paths crossed in a moment of time that changed us both, as well as the destiny of Berea College.

George Giffin was the man of the hour. He studied the plight of black people in America. Deep inside, he felt sadness and revulsion that people could be treated as second class citizens. When the struggle for civil rights reached the national news, George watched the police in Selma attack demonstrators with clubs, water, and ferocious dogs. He gathered together three friends, piled them into a small Volkswagen, drove to Selma and entered the fray in order to support Dr. Martin Luther King's struggle for equality.

I cannot say that George and I were close friends. We knew each other. The few times I spoke with him, he was soft, gentle, kind, and accepting. I cannot recall a time when he lifted his voice in a debate or conversation. He was never abrasive. He argued with facts and principles, never with hostility. He looked out at the world through kind eyes billowed by the power of a compassionate heart.

But George was a veritable Pitt Bull. When focused on a goal, he was tenacious. He did not entertain any idea of not succeeding in whatever task stood before him.

I began to get acquainted with George after he and his friends had returned from Selma. Announcement papers appeared on trees, bulletin boards, and entrances to buildings. The headlines read:

HEADS UP ALL STUDENTS!!!!!!

The opening paragraph hurled forth an invitation for any Berea student to join a group that George and his friends were forming to march in Montgomery.

"WOULD YOU LIKE TO MARCH ALONGSIDE THOUSANDS OF OTHER AMERICAN CITIZENS (MINISTERS, PROFESSORS, STUDENTS, ETC. FROM ALL PARTS OF THE NATION) TO THE CAPITAL BUILDING IN MONTGOMERY, ALABAMA, THIS COMING MONDAY?" (Students Who Just Returned from Selma) (1)

As further explanation, George wrote on the paper, "Scores of Berea students have already indicated a strong desire to join in this nation-wide pilgrimage to Montgomery, Alabama. Together with members of our faculty and administration, and with assistance from local ministers, we students are presently making all necessary arrangements for such a trip which will involve as many Berea students and faculty members as possible."

Opposition to George and the proposed march grew quickly on campus. While many students wanted the march to happen, many did not. The Berea administration did not want it to happen. The President let us know very quickly that permission to go to Montgomery would not be forthcoming.

On March 12, 1965, President Hutchins gave a directive to Kenneth H. Thompson, Associate Dean of the College, to send a letter to Danny Daniel, a member of the Committee to go to Montgomery. Entitled "Statement Concerning the Proposed March to the Capitol Building in Montgomery, Alabama, This Coming Monday," it was the official letter informing all of us where the Berea administration stood on the issue. It was the only communiqué ever sent to the students.

In it the President laid out the following requirements for all of us:

"1. This is not a College approved trip. Anyone going is on his own. No liability will be assumed by the College.

2. The College owned bus is not available for this trip.

3. Any student desiring to take part in this trip must take care of it as he would any other out of town permit.

4. Berea College will continue as usual and all classes are expected to meet at their regular time." (Thompson)

In saying that classes would continue as usual, he left a specter of possible academic punishment if any teacher chose to invoke it. At no time did he say that we could not go to Montgomery. However, Berea is a private institution. They could punish any student who broke their rules in any way they saw fit.

George's group took umbrage at the patronizing tone of the letter and all of us fumed at the idea of "in loco parentis." Our leaders called for a Sunday meeting of demonstration and prayer to President Frances Hutchins' house.

From the outset, the Berea group had believed in non-violence. In their letter to all marchers entitled, "Information Concerning Sunday Meeting of March and Prayer," Co-chairmen, Danny Daniel and Roy Birchard, wrote the following instructions for our group: "Upon arrival at the Hutchins home, the group will join hands and await further instructions. The program, it is anticipated, is to consist of prayer, singing of appropriate music and organized public speaking." They went on to outline our conduct during the march.

"Traditional procedure for non-violent demonstrations will be observed. Private property will be respected (special care is requested to avoid contact with the Hutchins' flower bed and the surrounding shrubby). Do not reply to any comments or provocation from the sidelines. Follow the march leaders, keeping on the line of march."

Since I had already been nailed for plucking a flower on campus in violation of the rule about not picking flowers on the Berea campus, I chuckled out loud. It was edifying to note that our esteemed leaders were concerned about respecting our college and its rules, all except for denying us permission to go to Montgomery.

The informational letter ended with a statement of purpose from our group. "United by a common purpose, we, members of the Berea College community, march today in order to witness to the wider Berea community our continuing and deep concern regarding the denial by the College of its historical commitment to the struggle for human rights and human dignity.

We believe that the motto of the College, 'God Hath Made of One Blood All Nations of Men,' demands of us that we actively pursue the search for equal rights for all citizens."

President Hutchins received us graciously at his home. Then, he once again denied us permission to go to Montgomery.

The student committee took the next step by raising funds to charter a private bus for the group. Many faculty members donated money as did churches and other interested adults. It took just a few days to raise over seven hundred dollars. The charge for the bus came to $680.40. One must remember that that sum was quite a lot in 1965.

The trip was set. No one cared any longer about permission to go. The student committee had accomplished the first leg of their goals. They sent out a final paper entitled, "Final Instructions, Rules, and Schedules for the Montgomery Trip." They instructed the men to, "...Please SHAVE as close to departure time (5:15). Take electric razors only (We shall share razors). You must have your Selective Service Card and your Driver's license on you at all times. Wear school clothes or "Better". (No blue jeans or shorts!)"

The committee made sure that we were not going to present ourselves as a bunch of "hippies" or "beatniks."

They instructed the women to, "...Wear comfortable 'marching' shoes. Wear school clothes (no slacks or Bermuda shorts!)...."

With non-violence and safety always in mind, the committee told everyone, "Do not bring anything which might be construed as a weapon (no knives, beer can openers, nail files, or hand razors)."

The instructions ended with the words, "Traditional procedure for non-violent demonstrations will be observed. Detailed instructions on the non-violent method will be given to you before we leave."

A Send-Off Committee for Pilgrimage to Montgomery, composed of Ann Beard, Audrey Berry, Jacoba Hurst, Rev. T.B. Cowan, and Nancy Latham, sent out a note with the following message: "To All Faculty and Staff, We hope you will wish to express support for your colleagues and students who are going to Montgomery.

Come for send-off service for the pilgrimage to Montgomery in front of Union Church at 5:15 p.m. on Wednesday, March 24th.

Bus and Cars leave at 5:30 p.m."

Night had already fallen when the bus and four cars of students pulled away from the triangle across from Boone Tavern Hotel. I rode in a station wagon car driven by Tom Fern, art teacher at Berea. These students rode in Tom Fern's car: Tom McClure, Omer Kiser, Howard Caldwell, Fred Epeley, and Tony Graham. There were three other "Buddy Cars" that followed along behind the bus.

George Giffin was a natural leader. I looked to him for direction and solace as we made our way to the rendezvous at St. Jude's School in Montgomery. When we disembarked the following morning, our entire group hovered around George as if he were Moses leading us to Mt. Sinai.

In the famous photo of our group assembled at St. Jude, taken by Mike Clark, George is standing behind the Berea banner. Throughout the years, I have studied his face and the faces of all the Berea students. George is calm, serene, and collected. A definite sense of great satisfaction emanates from his face. The long night and the long fight are over. The Berea group is happy, smiling, enthusiastic and extremely tired. On the expanse of greening grass in front of St. Jude, the lives of each Berean were changing forever. We had battled the college, fellow students, detractors as well as our own fears. We had raised our own money to be present here. We had been victorious.

When I saw how calm George was, I let go of my own fear. I marveled at how much he had accomplished. It is still astonishing today that a twenty-one-year old college student could organize such an undertaking and carry it out flawlessly. He had a supporting group, but he was unquestionably our leader.

On our stop at Collinsville, Alabama, on the return trip, George had cautioned all of us, "Mrs. Zadia Johnson's neighborhood is a black area. Remember this; we will be four cars of white men arriving at night in a Negro neighborhood. Mrs. Johnson is expecting us. Do nothing to alarm anyone in the area."

I graduated from Berea two months after our return from Montgomery. I never discussed the march with George or anyone on campus. I felt like I had done something wrong. Dean Thompson informed me that the college was withholding my diploma and that there were unresolved disciplinary issues to be dealt with. He told me that I had left campus without permission. He did not specifically allude to the trip to Montgomery. However, that was the only time I had left campus, except for Christmas vacation. In a cruel act of authority, he informed me two days before graduation (June 4th, 1965) that the College would let me have my diploma.

I never saw George again after I graduated. As a matter of fact, I have not seen him in fifty-two years. But I will never forget him and what he did for civil rights and how greatly he affected the lives of all of us who participated in the Montgomery experience.

Berea now honors outstanding alumni by hanging beautiful banners on lampposts across campus. Underneath their names, the college has written about their accomplishments.

Resolved: Let there be hung a magnificent banner bearing the name of George Giffin. Let it carry the words: Man of distinction, civil rights advocate, educator, and humanitarian. He led Berea students to march in Montgomery. He helped to change their lives, the destiny of Berea College, and our nation.

Hang that banner high!

MY CALL TO MARCH

I look out on the world now with the perspective of an old man. And I look back at Berea with the perspective of a senior citizen who has travelled many highways. I can see the events of my life there with more wisdom and understanding than I had as a youth. I no longer breathe with idealistic hope that I will find or create a perfect family for myself nor do I hold hope that America will resolve its differences and bond as one nation. Certainly bullies will not go away. I do know that there is equality under the law. Everyone can vote and participate in all phases of daily life. I am proud that I helped to bring that about. There are laws in effect that punish bullies, too. In retrospect, I now know that the Montgomery March was as much about me personally as about political and civil rights issues.

I came of age at a time of great idealism in America. Fired up by the election of John Kennedy, students came forth to volunteer for the Peace Corps and to reach out to help struggling peoples all over the world. The youth of America were no longer willing to accept the status quo of second class citizens. The youth of the time became hippies and preached love and peace in our time. They rose up against the conflict in Vietnam and the idea of war in general. Thinking that I was advocating for the rights of others, I rode the crest of the wave of idealism and tolerance. I failed to realize at the time that everything I did was for me.

Chloe and other African-American students opened my eyes to see that a person's skin color is irrelevant to everything. Friendship has no color markers and goodness in a person can be found among all the colors of the rainbow. It was a great leap forward for me to lay aside my upbringing and let people come to me as they are. All of us at Berea were a multitude of colors, but we had one thing in common. We were moving upward, out of, and away from poverty. When people live on the same economic and educational scale, they don't seem to make too much of an issue of race.

It was the abject poverty of Ottie's world that had sunk my hopes and dreams. When a person has no money or parental support, his options are severely limited. My presence at Berea came through my own courage to go ask for assistance.

My presence at the march in Montgomery was a culmination of many factors: Poverty, Ottie's world, being bullied, empathy with the suffering of black people, a desire to rise above what life had dealt me. I did not want my world to remain as it was. I was a prodigal son yelling to the world, "I will arise." No danger at the march could threaten me more than what I had already been through.

I only knew about ten of the fifty-eight students who went to Montgomery that day. Most were underclassmen and I was a senior. Two months after the event, I moved away.

The poverty that we students at Berea experienced left us with no bargaining chips. Our families carried no prestige or political clout. We were left behind at birth and spent most of our lives trying to catch up, or at least I did. I had always felt as if I were on the outside of life looking in. Bullies made certain that I did. My life had not been normal. I had only one parent. I never experienced a father in my home. We had no car. I walked everywhere I went or rode a bus. We did not celebrate lavish Christmases because what little money my mother could generate went to survival needs. I never had a birthday party nor could we even invite friends into our home. I did not date as a teenager because my family remained on the fringe of our community. I learned to drive a car when I was twenty-three.

Other students bullied and harassed me from elementary school right up to Berea. Students were very mean to me. I had no power, no one to support me, no means to stand equal to others. The opportunity to go to Montgomery changed my perception. I joined the act of defiance to go even when Berea had denied us permission. I stood with thousands of black men and women who had been treated as badly as I had, and, perhaps even worse. The march was my response to bullies, to the students who had called me a dancing monkey and had pitched coins at me simply because I had loved dancing and had been good at it. It was a response to Jethrene and the customers at the restaurant as well as to the swimmers at the city pool. I affirmed my equality and that of black people to be a part of this world on an equal basis. I sent a message to my detractors that I would never again be bullied by anyone. I walked the four miles asserting myself as a worthy human. Montgomery was the platform; my own growth in the family of man was the result.

The marchers with whom I walked were fighting for basic rights that everyone took for granted. As a white student, I already had the basic rights. I did not have the respect and acceptance of whites around me. Because I had befriended people of color, people had treated me as badly as they had treated the blacks. Sometimes, they had treated me even worse. Discrimination wounds the heart and kills the soul. There is an economic and color caste in this country that is as rigid and severe as the caste system of India. Whichever one a person is born into, he can rarely escape it. Berea was a major step in my journey upward out of Ottie's world and Montgomery was a decisive day in my growth as an adult.

I made the journey to Montgomery and presented myself with thirty thousand people because I had had enough. I chose to stand up and be counted.   My issues were the same as the blacks who were there. I had had enough of second-class status, of bullying, of people keeping me in an economic caste system that was destructive. I wanted the hope and idealism sweeping the decade of the sixties. The courage to participate in a civil rights' demonstration cleared my emotional wounds and strengthened my soul. I re-solved to treat everyone with love and respect and I would forever after demand a little of it for myself.

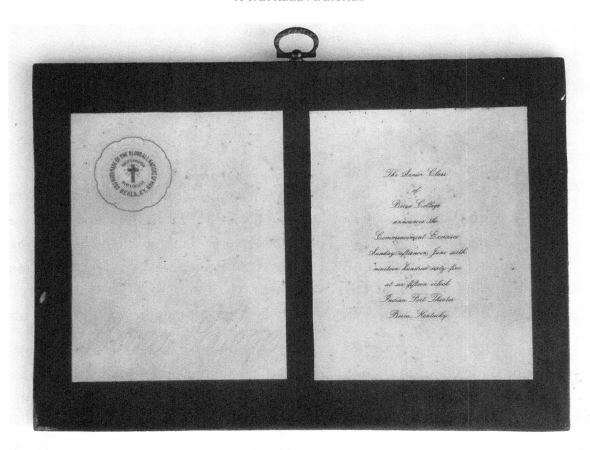

Formal invitation to Berea College graduation, 1965. (The Senior Class of Berea College announces the Commencement Exercises Sunday afternoon, June sixth nineteen hundred sixty-five at six fifteen o'clock Indian Fort Theater, Berea, Kentucky) Preserved by the author's sister (decoupage) who wrote the college to get a copy.

THE LONG ROAD HOME

In the beginning, I had escaped to Berea. In the ending, I was escaping from Berea. I rode in silence in the back seat of the car that my sister and Elaine Collett were driving, the one she had borrowed to bring my mother to graduation. Four years of my new life were ending, not with grace and satisfaction, but with a grinding pain of self-awareness. My dream that Berea would bring me a new start was yet to be realized. A new family and acceptance turned out to be only a dream.

All my friends throughout the four years had disappeared in the fury of a thunder storm that had deprived me even of the satisfaction of a feeling of accomplishment. When the lightning had flashed and the thunder had rolled, everyone had fled the ceremony. How symbolical it all was! The president had fled; the deans had fled; the faculty had run. Even our parents had turned their backs on us and had run for cover. No one had told the graduates sitting in metal chairs what to do. No one had seemed to know what to do. Berea had taught me a great lesson of life that day. It had taught me more in a few minutes about life than I had learned in four years of study. Books and lectures did not matter. Actions mattered.

In a great moment of illumination, I learned that all the college officials and faculty had done a lot of talking. In a moment requiring courage and decisions, they folded like a useless hand of cards cast wantonly on the card table. What I would do under the circumstances was left entirely up to me. Of course, that had always been the case. When I had decided to flee Ottie's world, I had boarded a Greyhound bus not caring much where it was going.

Elaine Collett sped her car down the wet highway from Indian Fort Theater back toward Berea. Rain sloshed across the windshield and spun wildly from underneath the car tires. I had wanted to say farewell to people I knew. It was not to be. The graduation class had had its fill of Berea and they were escaping back to former lives.

I never saw Chloe again. The memories and growth I had shared with her would remain as our legacy. Salome had long ago crossed the Atlantic to resume her life in Kenya. John and Alfred would live short lives and they would not return to mine. Wayne went back to his family and established a home and family in Kentucky and South Carolina. The ebb and flow of life on the campus to which I had grown accustomed faded rapidly away. I was on my way back to Ottie's world and house right back to where I had started. I held in my hand a Berea diploma and I held four years of memory in my heart.

It was exhilarating to realize that I was forever free from Mr. Rules and Regulations and his narrow perception of life. Gone were Miss Kaulner, Mrs. Kerfluffle, Jethrene, and the foolish women who had attempted to teach me French and Spanish. Like me, they were all pathetic characters on a Shakespearean stage "strutting and fretting" not to be heard any more.

The march to Montgomery and my fight for civil rights, not just for black people, but for all people who had been bullied and mistreated, had been the high water mark of my college education. I could have foregone college altogether. What I had learned in the Montgomery experience had been all I had needed to know of people and life. For one day, I had been a member of a family of thirty thousand. Everything had been in perfect harmony. We had all been equal.

I came to understand that life is an exercise in escaping. I had escaped to Berea in order to get out of Ottie's world. I was now escaping Berea for what was supposed to be the next haven. But there are no safe havens. One cannot escape himself or his issues. A safe haven is established, not by friends and family surrounding one, but by an individual, himself, when he stands to face and to clear his own issues of life. It would take me fifty years to act on that bit of wisdom.

Berea is only a memory. That is all that it should be. Other universities pulled me onward, tube fed me with their pabulum, bestowed on me diplomas and degrees. Not much changed. I was seeking to identify myself, but, I was like the mists that swirled around the peaks of the Appalachian Mountains that had given me life. I existed in the mists in a gossamer flow of time. I just had to learn to love the idea of me, for there would never be a reality of me. I am neither one thing nor another. I simply exist in the totality of life.

My Berea is no more. It changes with each freshmen class and dies with their exit at graduation. I have left my footprints on the skeins of time and place, however, and they cannot be erased. As long as I live, the story will go on.

The author on graduation day with his mother, Ottie, whose story he tells in his first book, GROWING UP IN OTTIE'S WORLD.

Vincit Qui Patitur

He Who Suffers, Conquers

The author with Dr. Chad Berry, Academic Vice President and Dean of the Faculty, Professor of History, Goode Professor of Appalachian Studies, at Boone Tavern Hotel in October, 2017, as Berea welcomed Mr. Epeley back home.

From your humble home in the Blue Ridge Mountains of North Carolina to the citadel of Berea College I came. You gave me a proud, Appalachian heritage, a desire to learn, and what little money you possessed in order to get started. I gave back to you through being successful. I send my love and best wishes to you across the skeins of Time and Space to let you know that your grandson made the journey. And he did not forget you!

REQUEST FOR AN HISTORICAL MARKER

Resolved:

Let there be established on the Berea campus an historical marker to those who participated in the Montgomery march. Place it on the grassy triangle opposite Boone Tavern Hotel, the spot from which students departed by bus and cars in March, 1965.

On one side of the marker, tell briefly what the march was about. On the opposite side, list the names of those who participated in the march.

The Montgomery march was an important event in the history of race relations at Berea College. It had a powerful effect on civil rights advancement at the national level.

Good men and women make good things happen. Berea College is filled with good administrators, faculty, alumni, and friends. May all these good people gather together to create a monument to remember our past. Let this monument be a testament that Berea College lives its magnificent motto, "God Hath Made of One Blood All Peoples of the earth."

EPILOGUE

RETURN OF A PRODIGAL SON

Half a century passed before I returned to visit the Berea College campus. My wounds were intense. My memories faded through the years, but I allowed them to fester in my mind. It was a mistake to do so. Emotional issues buried in the subconscious are much harder to resolve than if they had remained conscious.

I resolved to go back at least once to visit the places at Berea that had affected much of my life. But then circumstances arranged themselves in the most incredible way.

I called Rachel Vagts, Head of Special Collections and Archives, to get permission to use copyrighted materials owned by Berea College. I also asked her to find someone on the Berea campus that would read my manuscript before publication. She passed the manuscript to Dr. Dwyane Mack, Professor of History and Carter G. Woodson Chair of African American History. Dr. Mack called me for a long chat. He then spoke with Linda Strong-Leek, Vice President for Diversity and Inclusion, Associate Vice President for Academic Affairs about me and the fact that I had been an original marcher to Montgomery.

She began her letter with the words, "We would like to invite you to come back to Berea on October 17 and participate in our monthly panel discussion, Truth Talks..." She then suggested that Dr. Mack come to Morganton to meet me in person. He and his son had breakfast with me at Abele's Restaurant in Morganton.

The time for departing for Berea a second time had come.

Just like the first time I had left for Berea, I took I-40 to Knoxville and then I-75 northward to Berea. This time, however, I drove a new car and my pockets were stuffed with money. A distinguished career in education lay behind me. I was living a happy life.

I left the interstate at Corbin, and I intentionally drove old highway 25 the rest of the way. I wanted to recreate as much of my original trip as possible. Little had changed in fifty years along the old highway. Some new stores and houses had been built, and pockets of poverty were still evident.

The town of Berea had expanded to the interstate and it boasted of fast food eateries, motels, and gasoline stations. Old Town was now a tourist area. I wondered what had happened to the dumpsters Josiah, Melbert, and I had enjoyed years ago. The All Night Restaurant had been torn down a long time ago.

The old movie house was closed and abandoned, and new buildings had gone up all over campus. I saw the dome of Phelps-Stokes rising above the trees. My heart leapt with joy because this was the one building that had represented Berea for me. I parked my car on the highway in front of it and waited fifteen minutes for the chimes to ring. Its ringing welcomed me home. This building represented stability, Chloe, my arrival, and my discovery of self. It was the one constant that students could count on each Wednesday evening. My tulip magnolia was still growing beside it. The rule against picking flowers on campus was obviously a good one because my favorite tree had survived.

Parking my car in front of Boone Tavern Hotel, I checked into the hotel. It was my first time to stay at the hotel. Berea paid all my expenses. I crossed the street and stood on the exact spot where our little group had departed for Montgomery and to which it had returned. A voice in my head whispered, "You are standing on sacred ground. Tread lightly." I wondered how many students had crossed this very spot throughout the years and had never realized the energy that it carried. I doubted that many Berea students on campus today even knew that a group had marched in Montgomery.

At five-thirty, I met Dr. Mack in the Carter G. Woodson building which was originally the Snack Bar where I had spent hundreds of hours dancing and socializing when I had been at Berea. It had been rebuilt inside into a beautiful museum to Black History. Mike

Clark, who had made the famous photos of our march, and I participated with students in a panel discussion on race history and relations.

During the discussion, two distinguished gentlemen entered the room and sat down at the back. I recognized one as Dr. Lyle Roelofs, President of Berea College, and the other was Dr. Chad Berry, Dean of Faculty.

In closing my part of the panel, I told the story of how my graduation from Berea had been ruined by a sudden downpour of rain. I had never received my diploma officially. I had brought my diploma with me hoping that someone would present it to me formally.

"Would the president of Berea College please come forward and present me my diploma after fifty-two long years?" I asked.

The crowd roared its approval. Dr. Roelofs smiled as he stepped forward to present my diploma. He then took me to Boone Tavern for coffee and dessert.

The following morning, Dr. Chad Berry, Dean of Faculty, met me at Boone Tavern for breakfast. He asked me why I had not returned to Berea in fifty years. I had a chance to pour out my heart, to tell my story, to weep. Dr. Berry was filled with deep compassion. He assured me that I was considered and that the Berea of today would not tolerate what I had experienced in the 1960s. This fine man transformed my feelings and helped me to let go of the past. I express my deep gratitude to him.

In my stroll across campus, I saw that Howard Hall and Curtis House had been demolished and new dormitories rose proudly in their places. Pearsons Hall was still there as was the Draper Building. However, someone had committed a sacrilege. Pearsons Hall was now a women's dorm!

It was an emotional experience when I walked into Danforth Chapel where our group had met before marching to the president's house. I sat down and drank in the heavy silence. The lilting voices of our leaders from the past seemed to come alive and sweetly permeate the entire room. I could still hear them praising Berea and extolling us to act with dignity and pride. I felt that pride once again as I stared at the stain glass windows.

Walking into the sunlight from Draper Hall, I slowly strolled to the president's house across highway 25. Standing on the sidewalk, I stared at the white door that was still there. I could hear our group singing majestically, "We Shall Overcome." The huge sign stating, "God Hath Made of One Blood All Nations of Men," was etched in my memory. I could still see President Hutchins open the door and welcome our leaders in.

Then the great moment of atonement came. I walked to Lincoln Hall where the Dean's office had been. It was in that building that my punishments had been meted out. There is where the letter denying us permission to go to Montgomery had been written. There is where my folder with numerous infractions had been stored. In this ancient building, someone had denied my graduation and then they had reinstated it. I had hated this building for fifty years. It had represented the worst experience of Berea College for me.

As I stared at its ivy-covered walls, I was armed with a renewed respect for Berea engendered by Dr. Mack and Dr. Berry. I realized that in the present moment, I held all the power. I had outlived all my tormentors. I was having the last word. I was the guest of the college. I also held the trump card for all the memories stored in my head---self-forgiveness. I used that trump card in the most powerful way by uttering the words, "I forgive myself everything that happened on this campus. I reaffirm my love for this school."

I summoned the old memories and emotions in my mind and, one by one, I forgave myself for what I had done and for how I had felt about these events for fifty years. Those long-dead faculty and students had already answered to God for their actions, but I chose not to wait until I died to do so. No power on earth had been able to prevent our student group from marching in Montgomery. The after effects of what we had accomplished that day were evident all over America.

I stood for a moment remembering Chloe and I thanked her for being the vessel by which I had learned to accept black people. And my heart went out across the distant ocean to a great lady named Salome Nogola. Her philosophy of milkshakes made sense now. I promised myself a strawberry milkshake in her honor.

As I left the Berea Campus, I stopped my car and listened once more to the Phelps-Stokes chimes sounding out the hour. I got out of my car and broke a leaf from my favorite magnolia tree growing by Phelps-Stokes. I tucked its stem lovingly into my shirt pocket.

From across the years I thought that I heard the choir singing the stirring words from "Berea Beloved":

"And though we wander far away, thy chimes will ring for us each day."

The author, age 20

Berea College

WINDS OF CHANGE

The author wrote this poem on September 22, 2017, to commemorate the 52nd anniversary of the march. He expresses pride in his classmates and Berea College. He looks forward optimistically to full equality for all peoples.

WINDS OF CHANGE

 soft, south wind lifts gently from the black delta
plains of Alabama.

Winds of change

It caresses the red clay hills of Georgia and blows the smell
of ripened peaches northward

The majestic mountains of Carolina sway to its bidding

Blue grass in Kentucky undulates to its rhythm across
shale-covered earth

ppressed men and women with heads bowed begin
to awaken from centuries of slumber

At the birth of each new slave baby, old women had
asked, "Is it you, babe, is it you?"

Is you de one to set us free?"

"He's here," whispered the wind across the delta, the plains,
the red clay hills, and the sea

"I bring you good news."

"He can but lead you. Each must break the shackles
from his own hands and feet."

He's sending his voice urging us all to come

Come to Montgomery, follow your own inner sun

Walk the pathways, the byways, asphalt, and stones

Young and old, black and white

We must all enter into this worthy fight

Winds of change

The wind blew to Berea where students were awakening
from slumber

They rose up with heart to march with feet of thunder

When they were told, "No, you cannot go,

It's too dangerous for you are young."

"We must own our lives," they said, "our own songs will
be sung."

D efiant and brave, valiant and unafraid

They moved southward in the darkness of night

Love in their hearts, hope in their dreams

They would heal the hurt and make everything right.

On the morrow they joined thousands

Marching through the heart of a city

Like a mighty army they came

To trample racism and destroy all pity

A great shout of "Lord, I'm free" rose upon the wind

It touched the heart of a nation

And it brought winds of change

B erea students rode home, tired and alone

There was no homecoming on campus

No drums or bugles playing

Their friends and companions were gone

Gone to classes, gone to breakfast, all hidden away

Most important in their minds was what they had to do that day

We have wrought change.

Be patient.

Persevere,

roared the wind,

"You are all heroes."

Fifty years from this time

Many in the Berea family will say, "I consider myself cheated

That I did not go with you on your glorious day."

Fred E. Epeley

September 22, 2017

MESSAGE FROM THE AUTHOR

Fred Eli Epeley

I leave my love and best wishes to Berea students, administration, and faculty as well as to all the youth of today. John F. Kennedy told people of my time that the torch had been passed to a new generation of Americans. We held that torch high and worked toward better race relations in our country.

My generation now passes the torch to you. Do not use the torch to burn down our nation. Hold it high. Let it be as a lamp unto your feet as you continue our work. Work toward your goals with love and non-violence.

May you first believe in justice. Then, may you have every reason to believe in yourself. Join your hands in mine as we loudly proclaim:

THE WORLD IS MY COUNTRY! ALL MEN AND WOMEN ARE MY BROTHERS AND SISTERS! GOD HATH TRULY MADE OF ONE BLOOD ALL PEOPLES OF THE EARTH! LET US LIVE IN PEACE AND HARMONY! WE SHALL OVERCOME!

"I HAVE A DREAM."

Martin Luther King

The Dreamer

BIBLIOGRAPHY

Cable, William M. And Wilfred Johnston. "Berea Beloved." Berea College

Special Collections and Archives, Berea, Ky. 1929.

Clark, Mike. "God Hath Made of one Blood All Nations of Men." Photo. Berea

College Special Collections and Archives, Berea, Ky. 1965.

Corbett, Frank. "Poster Number 2. Berea College Special Collections and

Archives, Berea, Ky. 1965.

Hapgood, David. "A Week with the Peace Corps." (A private, unpublished letter

to Richard H. Nolte of the Institute of Current World Affairs explaining

his participation with Berea College Peace Corps Training Center.)

Instiltute of Current World Affairs. 1963.

Hutchins, Dr. Francis. "Letter from Dr. Francis Hutchins to Mrs. R. W. Rueter."

Berea College Special Collections and Archives, Berea, Ky. 1964.

Meisler, Stan. Interview on Internet. Peace Corps Writers. November, 2010.

"Number l." Anonymous Poster. Berea College Special Collections and

Archives, Berea, Ky. 1965.

"Number 111." Anonymous Poster. Berea College Special Collections

And Archives, Berea, Ky. 1965.

"Students Who Just Returned From Selma." George Giffin. Letter. Berea College Special Collections and Archives, Berea, Ky. 1965.

Thompson, Kenneth H. "Copy of Letter Received by Danny Daniel from Dean Kenneth H. Thompson." Berea College Special Collections and Archives, Berea, Ky. 1965.

Made in United States
Orlando, FL
29 March 2022

16284472R00167